Module A

FOUNDATIONS OF BEHAVIOR SUPPORT

A Continuous Improvement Process

Module 1 of 6 in *Foundations: A Proactive and Positive Behavior Support System* (3rd ed.)

Randy Sprick
Mike Booher
Paula Rich

RANDY SPRICK'S

safe & civil
SCHOOLS

Practical Solutions, Positive Results!

Published in the United States by
Pacific Northwest Publishing
21 West 6th Ave.
Eugene, Oregon 97401
www.pacificnwpublish.com
ISBN: 978-1-59909-069-6

Part of *Foundations: A Proactive and Positive Behavior Support System* (3rd ed.)
ISBN: 978-1-59909-068-9

Cover by Aaron Graham
Book design and layout by Natalie Conaway

Pacific
Northwest
Publishing

Eugene, Oregon | www.pacificnwpublish.com

Any resources and website addresses are provided for reader convenience and were current at the time of publication. Report any broken links to info@pacificnwpublish.com.

DOWNLOAD CD CONTENT

Go to cdcontent.pacificnwpublish.com and enter access code **59909-069-6-forms** to download forms, PowerPoints, and other resources. Enter access code **59909-069-6-samples** to download samples.

48600000189713

CONTENTS

CONTENTS

iv

ABOUT THE AUTHORS

Randy Sprick, Ph.D.

Randy Sprick, Ph.D., has worked as a paraprofessional, teacher, and teacher trainer at the elementary and secondary levels. Author of a number of widely read books on behavior and classroom management, Dr. Sprick is director of *Safe & Civil Schools*, a consulting company that provides inservice programs throughout the country. He and his trainers work with numerous large and small school districts on longitudinal projects to improve student behavior and motivation. Efficacy of that work is documented in peer-reviewed research, and *Safe & Civil Schools* materials are listed on the National Registry of Evidence-Based Programs and Practices (NREPP). Dr. Sprick was the recipient of the 2007 Council for Exceptional Children (CEC) Wallin Lifetime Achievement Award.

Mike Booher, M.Ed.

Mike Booher, M.Ed., worked as a school psychologist and supervisor of psychological services in the Guilford County Schools (North Carolina) for 33 years. While in Guilford, he served for 8 years as a project coordinator, trainer, and coach for Guilford's implementation of the *Safe & Civil Schools* Foundations and CHAMPS programs. He coordinated the district's school-based intervention teams who responded to teacher referrals of students having academic and/or behavioral challenges, and provided training and coordination for the district's intervention services for a school in crisis or a student in a suicidal crisis. From 2000 to 2005, Mr. Booher served as a clinical instructor in School Psychology at UNC–Chapel Hill. He has worked as a national trainer and consultant for *Safe & Civil Schools* since 2005.

Paula Rich, B.Mus.Ed., M.Mus.

Paula Rich, B.Mus.Ed., M.Mus., has been a substitute teacher in public schools, was a freelance musician, and taught private music lessons for many years in the Boston, Massachusetts, area. Since joining Pacific Northwest Publishing in 2006, she has contributed original stories and poems to the *Read Well* curriculum for second-grade readers and has edited several of Randy Sprick's staff development and behavior management books and papers. She was instrumental in developing Connections, Pacific Northwest Publishing's online check-and-connect program.

SAFE & CIVIL SCHOOLS

THE SAFE & CIVIL SCHOOLS SERIES is a comprehensive, integrated set of resources designed to help educators improve student behavior and school climate at every level—districtwide, schoolwide, within the classroom, and at the individual intervention level. The findings of decades of research literature have been refined into step-by-step actions that teachers and staff can take to help all students behave responsibly and respectfully.

The hallmark of the *Safe & Civil Schools* model is its emphasis on proactive, positive, and instructional behavior management—addressing behavior before it necessitates correction, collecting data before embarking on interventions, implementing simple corrections before moving to progressively more intensive and time-intrusive ones, and setting a climate of respect for all. As a practical matter, tending to schoolwide and classwide policies, procedures, and interventions is far easier than resorting to more costly, time-intrusive, and individualized approaches.

Foundations and PBIS

Positive Behavioral Interventions and Supports (PBIS) is not a program. According to the U.S. Department of Education, PBIS is simply a framework to help provide "assistance to schools, districts, and states to establish a preventative, positive, multi-tiered continuum of evidence-based behavioral interventions that support the behavioral competence of students" (A. Posny, personal communication, September 7, 2010). That framework perfectly describes *Foundations. Foundations* provides instructions for implementing such an approach—with detailed processes and hundreds of examples of specific applications from successful schools. Furthermore, *Foundations* provides step-by-step guidance for involving and unifying an entire district staff to develop behavior support procedures that will prevent misbehavior and increase student connectedness and motivation. *Foundations* moves well beyond a simple matrix into how to guide and inspire staff to take ownership of managing and motivating all students, all the time, every day.

SAFE & CIVIL SCHOOLS

Resources in the series do not take a punitive approach to discipline. Instead, *Safe & Civil Schools* addresses the sources of teachers' greatest power to motivate: through structuring for student success, teaching expectations, observing and monitoring student behavior, and, above all, interacting positively. Because experience directly affects behavior, it makes little sense to pursue only the undesired behavior (by relying on reprimands, for example) and not the conditions (in behavioral theory, the antecedent) that precipitate experience and subsequent behavior.

The *Safe & Civil Schools* Positive Behavioral Interventions and Supports (PBIS) Model is listed in the National Registry of Evidence-based Programs and Practices (NREPP) after review by the Substance Abuse and Mental Health Services Administration (SAMHSA).

Inclusion in NREPP means that independent reviewers found that the philosophy and procedures behind *Foundations, CHAMPS, Discipline in the Secondary Classroom, Interventions,* and other *Safe & Civil Schools* books and DVDs have been thoroughly researched, that the research is of high quality, and that the outcomes achieved include:

- Higher levels of academic achievement
- Reductions in school suspensions
- Fewer classroom disruptions
- Increases in teacher professional self-efficacy
- Improvement in school discipline procedures

For more information, visit www.nrepp.samhsa.gov.

The most recent evidence of the efficacy of the *Safe & Civil Schools* PBIS Model appeared in the October 2013 issue of *School Psychology Review.* "A Randomized Evaluation of the *Safe and Civil Schools* Model for Positive Behavioral Interventions and Supports at Elementary Schools in a Large Urban School District," by Bryce Ward and Russell Gersten, shows how the *Safe & Civil Schools* PBIS Model improves student behavior and school climate. Thirty-two elementary schools in a large urban school district were randomly assigned to an initial training cohort or a wait-list control group. Results show reduced suspension rates, decreases in problem behavior, and evidence of positive academic gains for the schools in the training cohort.

Observed improvements persisted through the second year of trainings, and once the wait-list control schools commenced *Safe & Civil Schools* training, they experienced similar improvements in school policies and student behavior.

 Download and read the full article at:
www.nasponline.org/publications/spr/index.aspx?vol=42&issue=3

Safe & Civil Schools acknowledges the real power educators have—not in controlling students but in shaping their behavior through affecting every aspect of their experience while they are in school: the physical layout, the way time is structured, arrivals and departures, teaching expected behavior, meaningful relationships with adults, and more. These changes in what adults do can create dramatic and lifelong changes in the behavior and motivation of students.

ACKNOWLEDGMENTS

As lead author, I owe a huge debt to many people who have guided the development and revision of *Foundations* over the past three decades. Betsy Norton, Mickey Garrison, and Marilyn Sprick were instrumental in the development and implementation of *Foundations* long before the publication of the first edition in 1992. Dr. Jan Reinhardtsen received the very first federal grant on the topic of positive behavior support and, with Mickey, implemented the first edition of *Foundations* as the basis for Project CREST in the early and mid-1990s. Jan also came up with *Safe & Civil Schools*, which became the name of our staff development services. Dr. Laura McCullough implemented a brilliant state-level Model School project in Kentucky, followed by the Kentucky Instructional Discipline System (KIDS) project that taught me so much about the importance of training and coaching to assist schools with implementation of both schoolwide and classroom behavior support.

I want to thank my coauthors of the different modules within this edition. Susan Isaacs, Mike Booher, and Jessica Sprick are outstanding trainers of *Foundations*, and their respective expertise has added depth to the content that makes this edition more practical, rich, and fun than previous editions. Paula Rich has provided both organizational skill and writing expertise to weave together a vast amount of content with many school- and district-level examples to create a highly accessible and user-friendly resource.

Thanks to the awesome staff of Pacific Northwest Publishing: Aaron Graham and Natalie Conaway with design, Sara Ferris and K Daniels with editing, Matt Sprick for directing both video and print development, Sam Gehrke for video editing, Robert Consentino and Jake Clifton for camera and sound, and the rest of the Pacific Northwest Publishing and *Safe & Civil Schools* staff—Jackie Hefner, Karen Schell, Sarah Romero, Kimberly Irving, Brandt Schram, Caroline DeVorss, and Marilyn Sprick—for their great work.

Implementation of *Foundations*, *CHAMPS*, and *Interventions* would not have thrived without the skill and dedication of great staff developers and trainers: Tricia Berg, Mike Booher, Phyllis Gamas, Laura Hamilton, Andrea Hanford, Jane Harris, Susan Isaacs, Debbie Jackson, Kim Marcum, Bob McLaughlin, Donna Meers, Carolyn Novelly, Robbie Rowan, Susan Schilt, Tricia Skyles, Pat Somers, Karl Schleich, Jessica Sprick, and Elizabeth Winford as Director of Professional Development.

ACKNOWLEDGMENTS

Fresno Unified School District and Long Beach Unified School District in California allowed us to visit with the Pacific Northwest Publishing video crew to capture the excitement, professionalism, and commitment of school and district personnel. These districts have taught us so much about the importance of common language and district support in creating a sustainable implementation.

Lastly, I want to the thank the schools and districts that have implemented *Foundations* over the years and graciously shared their lessons, posters, staff development activities, forms, and policies that you will find as examples throughout the print and video presentations. These real-world examples will help your implementation process by illustrating how other schools and districts have successfully implemented and sustained *Foundations*.

—R.S.

HOW TO USE FOUNDATIONS

This third edition of *Foundations* is constructed as six modules to accommodate schools that are just beginning their implementation of multi-tiered systems of behavior support (MTSS) as well as schools that already have some, but not all, pieces of behavior support firmly in place. For example, a school may have done great work on improving behavior in the common areas of the school but very little work on intentionally constructing a positive, inviting climate or addressing conflict and bullying in a comprehensive way. This school could go directly to Module C: *Conscious Construction of an Inviting Climate*, and after implementing those strategies, move to Module E: *Improving Safety, Managing Conflict, and Reducing Bullying*.

Each module incorporates multiple resources to assist you: video presentations on DVD, the book you are reading now, and a CD with forms and samples. The videos can guide a building-based leadership team through implementing *Foundations*. The same content is available in print format; we provide eight copies of this book for each module, one for each member of the leadership team. Teams can decide which content delivery form works best for them—video or print.

Each book comes with a CD that contains reproducible forms, examples of policies and procedures from real schools that have implemented *Foundations*, and other implementation resources. The CD also includes PowerPoint presentations that correspond directly to the video and print content. Your leadership team can use these presentations to deliver the most relevant *Foundations* information to the entire staff.

Beginning Behavior Support

For schools and districts that are just beginning with behavior support or are unsure where to begin, we suggest starting with Module A: *Foundations of Behavior Support—A Continuous Improvement Process*. This module is the foundation of *Foundations*. It describes the importance of a well-designed leadership team, a formalized continuous improvement cycle, how to use multiple data sources to drive that cycle, and how to involve and unify the staff in implementation. Without laying this groundwork, any specific work on procedures, such as improving the cafeteria, is unlikely to be effective or sustainable.

HOW TO USE FOUNDATIONS

Once your team is collecting and analyzing data, you will probably move through Modules B–F (described below) in order. You'll work on the common areas of the school, then positive climate, and so on. Once a module has been implemented, you are not done with that module. For example, after implementing the procedures in Module B for a couple of common areas and a couple of schoolwide policies, such as dress code, you may move on to Module C to work on improving school climate. However, you will concurrently continue to implement Module B procedures for additional common areas and schoolwide policies. Working through all six modules will take about two to five years of development and implementation.

MTSS in Progress

Schools and districts that have been effectively implementing other approaches to PBIS should follow these guidelines when implementing *Foundations*.

You may be able to use the modules in a nonlinear fashion if your school has a highly functional team, uses multiple data sources to involve the entire staff in continuous improvement of behavior support, and has worked to improve several common areas or schoolwide policies. To self-assess where to begin, a resource for each module called the Foundations Implementation Rubric and Summary is included in Appendix A of the book and on the CD. The rubric can help your leadership team assess which modules have information useful to your school at this time and help you make judgments about where to begin. Print the rubric, work through it as a team, and summarize your findings, and you will see patterns emerge. (Instructions are included with the rubric.)

For example, if all the conditions described at the beginning of this paragraph are in place, you will probably find that you are already implementing many of the procedures delineated in Modules A and B. One school may have an urgent need to go directly to Module E because the school has no programs or policies to address conflict and bullying, whereas another school may go directly to Module D because staff are very inconsistent about when and how to use disciplinary referral to the office. Another school may go directly to Module F because their schoolwide structures are relatively well established, but they have yet to address classroom management or the integration of universal, targeted, and intensive interventions.

HOW TO USE FOUNDATIONS

Appendix B of each module presents an Implementation Checklist for that module. The Implementation Checklist details the summarized items on the rubric. You will use this tool as you near completion on any module to ensure that you have fully implemented it, and it's also useful for reviewing the implementation every three years or so. The checklist can identify strengths to celebrate and catch gaps in your implementation that you may be able to fill before a major problem emerges.

OVERVIEW OF MODULES

The modules in *Foundations* are designed to be used sequentially by a school or district that is just getting started with behavior support. However, if a school or district is already implementing a team-based, data-driven approach to continuous improvement of climate, safety, discipline, and motivation, the modules can be used in any order.

This module, **Module A:** *Foundations of Behavior Support—A Continuous Improvement Process,* covers the essential processes for involving the entire staff in developing, implementing, and sustaining positive behavior support. It includes detailed information about establishing a building-based leadership team (Foundations Team) to represent the entire staff. This module advises the team on how to collect and analyze data, identify and rank a manageable number of priorities for improvement, and guide the staff in revising, adopting, and implementing new policies and procedures for each priority. This process creates a cycle of continuous improvement that empowers and unifies the entire staff.

- Presentation 1: Foundations: A Multi-Tiered System of Behavior Support
- Presentation 2: Team Processes
- Presentation 3: The Improvement Cycle
- Presentation 4: Data-Driven Processes
- Presentation 5: Developing Staff Engagement and Unity
- Appendix A: Foundations Implementation Rubric and Summary
- Appendix B: Module A Implementation Checklist
- Appendix C: Guide to Module A Reproducible Forms and Samples

Other modules in *Foundations: A Proactive and Positive Behavior Support System* are:

Module B: *Managing Behavior in Common Areas and With Schoolwide Policies* delineates processes for ensuring that common areas (arrival, cafeteria, hallways, and so on) and schoolwide policies (dress code, electronics use, public displays of affection, and so on) are structured for success and that expectations for behavior are directly taught with clarity and repetition to students. In addition, this module includes detailed information for all staff about how to provide positive and systematic supervision and how to correct misbehavior calmly, consistently, and respectfully.

- Presentation 1: Laying the Groundwork for Consistency in All School Settings
- Presentation 2: Structuring Common Areas and Schoolwide Policies for Success
- Presentation 3: Teaching Expectations to Students

- Presentation 4: Effective Supervision, Part 1—Protect, Expect, and Connect
- Presentation 5: Effective Supervision, Part 2—Correct and Reflect
- Presentation 6: Supervising Common Areas and Schoolwide Policies—for All Staff
- Presentation 7: Adopting, Implementing, and Monitoring Improvements to Common Areas and Schoolwide Policies
- Appendix A: Foundations Implementation Rubric and Summary
- Appendix B: Module B Implementation Checklist
- Appendix C: Guide to Module B Reproducible Forms and Samples

Module C: *Conscious Construction of an Inviting School Climate* guides the entire staff in creating and sustaining a school environment that makes all students feel welcomed and valued. This process includes developing Guidelines for Success, a set of behaviors and traits that provides a common language and common values among staff, students, and parents. This module explains how and why to maintain at least 3:1 ratios of positive interactions and covers the importance of regular attendance and strategies for improving attendance. Strategies for meeting the basic human needs of all students are also discussed. Finally, the module outlines how to welcome and orient staff, students, and families who are new to the school in a way that connects them to the school community.

- Presentation 1: Constructing and Maintaining a Positive Climate
- Presentation 2: Guidelines for Success
- Presentation 3: Ratios of Positive Interactions
- Presentation 4: Improving Attendance
- Presentation 5: School Connectedness—Meeting Basic Human Needs
- Presentation 6: Programs and Strategies for Meeting Needs
- Presentation 7: Making a Good First Impression—Welcoming New Staff, Students, and Families
- Appendix A: Foundations Implementation Rubric and Summary
- Appendix B: Module C Implementation Checklist
- Appendix C: Guide to Module C Reproducible Forms and Samples

Module D: *Responding to Misbehavior—An Instructional Approach* focuses on the vital importance of an instructional approach to correction in reducing future occurrences of the misbehavior. It provides information on training and inspiring all staff to correct all misbehavior by giving students information about how to behave successfully and by using the mildest consequences that reasonably fit the infractions. Module D describes how to get consensus among staff about when (and when not) to use office discipline referral. It provides menus of corrective techniques for mild and moderate misbehavior, from gentle verbal correction to time owed after class to restorative justice strategies. All staff learn strategies for de-escalating emotional situations, and administrators are introduced to a comprehensive game plan for dealing with office referrals and for implementing alternatives to out-of-school suspension. This module includes sample lessons for students on how to interact with people in authority.

- Presentation 1: The Relationship Between Proactive Procedures, Corrective Procedures, and Individual Student Behavior Improvement Plans
- Presentation 2: Developing Three Levels of Misbehavior
- Presentation 3: Staff Responsibilities for Responding to Misbehavior
- Presentation 4: Administrator Responsibilities for Responding to Misbehavior
- Presentation 5: Preventing the Misbehavior That Leads to Referrals and Suspensions
- Appendix A: Foundations Implementation Rubric and Summary
- Appendix B: Module D Implementation Checklist
- Appendix C: Guide to Module D Reproducible Forms and Samples

Module E: *Improving Safety, Managing Conflict, and Reducing Bullying* guides the Foundations Team in assessing school strengths and weaknesses related to safety, conflict, and bullying. The module begins by examining the attributes of safe and unsafe schools and offers suggestions for moving your school toward the evidence-based attributes that contribute to safety. One potential risk to safety is poor conflict management, so this module includes a simple conflict resolution strategy that students can use to manage conflict in peaceful and mutually beneficial ways. Bullying is another serious risk to safety. Module E provides a step-by-step process for analyzing strengths and gaps in your school's bullying policies and procedures as well as suggestions and examples for turning gaps into strengths. This module includes lessons for students on safety, conflict, and bullying prevention and intervention.

- Presentation 1: Keeping Students Safe From Physical and Emotional Harm
- Presentation 2: Attributes of Safe and Unsafe Schools
- Presentation 3: Teaching Conflict Resolution
- Presentation 4: Analyzing Bullying Behavior, Policies, and School Needs
- Presentation 5: Schoolwide Bullying Prevention and Intervention
- Appendix A: Foundations Implementation Rubric and Summary
- Appendix B: Module E Implementation Checklist
- Appendix C: Guide to Module E Reproducible Forms and Samples

Module F: *Establishing and Sustaining a Continuum of Behavior Support* outlines how the Foundations Team can analyze and guide an integration of universal prevention, targeted support, and intensive support for students. This process includes adopting and supporting a schoolwide or district approach to classroom management that creates a common language and ensures that teachers, administrators, and support staff are on the same page about classroom organization and management. For students who need individual support, this module provides staff training in early-stage interventions and a variety of problem-solving structures that match the intensity of student need to the intensity of school- and district-based resources. Finally, Module F provides guidance in sustaining *Foundations* at the building and district level so that effective procedures are maintained and improvement continues, even when school administration changes.

- Presentation 1: The Vision of a Continuum of Behavior Support
- Presentation 2: Supporting Classroom Behavior—The Three-Legged Stool
- Presentation 3: Articulating Staff Beliefs and Solidifying Universal Procedures
- Presentation 4: Early-Stage Interventions for General Education Classrooms
- Presentation 5: Matching the Intensity of Your Resources to the Intensity of Student Needs
- Presentation 6: Problem-Solving Processes and Intervention Design
- Presentation 7: Sustainability and District Support
- Appendix A: Foundations Implementation Rubric and Summary
- Appendix B: Module F Implementation Checklist
- Appendix C: Guide to Module F Reproducible Forms and Samples

Foundations: A Multi-Tiered System of Behavior Support

ONE

CONTENTS

Introduction

Task 1: What Is Foundations?

For the Foundations Team and all staff

Task 2: Change Student Behavior With STOIC

For the Foundations Team and all staff

Task 3: Decide How Foundations Will Be Structured in Your School

For the Foundations Team and all staff

INTRODUCTION

Foundations is a process for guiding your entire staff through construction and implementation of a comprehensive approach to behavior support. The *Foundations* approach is proactive, positive, and instructional. The goal is to reduce all behavioral and motivational barriers to learning by:

- Reducing misbehaviors such as disruption, disrespect, and bullying
- Promoting safety and prosocial behavior
- Supporting both academic instruction and social-emotional learning
- Establishing a positive climate
- Enhancing staff consistency in teaching expectations and correcting misbehavior

Foundations guides you in this work within the framework of Multi-Tiered Systems of Support (MTSS) or Response to Intervention (RTI), and it emphasizes universal support and prevention—working with all students throughout the common areas of the school and within every classroom to promote responsible and highly motivated student behavior.

Foundations encompasses six major content areas that we present in modules. The modules are built so that if you have already been implementing some aspects of positive behavior support, you don't necessarily have to work through that concept again—you can go directly to the content most relevant for you. Each module is made up of presentations structured as a series of tasks. Your leadership team or your whole staff undertakes these tasks to construct and implement the different components of behavior support.

Each module is provided in both video and book format. This allows you to choose the most convenient way to present the material to the team and staff. Each team member receives a copy of the book, and each copy includes a CD of reproducible forms, sample policies, sample lessons, and so on that will help you develop policies and materials for your own school. In the past 20 plus years of *Foundations* trainings, many schools have shared their wonderful ideas with us, and we thank them for allowing us to share them with you.

The CDs also contain PowerPoint presentations that correspond directly to the content of each module. You can use these PowerPoints for staff training and review, and you can modify the slides to match the unique needs of your school.

The modules are built around the concept of a multi-tiered continuum of behavior support. Each module corresponds to a tier of the Foundations continuum shown in Figure 1a on the next page.

Figure 1a *The Foundations continuum of behavior support (A-10)*

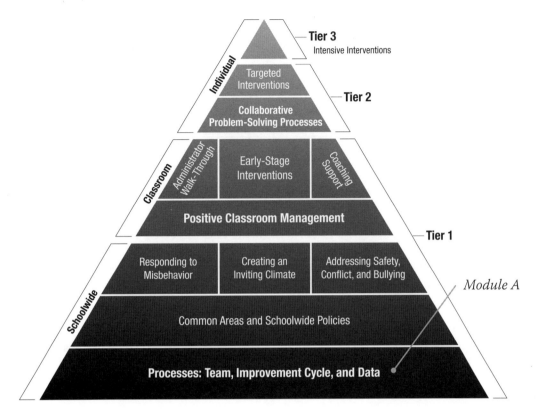

You may think of *Foundations* as a construction process. The finished building is analogous to a staff unified in implementing proactive and positive instructional approaches to discipline that enhance student behavior and motivation. The foundation of the building is this module, Module A, so you'll want to begin here. Module A describes how to establish a leadership team and develop a data-driven continuous improvement cycle that involves the entire staff in setting priorities and implementing improvements.

Module B explains how to achieve clarity and consistency with expectations and corrections in the common areas of your school and with schoolwide policies.

Module C discusses the conscious construction of a positive, welcoming, and inviting climate, and is supported by Modules D and E—Module D clarifies how and why to establish a system that ensures consistent and unified staff responses to misbehavior, and Module E suggests policies and procedures to ensure safety, help students resolve conflicts, and prevent bullying.

All of the schoolwide work in the first five modules supports effective classroom management and efforts to implement behavior support plans for students with the greatest social, emotional, and behavioral challenges, the topic of Module F.

You might want to jump directly to Module F for guidance on working with your most challenging students. But we recommend that you ensure that your universal supports are in place first. If you go to Module F too soon, you might end up with so many students on individual behavior improvement plans that you overwhelm classroom teachers—they are so busy keeping track of the different techniques they need to use for individual students that they can't run their general management plan or provide good instruction.

⮞ FOUNDATIONS RECOMMENDATION ⮜

Ensure that universal supports are fully in place before you begin work on individual behavior improvement plans.

So the goal is to integrate all of Modules A through F so that the number of students who need individual support is minimal and not burdensome to either general education or special education teaching staff.

Module A Overview

What's in Module A? Presentation 1 provides an overview of *Foundations* and gives a clearer sense of the construction project you are beginning. Task 1 explains the *Foundations* approach. Task 2 discusses how behavior can be changed and describes the mechanisms used throughout *Foundations* that can have a positive effect on student behavior. Task 3 is a nuts-and-bolts explanation of how to get started with *Foundations*. The entire staff will find this task useful.

Presentation 2 describes why and how to form a leadership team to represent and unify the staff in your efforts to improve discipline, safety, climate, and all other aspects of behavior support. Think of this team as the architects and managers of your construction project and the whole staff as the builders—they will work together as a coordinated unit to build a positive, proactive, and instructional climate.

Presentation 3 explains the continuous Improvement Cycle. This concept is used by the team and the entire staff to review meaningful data, prioritize a manageable number of things to work on at any given time, develop revision proposals to present to the staff for adoption, implement adopted policies and procedures, and ensure that improvement efforts never end.

Presentation 4 is about the importance of collecting and analyzing data from multiple sources to drive the Improvement Cycle.

Presentation 5 suggests ways to create and enhance staff buy-in to the *Foundations* process. All staff members must actively work together to positively influence the culture, climate, safety, and discipline of your school. If everyone does a little, no one has to do a lot. Presentation 5 also includes suggestions for administrators on their role in guiding these processes.

You begin the construction process by working through this module. You build the foundation that all of your behavior support practices will rest on. But, as with any building, you will never be completely finished. Maintenance is required, bedrooms need repainting, bathrooms need remodeling, kitchens need updating. Schools are such complex places and the needs of your students are so varied and unquestionably complex that maintenance is a constant consideration. You will keep asking questions like: Is this policy doing what we need it to do? Can this common area function more efficiently?

You are building a unified staff committed to making the school a safer, more orderly, more motivated, and generally better place for all students each year. John Foster Dulles once said, "The measure of success is not whether you have a tough problem to deal with, but whether it's the same problem you had last year." That's a great theme for *Foundations*—every year, make your school a little bit better. You can achieve that goal by creating a process of continuous improvement so that your school is the best possible environment for every student, no matter his or her needs.

 The measure of success is not whether you have a tough problem to deal with, but whether it's the same problem you had last year."

JOHN FOSTER DULLES
(1888–1959), former U.S.
Secretary of State

Presentation 1 Overview

Presentation 1 provides more details on the construction process you are about to undertake.

Task 1: What Is *Foundations?* provides an overview of the *Foundations* concept, explains why rules and punitive consequences by themselves don't work, and discusses where *Foundations* fits in the context of other approaches to behavior support.

Task 2: Change Student Behavior With STOIC explains how to change behavior by manipulating five variables: Structure, Teach expectations, Observe and monitor, Interact positively, and Correct fluently.

Task 3: Decide How *Foundations* Will Be Structured in Your School suggests ways to organize the MTSS teams in your school so that both behavior and academics get the attention they need. It also describes how to form the Leadership Team that will guide the *Foundations* process.

Thank you for allowing us to join you in this construction process. We hope that your journey will be fun and deeply gratifying for you, your staff, and, of course, the ultimate beneficiaries—your students and their families.

All of the subsequent presentations include Action Steps that follow each task and provide guidance about how to archive your completed work. Because the first two tasks in this presentation mainly cover background information for the Leadership Team, they do not include Action Tasks. Task 3 is about getting started with the *Foundations* process and will end with some specific suggestions about how to use all six of the *Foundations* modules.

TASK 1

What is *Foundations*?

Foundations is about improving all aspects of behavior in your school, including climate, safety, discipline, behavior support plans, and student connectedness. Everything that is not directly related to academic instruction can fit within this broad view of behavior and discipline.

Although school personnel are under tremendous pressure for academic accountability—academic test scores are public knowledge, they are used to rank your school against other schools, and so on—you shouldn't limit your improvement efforts to academics. If you work only on increasing the pressure of academic instruction, you will plateau. For example, if some students do not feel safe, their worry about safety detracts from their focus on learning. If many students are emotionally disconnected from the school and their teachers, they are less likely to strive to do their best work.

Improving the climate, safety, and discipline aspects of your school along with academics can reduce barriers to academic success such as disruptions, disrespect, off-task behavior (students disengaged and wasting time), student apathy (doing the minimum to get by), bullying, cliques, and so on. These barriers prevent students from being able to achieve academically to the degree that they should. One of those barriers is that misbehavior can *drive your staff crazy*. When a student says, "You can't make me," staff can feel helpless and out of control, and they realize that the student is correct. They can't *make* a student do anything. Then it is too easy to react to the misbehavior with frustration and anger.

Any student who says, "You can't make me," wants to fight at that moment. And any effort to try to make the student do something at that moment gives her exactly what she wants. If you aren't careful, frustration can force you to put all of your energy into rules and punitive consequences.

Rules and consequences are necessary—in fact, we devote an entire module (Module D) to that topic. But rules and punitive consequences have severe limitations—mainly that, especially with your toughest kids, they just *don't work*.

Some percentage of the children in your school have developed to an art form what we call the *So What?* response. Despite your best efforts to apply consequences for misbehavior, some students will respond with some variation of this: "So keep me in from recess. Shoot, I haven't had a recess in 3 years. So what? Call my mommy. You think you've been hearing bad language from me? Wait until you get in touch with her. You'll hear yourself some language."

Consider in-school suspension: Is being confined in a small room with eight close friends really an effective corrective consequence?

And what is the ultimate consequence for out-of-control, we-can't-take-it-anymore, severe misbehavior? Out-of-school suspension. But for most kids, out-of-school suspension is a 3-day, no-accountability vacation. It is a reward, not a consequence.

Wouldn't it be nice to apply a consequence and hear the student say, "Thank you. I've learned my lesson. I will never misbehave again"? Well, you won't learn any magical consequences in *Foundations* (or in any other set of behavior support materials) that have that power. For every consequence that you can legally and ethically apply, there is the potential for students to respond, "So what? Big deal. Who cares?"

Consequences are not bad or wrong. They're a necessary part of a well-run behavior plan, but by themselves they have never worked to change the behavior of those students with the greatest social, emotional, and behavioral challenges. Consider a historical perspective: Graduation rates in 2010 were approximately 76%. (Depending on the source, graduation rates range from about 74% to 80%.) So with at least one out of four, perhaps one out of five children, consequences by themselves aren't enough to make them behave successfully within our system. In 1946, only 48% of students graduated, and in 1900, only 6% graduated. If consequences for misbehavior were so effective, wouldn't children be more successful in our system? Consequences just don't work. (We are not saying that punitive consequences were the reason students dropped out, merely that if consequences were effective, they would have solved every motivation or behavior problem, and that is clearly not the case.)

These historical graduation rates highlight another point—that you are expected to accomplish something that school personnel have never been asked to do before, and that is to successfully teach *every* student. Low graduation rates in 1946 and 1900 were not alarming because there were plenty of jobs on farms and in factories, but those jobs do not exist anymore.

Administrators feel tremendous pressure to avoid using out-of-school suspension because it's so associated with high dropout rates. And everyone feels pressure from federal and state regulations and district policies to reduce the dropout rate. To economically (and legally) survive in the culture of the United States, people need to earn at least a high school diploma, so you have to try to keep students in school who in earlier times would have left school for the workplace. Many of those students will exhibit challenging misbehavior, and simple consequences will not be enough to keep them productively engaged in school.

Make students your allies, not your adversaries.

Overreliance on reactive, punitive consequences can also set an adversarial tone, making students enemies, not allies, in your efforts to improve behavior. The following example is adapted from a Dallas newspaper article titled, "Which Prom Are You Going To?"

> *The most popular question at the high school this month won't be, "Who are you taking to the prom?" or "What are you wearing?" The most pressing question will be, 'Which prom are you going to?" Irked by a school rule that bars many students from the school-sponsored prom, a group of students is planning an alternative prom to compete with the official prom on April 24. The high school principal, to encourage classroom attendance, decreed that students who collected eight absences, excused or not, between November 10 and March 31 can't attend the prom.*

Now this school is doing something that we encourage in *Foundations*—they're using data to set a priority for improvement. Test scores were slipping, so they examined the excused and unexcused absences and attributed some of the low scores to these absent students and the instruction they missed. So the principal established the rule that if a student collects eight absences, he or she cannot attend the prom. But keep reading to see what can happen when this kind of punitive consequence is the only approach used to try to change behavior. The article continues:

> *That didn't sit well with seniors Ian and Peter, who launched the alternative-prom idea with the help of their friends. "It was a joke at first," said Ian, 17. But as more and more students couldn't attend the prom because they exceeded the eight-absence limit, Ian and Peter began to get serious about the party. By February, the party was too big to be held in a home, so they investigated renting a ballroom. By March, so many people had bought tickets to the alternative prom that they not only rented a ballroom, they hired a band—and it was a better band than the one hired for the school-sponsored prom.*
>
> *"Then we just said, let's do it. They can't stop us," added Peter, aged 18. "We're teenagers with time."*

They are teenagers with time. If you engage in behavioral practices that make students your adversaries, not your allies—if you just draw battle lines—you will lose. Because there are so many more of them than there are of you, and they have so much more time to think about the battle, you will lose the battle.

Shouldn't students just behave?

Use of consequences by themselves has significant limitations. They don't work and might make the student body our enemies, not our allies. At this point, some of you might be thinking: But shouldn't students just behave responsibly? Shouldn't they just shape up? Well, yes, of course. But by the same logic, shouldn't we also have clothes that wash themselves?

We wish for many things. In an ideal world, things would be different. Politicians would work together for the common good. Businesspeople would be ethical and make products that last. Airlines would accommodate every size of customer in comfortable seats.

But we have to accept reality. Some politicians do not get along, some businesspeople are unethical, and airline seats are not comfortable for all passengers. And not all students are highly motivated, have a great work ethic, can handle frustration, and are in a cooperative mood every single day. Theodore Roosevelt offered some timeless advice that applies here: "Do what you can, with what you have, where you are."

Rules and consequences by themselves are unlikely to change behavior. If they could, you would never have behavioral or motivational problems. But you can reduce behavioral problems and increase motivation by surrounding consequences with clear expectations, a safe, positive climate, and caring adults.

How does *Foundations* approach behavior support?

Another major concept to consider is how *Foundations* compares with other approaches to behavior support. There are three basic approaches:

Traditional: Traditional consists mainly of rules and consequences—that is, a code of conduct. The rules usually specify what *not* to do, leaving hidden many norms about what is expected.

Basic: Expectations for behavior are clearer in a good basic behavior support approach, especially for the common areas of the school. The school might have developed a behavior matrix—how to be safe, respectful, and responsible in each common area and with each schoolwide policy. The basic approach might have some broad-based goals and expectations.

Advanced: *Foundations* is an advanced behavior support approach. Expectations for behavior in common areas and with schoolwide policies are even clearer than what a simple matrix can provide; students are taught lessons about dress code, appropriate language, electronics policies, bullying policies, and so on. Each teacher also clarifies his or her unique classroom expectations—what does it take to be successful in

Room 9? Staff also have clear expectations about their roles in supporting schoolwide policies in common areas.

The traditional approach specifies broad rules—what you can't do—and a long menu of consequences that the system can legally and ethically provide when a rule is broken. It's not a bad approach, just not enough. Basic behavior support might recommend or require a positive reward system or token economy system. With *Foundations*, we emphasize careful supervision and monitoring along with lots of positive feedback to students. Staff build constructive relationships with students so that students want to be allies rather than adversaries, and they use schoolwide rewards when necessary (but many *Foundations* schools can get by without reward systems).

The traditional approach also features mainly negative, reactive responses to misbehavior. Staff hand students over to the administrator, who acts as the enforcer of the expectations. With basic behavior support, you reduce the reactive responses and blur the line between what the administrator is responsible for enforcing and what staff are responsible for. One weakness of many basic behavior support implementations is that the approach is viewed largely as a special education initiative. With *Foundations*, the goal is that all staff view schoolwide behavior management and support as a collective responsibility. Staff are encouraged to think, "We all have roles to play. We all need to be active problem solvers. We are all in this together."

Data are not a focus of the traditional approach. If data are considered at all, they are academic data. Basic behavior support emphasizes data analysis, but many schools focus on office discipline referrals and so the leadership team decides improvement priorities based mainly on office discipline referral data. The goal of *Foundations* schools is to use multiple data sources: surveys of staff, students, and parents; observations of common areas; office discipline referrals; and data from detention and other corrective strategies. The leadership team summarizes multiple data sources and shares the information with the entire staff so the staff collectively can determine which aspect of the school to work on next.

Traditional behavior support does not emphasize continuous improvement. With basic behavior support, the leadership team drives a continuous improvement process, but it may or may not have a formal focus on involving the entire staff. With *Foundations*, the leadership team strives to engage all staff members in all aspects of a formal continuous improvement process and unify the staff to create a sense of ownership in the process.

The traditional approach is very staff-centric and a bit arrogant: "We do what we do, and if it does not meet a student's needs, that's the administrator's problem." The administrator uses mainly out-of-school suspension to more or less get rid of challenging students. The basic behavior support approach is much more student-centric and attempts to meet the needs of students. A well-implemented *Foundations* school, however, is *altruistically* staff-centric: What can we do collectively, as a staff, to meet the needs of all of our students?

Understand the vision of *Foundations* through statements of staff beliefs.

To explain our vision of *Foundations*, we share some belief statements that form the basis of all of the modules in the program. These beliefs are ours—the authors of *Foundations* and all the *Safe & Civil Schools* trainers—and we hope over time they will become the basis of your own set of beliefs. One of the presentations in Module F is about developing staff beliefs and includes several examples from schools that have implemented *Foundations*. In the following example, the name *Foundations School* represents any school.

Staff Beliefs

The staff of *Foundations School* are committed to providing welcoming and supportive educational settings where all students can thrive.

We believe that staff behavior creates the climate of the school and a positive, welcoming, and inviting climate should be intentionally created and continuously maintained.

All student behaviors necessary for success need to be overtly and directly articulated and taught to mastery. If you want it, teach it.

We believe that all students should have equal access to good instruction and behavior support, regardless of their skills or backgrounds.

We believe clarity of expectations and consistency of enforcement are essential for all common areas and schoolwide policies.

We further believe that punitive and corrective techniques are necessary but have significant limitations. Misbehavior presents teaching opportunities.

And everyone, even students who make poor choices, should be treated with respect.

Foundations is a process, not a canned program.

An example of a canned program is when every teacher at an elementary school is required to use the same reinforcement system of placing a marble into a jar as a reward for meeting expectations. When the jar fills up, the class earns a prize. Marbles in a jar is a fine technique and is useful for some teachers, but not for others.

Here's another example of a canned approach: Every teacher writes students' names on the board as a consequence for misbehavior, with checkmarks for each additional infraction. If a student earns three checkmarks, the student is sent to the office. That strategy fits the style of some teachers; it doesn't fit the style of others. *Foundations* is not a canned program.

Foundations is also not a quasi-canned approach. Here's an example of a quasi-canned approach: You're told to clarify expectations, so you develop a matrix—how to be safe, respectful, and responsible in each common area. That's a fine procedure, but it might not be enough. You have to clarify your expectations *and* you have to teach age-appropriate lessons. Another example of a quasi-canned system is when you're told your school must reward appropriate behavior by handing out tokens that go into a lottery for a prize. That system is useful in some schools; it's not necessary in others.

If you are told you must use office discipline referrals as your main data source, that's a quasi-canned approach. Office referrals are a useful data source, but not the only one.

Foundations guides you in adapting evidence-based procedures to meet the needs of the students in your school as delivered by your staff. Every step of the way are examples of how schools have implemented components of the program. The CD for each module contains sample lessons, posters, and policies that schools have developed, forms they've used, and templates for action, all of which can make it easier for your team to adapt our recommendations to fit the needs of your school.

Here's a construction analogy: Most people (unless they are architects) who are designing a new home don't sit down with a blank sheet of paper. They buy a book of house plans, quickly look through the plans, and find one that is close to what they have in mind. They modify and tweak the plan until it is exactly what they want. Like a book of house plans, *Foundations* provides many examples of how different schools have constructed their safe, welcoming climate. Everything is framed within a multi-tiered system of continuous behavior support, with the greatest emphasis on universal.

The goal of this MTSS is that no student falls through the cracks of our system. A graduation rate of 75% to 80% means that one in four or one in five students are not graduating. That does not represent mere cracks in our system—students are falling into vast, gaping chasms. The goal of the *Foundations* continuum is to build a system that meets the behavioral and social-emotional needs of all students so that no students fall through the cracks.

Foundations describes a continuum with no chasms and even no cracks. Each section of this MTSS is covered by one of the *Foundations* modules. We hope that these modules will guide you in creating a system where all of your students have support, even those with the most challenging behaviors and the most significant emotional or social difficulties. Your school can be a great place for all students.

TASK 2

Change student behavior with STOIC

Some people tend to look at students with chronic misbehavior or a challenging class and think, "That's just the way the kids are. They'll never really change." We beg to differ. Behavior can be changed, and in this task we present a framework for working on change.

A theme that runs throughout *Foundations* is the concept that all adults should be problem solvers. Chronic misbehavior should be viewed as a puzzle to be solved (What variable can I manipulate that might have a positive impact?) rather than a threat that needs to be removed (This student is interfering with my ability to teach effectively).

The acronym STOIC provides guidance for fitting those puzzle pieces together, whether you're trying to change the behavior of an individual student, positively affect the collective behavior of a class, or improve the behavior of the whole student body in the cafeteria. STOIC provides a framework for designing comprehensive interventions. (Figure 1b on the next page shows a STOIC poster you can print from the Module A CD.)

STOIC stands for Structure, Teach, Observe, Interact positively, and Correct fluently. Whenever you face behavioral challenges, you can rearrange those five variables to try to solve the problem.

STRUCTURE FOR SUCCESS	**S**TOIC

We begin our explanation of the five STOIC variables with **Structure**. Structure is important in many areas of life. We use a restaurant analogy to illustrate:

Let's say you've heard about a great new restaurant, Chez Structure. You reserve a table for 7 p.m. Friday night. When you and your family arrive, the restaurant is crowded, but you are seated promptly by a polite hostess. The server is attentive and respectful, the atmosphere is pleasant, and the food arrives quickly and is delicious. You have a wonderful, memorable evening with your family.

Now compare Chez Structure with Chez Chaos, a restaurant that hasn't worked on structure. Imagine you arrive at Chez Chaos with the same dining companions. Assume for this thought exercise that the food is the same quality at both restaurants. The restaurant entrance is so crowded that you have difficulty reaching the door. As you work your way through the crowd, disgruntled people say, "Where are

Figure 1b *STOIC poster (A-15)*

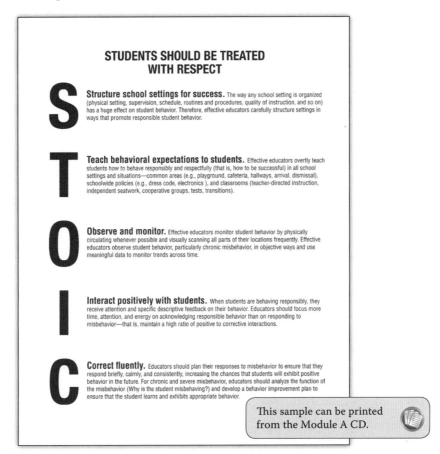

you going? We've been waiting for 30 minutes. Get in line." It seems that people with reservations have been waiting as long as those without reservations.

When you finally reach the maître d' station, the man doesn't even look up at you. You say, "Excuse me, my reservation is for 7." The maître d' replies, "It's 6:45. Your reservation is for 7. We'll get to you when we can." So you wait and are finally seated at 7:45. The tables are packed closely together, the server is slow and rude, and you have to almost shout to converse with your companions. When your meals arrive, they come with the incorrect side dishes. The food that should be hot is cold, and the food that should be cold is lukewarm. Throughout the evening, you notice that other diners are having an equally frustrating experience.

What would you remember as you reflect on these two experiences? For Chez Structure, you would probably remember the interactions with your family, the great food, and what a generally pleasant evening it was. You probably wouldn't think about how well the restaurant was structured (although it was), because people often don't notice when a setting is structured well. Good structure allows you to focus on important things—in a restaurant, that's good companionship and great food. When students reflect on their school experience, they should think of their healthy peer and adult relationships and the exciting and engaging curriculum that led to their mastery of skills.

What would you remember about Chez Chaos? Probably the bad structure: the wait, the noise, the rude treatment from staff, the slow service, the cold food. What do students remember about a badly structured school? The bullying, the rude treatment from other students, the unhelpful statements from staff, the long lunch lines.

How does the importance of structure apply to schools? We have visited middle schools of 750 students that schedule three lunch shifts of 250 students each. At School A, the cafeteria is structured so well that on a typical day no student spends more than 2 or 3 minutes in the lunch line. In School B—with the same number of students and the same lunch schedule—students might spend 20 minutes in the lunch line because the school hasn't analyzed and optimized their cafeteria procedures and setting. The students know that if you're not the first one out the door at the end of third period, you'll be at the end of a 20-minute lunch line. So getting to lunch becomes an aggressive, competitive event among the 250 students on each lunch shift, and that tension and excitement ratchets up the emotional tone of the school. Well-structured cafeteria procedures could mitigate those negative aspects of the lunch period.

Working on structure is a theme that runs through all *Foundations* modules. Module B, Presentation 2 focuses on structuring common areas and schoolwide policies.

TEACH EXPECTATIONS   STOIC

Another puzzle piece that you can manipulate to positively affect student behavior is the T of the STOIC acronym: **Teach expectations.** Explicitly teaching expectations for all common areas and schoolwide policies is important because your school embodies a complex and unique mix of policies, procedures, expectations, rituals, and traditions.

If you've been at your school for a long time, you might have grown so accustomed to the status quo that you assume that all elementary schools of 500 students organize lunch the way you do. But every school is unique. One of the goals of teaching expectations is to impart such clear, useful, interesting lessons about how to be successful that there are no hidden norms.

Here's an example of a potential hidden norm. I (Randy) grew up in the Pacific Northwest, where interactions between children and adults are relatively casual. Teachers and administrators are always in authority, but students rarely refer to the principal or a teacher as *ma'am* or *sir*. If I, as a teenager, had moved to one of the southern states where *sir* and *ma'am* are an expected part of the culture, and the principal said to me, "Good morning," I would have replied, "Good morning." If *sir* was a norm in that school, the administrator might have said to me, "Good morning, what?" I would have replied, without intending to be rude, "Good morning . . . ummm . . . how are you?" The administrator might think I was being a smart aleck, but I just didn't know that I was supposed to address an adult male as *sir*. It is not a norm in the Pacific Northwest. So think about the expectations for your school and whether there are any hidden norms related to any cultural groups. Make your expectations overt.

Teaching expectations is important in the classroom, too. Every teacher should realize that his or her classroom is an idiosyncratic mix of rituals, policies, and traditions. The longer a student has been in school, the less that student knows about your classroom management plan. Especially when students have been with several different teachers, each with unique classroom rituals and procedures, they need direct instruction on the expectations for the current classroom. Their previous teachers probably did things differently.

If you have traveled to a foreign country, you know how difficult everyday tasks can be when you don't know the expectations—Are tips expected? Where and how do you buy bus tickets? What hand signals should you avoid using? How do you say "Please" and "Thank you?" But the more you know ahead of time, the more people support you, and the more guidance you receive in how to fit within the norms of the country, the more comfortable, pleasant, and fun your travels are. Similarly, the more support and guidance students have about behavioral expectations, the better their school experience will be. Students should never have to guess what we want from them. Teaching expectations is absolutely critical. This theme runs throughout the *Foundations* modules. Module B, Presentation 3 presents detailed information about teaching expectations for common areas and schoolwide policies.

OBSERVE AND MONITOR   ST**O**IC

The O in STOIC stands for **Observe**—that is, supervise and monitor. Here's an analogy: On a highway with little traffic, no ice or snow, and no visible state trooper, most people exceed the speed limit. In a 65-mph zone, people tend to have a default speed—the speed they are comfortable driving and they think they can get away with. For some, it's 72 mph; for others, it might be 80 mph. But if a state trooper's car appears on the horizon, almost everyone slows down to the speed limit. The act of being observed by someone in authority prompts people to follow the rules.

Here's another analogy: For most people, their houses are always cleanest immediately before company arrives. This axiom has nothing to do with rules or consequences—when people you like and respect are observing you, you want to put your best foot forward.

So it's essential that all physical locations of your campus are supervised (to reduce rule breaking, similar to speeding on the highway) and that staff build positive relationships with students (so students want to "keep their houses clean"). Most people, when observed by someone in authority, want to follow the rules more closely. Any unsupervised areas of your school—a hallway, a landing, a portion of the playground—are areas where your most problematic students are likely to go to exhibit behavior such as bullying, harassment, and illegal activities. The act of being observed prompts most people to follow the rules and try to behave responsibly.

Having adults present isn't always enough—supervising adults must be attentive, and there must be enough of them. If three playground supervisors are standing together talking to each other, nobody's watching the children. If the supervision is not *active*, many students will push the limits, just like adults do when there's no state trooper on the highway. In high schools that we visit, there are often not enough adults in the hallways. The more adults present in common areas, the fewer the problems that occur. No areas of the school should be perceived by students as adult-free no-man's-land. We address the topic of supervising common areas and schoolwide policies in detail in Module B, Presentations 4, 5, and 6.

INTERACT POSITIVELY   STOIC

The I in STOIC stands for **Interact positively**. It's wonderful when the playground supervisors are circulating through the setting and plenty of adults are in the hallway, but even that is not enough—those adults need to provide both contingent and noncontingent positive attention to students and build relationships with them.

Imagine our restaurant, Chez Chaos, again. This time the structure is great, but every staff member is surly, rude, and brusque. Even though the food is delicious and the service is efficient, your unpleasant interactions with the staff overshadow and tarnish the good aspects of your evening. In school, students should experience well-structured classrooms and schoolwide procedures, clear expectations, and adequate supervision, but they also need to hear from staff comments such as:

- Good morning! It's nice to see you today.
- Hey, Charlie, I like your painting that's on exhibit in the library.
- Leticia, let me know if you need any help with the social studies assignment.
- Raul, I heard you set a new school record at the swim meet. Congratulations!

These interactions build relationships, model appropriate social behavior, and tell students that you notice them and enjoy talking with them. So while you're supervising, you can provide meaningful, positive feedback and supportive, friendly interactions to make every child, even the shyest, quietest child, feel valued. Module B, Presentations 4 and 6 suggest appropriate ways to interact with students, and Module C, Presentation 3 details strategies for providing lots of positive interactions.

Misbehavior will occur, despite good structure, effective teaching of clear expectations, active supervision, and positive interactions with students. So the C in STOIC represents **Correct fluently**. There's an art to correcting well, and the art lies in the fluency of the correction—corrections need to be given calmly, consistently, immediately, briefly, and respectfully. The corrective technique that you use for any given misbehavior is less important than doing *something* to correct the misbehavior in the earliest stage, and doing so consistently and respectfully.

Let's revisit the highway analogy. Imagine that your state has the budget to post state troopers at every milepost along the highway. The troopers pull over every car that exceeds the speed limit. They do not issue fines, but just warn the drivers. You are driving 66 mph in a 65 mph zone, so you are stopped and warned. Two miles later, you are stopped and warned again for driving 65.5 mph. You soon realize that you'll get to your destination much faster by driving the speed limit than by exceeding the speed limit and getting stopped every mile or so. It is not the severity of the correction—you don't have to pay a fine or do anything other than listen to the trooper's warning—that convinces you to follow the rule; it's the *certainty* that you will be corrected every time you drive faster than the speed limit. Module D specifically addresses correction; we recommend adopting instructional approaches to responding to misbehavior that are implemented calmly and consistently by all staff.

Overcome obstacles to improving behavior.

STOIC is a tool that can make changing behavior simple. Structure, Teach, Observe, Interact positively, Correct fluently. *Foundations* guides you in the relentless manipulation of those five puzzle pieces to attain the best possible result. But if changing behavior is conceptually so simple, why aren't most schools doing it? Well, you are likely to encounter some significant obstacles to improving behavior. Throughout *Foundations,* we suggest how to overcome these obstacles.

Obstacle: Overdependence on punitive or reactive techniques

When you are frustrated by students' behavior, it's easy to think the answer is just more and increasingly severe corrective consequences. As we described in Task 1, however, consequences alone don't work. You have to alter your mindset to think about affecting behavior by changing the structure of settings, teaching more effectively, supervising more actively, providing better positive feedback, and building relationships so students *want* to behave appropriately, in addition to correcting fluently.

Obstacle: Overdependence on role-bound authority

Wouldn't it be nice if teachers could get students to behave by saying, "Do this because I'm the teacher and I say you have to do it"? Some staff hang on to this concept of role-bound authority, but it's increasingly unlikely that students will comply just because an authority figure tells them to do so. An extension of role-bound authority is the teacher who says, "If you don't do it for me, I'm sending you to the principal."

Think back to your student days. If you were sent to the principal's office, it was a horrible experience, not so much because of the principal's response but because of how your family reacted. You parents questioned you about your behavior and might have grounded you for a time or assigned a consequence such as no television. But the most painful consequence was knowing you had disappointed your parents. In addition, you understood the hierarchy of school—the principal is at the top, followed by teachers and other staff, with you at the bottom.

Consider the at-risk child's perception of the same situation. We are all at the same level—the teacher, the student, and the principal. Getting sent to the office is not a vertical move up the hierarchy— it's a lateral move, a change of scenery. It's a chance to sit in the most fast-paced, active environment known to schoolchildren, the front office. A kindergarten student who is regularly sent to the office probably thinks that's just how school works: "I start out in this room, and then later in the morning I go to a different room and talk to the principal—that's my schedule." Role-bound authority works only when students understand the symbolism of a hierarchy, and many at-risk students don't.

*E*xample From the Field

> A principal from an elementary school in Texas told us a story that surely falls into the category of "You can't make this stuff up."
>
> The principal had just welcomed a new kindergarten student to the school and had taken him to the classroom, where the teacher began to introduce the student to the classroom routines. A half hour later, the teacher called and said the student was extremely disruptive and out of control. The teacher took the other students into the hallway, and the principal returned to the classroom. The student did not respond to any type of verbal instruction or de-escalation technique, so finally the principal gently captured him and walked him down to the office, with the student screaming the whole way. The principal waited for the student to calm down, then he leaned over a bit to talk to the child. The child grabbed the man's necktie and began to swing on it as though it were a tire swing! As he ended the story, the principal said, "This kid not only didn't

understand role-bound authority, he thought I was playground equipment, for goodness' sake!"

Role-bound authority is great when students recognize it, but when they don't, we can't overly depend on it.   —R.S.

Obstacle: Tendency to blame others

A tendency to blame others is also a potential stumbling block to changing behavior. "If the special education staff (or principal, paraprofessional, parents, and so on) would just do this . . ." That kind of thinking is counterproductive. Everybody has to pull together. If everyone does a little, no one has to do a lot. Conversely, if everyone does *not* pitch in to do a little, no person, team, or subgroup of staff can make up for a staff body that is not consistent or unified.

Obstacle: Overdependence on emotional intensity

Some staff may depend on emotional intensity to get their messages across to misbehaving students. When the usual consequences for misbehavior don't work— the student's attitude is "So what? Big deal. You can't make me"—some staff think injecting emotion into the situation will get the student to behave. But emotional intensity can escalate situations, and when a child is seeking power, an adult's emotional response is probably reinforcing.

Obstacle: Tendency to do it the way it has always been done

Another potential obstacle to improving students' behavior is the tendency for staff to resist change—"We've always done it this way." If you're going to work on, for example, dismissal, try to visit at least five other schools of your size that have about the same number of buses you have. Observe dismissal for about 10 minutes at those schools, and you'll get some great ideas for structuring dismissal. Some staff think that the way your school structures dismissal is the way all schools structure dismissal, but of course it's not. Each school is unique.

Obstacle: Lack of consistency and unity among staff

When staff are not united and consistent in how they teach and enforce expectations and correct misbehavior, they cannot expect student behavior to improve substantially. An example that applies to any schoolwide policy or procedure is that you are better off with no dress code at all than a dress code enforced by only seven out of ten of your staff members.

Divisions among staff can contribute to the tendency to blame others. We have seen staff meetings where male and female teachers sit on opposite sides of the room and communicate very little with the other group. You have to work at breaking down those kinds of divisions because they affect the consistency with which staff teach expectations, respond to misbehavior, and supervise common areas. When staff communicate with each other, they can understand the pressures and concerns of all staff roles. They will be less likely to blame others and more likely to actively participate in and contribute to creating a positive climate and consistent enforcement of expectations.

Solve the puzzle of misbehavior with STOIC.

Behavior can be changed by continually using and manipulating these five conceptually simple principles: **Structure, Teach, Observe, Interact positively, Correct fluently**. It can be difficult for individual staff members to implement these principles regularly, and it can be even more difficult for the staff as a whole to implement them. But it can be done. When all staff begin to view misbehavior as a puzzle rather than a threat, and when they relentlessly and collectively manipulate the STOIC pieces of this puzzle, they can change behavior. We have seen it. You as a staff can do it. In the next task, we'll talk about how to get started.

TASK 3

Decide how *Foundations* will be structured in your school

In this task, we discuss how to begin using the *Foundations* materials. You need to make two major decisions before you get too far into the process. First, determine how this behavior improvement process fits within your academic tiered systems of support or response to intervetion (RTI). What are the relationships between behavior and academics? Second, form your *Foundations* leadership team and ensure that all staff are represented. These two actions are the focus of this task.

Determine how *Foundations* fits within your academic tiered systems of support or RTI.

Most schools in most states are using either response to intervention or response to instruction (RTI) or multi-tiered systems of support (MTSS) as their framework for school improvement efforts. These processes are based on a continuum of universal, targeted, and intensive support. In many states the emphasis has been entirely on the academic side, and schools are just beginning to apply RTI and MTSS to behavior. It is essential to understand that academics and behavior are integrally related—you can't have one without the other, and one is not more important than the other. So think about how to organize your school politically so that the entire staff can work concurrently on both academics (instruction, curriculum, and assessment) and behavior (safety, climate, and discipline).

Single MTSS team. One possible organizational structure is a single MTSS (or RTI) team that unifies the staff and guides them in both academic and behavioral improvements (see Figure 1c). The single MTSS team structure works best in very small schools of about 300 or fewer students. When one team tries to work on both academics and behavior in larger schools, one of those areas tends to suffer. For example, if the team is already good at optimizing the academic side of the school, the behavior side might not get as much attention—people tend to work on what they already do well. If you already have a leadership team that functions well, that team can guide the *Foundations* processes. (Throughout *Foundations* we refer to the leadership team as the Foundations Team, but you may call it the MTSS Team, the RTI Team, the School Improvement Committee, or any other appropriate name.)

We recommend two other team structure models instead of the single-team structure (unless you don't have enough personnel for more than one team).

Figure 1c   *Single-team structure for small schools (fewer than 300 students)*

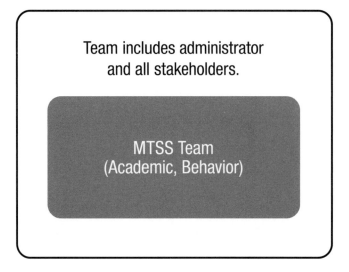

Two separate MTSS teams. You might form two separate but interrelated teams—one MTSS team for academic and one MTSS team for behavior (see Figure 1d). The instructional leader of the school—that is, the principal or another top administrator—serves on both teams.

Figure 1d   *Team organization for a medium school (300–800 students, principal, may or may not have an assistant principal)*

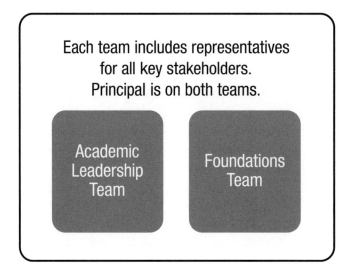

One large urban district that implemented *Foundations* took the extra step of requiring team membership for all principals; they said that building principals *must* be on the MTSS academic and behavior teams, although principals can delegate the leadership positions for other teams and committees. This district also requires a school counselor (or a staff member with a similar role) to be on both teams. Other team members serve on only one team.

One of the most precious commodities for the teams is time to talk to the whole staff at staff meetings, to conduct inservice for staff on early-release days, and to work with staff during professional development days. When the administrator is on both the academic and behavior teams, he or she can ensure that both sides get the time they need with staff and that the side that needs more attention at that moment is prioritized. Sometimes friendly competition develops between the teams, adding some fun, humor, and motivation to the work. This team structure has been very effective for the schools we've worked with.

One MTSS team with two separate task forces. Another organizational structure we recommend consists of one large MTSS team in which some members are on a behavior task force and some members are on an academic task force (see Figure 1e). The meeting schedule might be something like this: The academic and behavior teams meet separately each week for 3 weeks, then everyone meets together during the fourth week to talk about any issues with coordinating the two sides of the work.

Figure 1e   *Team organization for a large school (800 or more students, principal, and two or more assistant principals)*

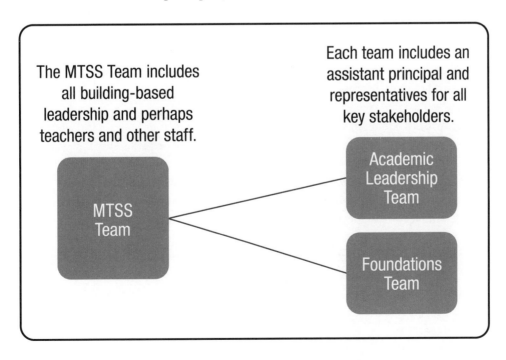

The MTSS Team includes all building-based leadership and perhaps teachers and other staff.

Each team includes an assistant principal and representatives for all key stakeholders.

MTSS Team

Academic Leadership Team

Foundations Team

Administrators, probably with staff input, can decide which organizational structure—single team, separate behavior and academic teams, or one team that comprises both behavior and academic teams that work largely independently—will work best for their school or district.

Regardless of the structure you choose, the key point is that behavior and academics are the chicken and egg of school improvement. You need to ensure that academic improvement and behavior improvement are integrated, and determining the make-up of school improvement teams is an essential step.

Most state departments of education and regional service centers can provide assistance in integrating academic and behavioral aspects of MTSS. For classroom teachers, these two sides truly are inseparable. The best classroom teachers pair great academic instruction with great behavior management, resulting in students who are highly motivated to succeed academically.

Form your *Foundations* leadership team and ensure that all staff are represented.

The second major decision you need to make before actively implementing *Foundations* is how to form your Foundations Team, the group that will guide these processes. The team will construct the entire base of behavior support as described in Module A. We recommend the following procedure:

- **Set up Foundations Team.** The administrator and several teacher leaders, perhaps your current MTSS leadership team, and possibly the entire staff work through the process of setting up the Foundations Team by reviewing Module A, Presentation 2, especially the Introduction and Task 1, which is all about who should be on the team, how to form the team, and how the team formally represents the staff.

  How does the team represent the staff? Every staff member should know which team member they can talk to about behavior problems. If students have been throwing paper towels on the floors in the restrooms, the custodians should be able to talk directly to their representative about re-teaching restroom expectations. If the cafeteria lines have been getting long, the food service staff should be able to talk to their representative about restructuring lines. If there's a widespread problem with students not bringing homework to class, classroom teachers can talk to their representatives about working on the problem. So when forming the Foundations Team, remember that the team needs to communicate with the entire staff and that every staff member should feel connected to the team.

- **Work through the rest of Module A.** Once the Foundations Team is formed, team members work through Module A, Presentation 3, which is about the continuous Improvement Cycle; Module A, Presentation 4, which is about using data to drive the Improvement Cycle; and Module A, Presentation 5, which discusses how the team can ensure that the entire staff is involved in these processes.

- **Begin work on common areas and schoolwide considerations (Module B).** Once your team processes are solidified and you have a plan to collect data, you'll probably begin Module B, which is about managing behavior in common areas and related to schoolwide policies. The Foundations Team involves the entire staff in identifying all of the common areas and schoolwide policies and ranking them: What area or policy needs improvement most urgently? What is the next most urgent area or policy? What does the data show regarding common areas or schoolwide policies that have problems? The team responds to staff interest about what the priorities are for improvement and in what order they should be addressed.

- **Work through the other Foundations modules.** You will probably work through them in order, but not necessarily. Data will drive these processes:

  - Module C: *Conscious Construction of an Inviting School Climate*
  - Module D: *Responding to Misbehavior—An Instructional Approach*
  - Module E: *Improving Safety, Managing Conflict, and Reducing Bullying*
  - Module F: *Establishing and Sustaining a Continuum of Behavior Support*

Completing all the modules will take a minimum of 2 years and perhaps more likely 3, 4, or even 5 years—and even then the work is not really finished. You will continually evaluate efficacy and identify and close gaps in meeting student needs for safety, school connectedness, and motivation.

If you are just starting *Foundations*, during the first year you need to form the team, collect and analyze data, and select one or more common areas or schoolwide policies as your first priority. If you are relatively conservative in how much you choose to do, you will work on one common area and develop Guidelines for Success, three to five rules that represent character traits students should aspire to. During the second year, you will probably work on one or more common areas or schoolwide policies, define responses to misbehavior, and begin working on classroom management. During Years 3, 4, and 5, you will move on to some of the other modules.

If you have the resources and time to be a little more ambitious, you might work on two or three common areas, one or two schoolwide policies, Guidelines for Success, responding to misbehavior, and classroom management during the first year.

During the second year, you might finish and archive all of your common area and schoolwide policies and work through the modules on individual students, bullying prevention, and so on.

We have seen schools have great success with the conservative approach, spreading the content out over 3, 4, or 5 years. We've also seen schools have equally great success with an ambitious approach, instituting all of this content within 2 years. There is no one right way to do this work and no correct pace other than steady, continuous improvement that involves the entire staff.

If you've already worked through some of the processes we suggest, either through *Foundations* or Positive Behavioral Interventions and Supports (PBIS), you might want to use the Foundations Implementation Rubric and Summary (see Appendix A), which you can print from the Module A CD. (It's also discussed in Module F, Presentation 7.) This rubric guides you through descriptions of all of the key content in *Foundations* so that you can identify the status of each piece in your school, from Preparing to In Place.

The completed rubric allows you to identify those modules with the most useful and timely information as you continue the process of constructing behavior support in your school. As you complete the rubric, err on the side of being critical of your implementation rather than congratulatory. Teams that do not analyze their implementation very deeply tend to give themselves higher scores than they probably should, thinking that their work on a rubric item is fully in place when it is not.

We suggest that you work through the Foundations Implementation Rubric by having individual team members rate the items for Module A, then as a team discuss your individual responses and come to a group consensus for all Module A items. Then go through the same steps for the sections of the rubric that correspond to Modules B, C, D, E, and F. The Foundations Rubric Summary is a one-page form you can use to summarize and compare all your findings.

For any sections that have low scores for all items, start working on the corresponding module as suggested in the introduction to that module. Once you have covered all of the content of this continuum and your Foundations Implementation Rubric ratings are largely In Place, consider establishing a maintenance schedule. For example, review and work on Modules A and B during the first year of maintenance, Modules C and D during the second year, and Modules E and F during the third year.

Task 3 Action Steps & Evidence of Implementation

Action Steps	Evidence of Implementation
1. Determine how *Foundations* fits within your academic tiered systems of support or RTI. Determine the team structure: • Single team for both academics and behavior • Separate behavior and academic teams with the administrator serving on both • One team that comprises behavior and academic task forces that for the most part work independently	Foundations Process: Team Composition
2. Set up a process for forming your Foundations Team. Consider having the entire staff or a current leadership group view Module A, Presentation 2, Introduction and Task 1 to learn about forming the team.	Foundations Process: Team Composition

Team Processes

DOCUMENTS*

- Foundations continuum of behavior support (A-10)
- Sample record of team composition and representation (A-16)
- Sample team purpose statement (A-17)
- The CRUISE Team PowerPoint presentation (A-19)
- Sample team logo and team purpose statement (A-18)
- Foundations Team Meeting: Agenda and Minutes (A-03a, b, c); Three versions available
- Sample documentation of meeting rules (A-20)
- Are You an Effective Team Builder? form (A-04)

* All documents listed are available on the CD. Other documents that are not shown in this presentation are also available on the CD (see Appendix C for a complete list).

INTRODUCTION

Presentation 2 focuses on the team that will guide all aspects of the *Foundations* process. Let's review some of the key concepts from Presentation 1:

- *Foundations* is a data-driven process for improving all aspects of behavior: discipline, motivation, safety, climate, student connectedness and engagement with the school, bullying, and so on.

- One of the major goals is to create and sustain a continuum of positive behavior support at the schoolwide, classroom, and individual student levels to ensure that your school is a great place for ALL students—talented high achievers, students with academic or emotional-behavioral challenges, and average students. The visual in Figure 2a illustrates this continuum.

- Staff consistency is essential to achieving this continuum. All staff members must be on the same page in regard to implementing all aspects of positive behavior support.

- Continuous improvement is essential and should become part of the school culture. You are never truly done with your improvement efforts. Your school is good now; it should be better next year and even better the year after that.

- The Foundations Team is key to creating and sustaining this continually improving continuum of behavior support.

Why is the leadership team critical? One of the most important broad goals of the team is to develop consistency among all staff members about expectations, corrections, and supervision. Students need consistent information about every school policy and procedure. If only seven out of ten staff members enforce the dress code, students get cloudy information about what is and isn't allowed and even about whether there are consequences for disregarding the rules. The culture and climate of the school are defined by the daily actions of the staff, so actions need to be consistent and unified in positive ways that communicate high expectations to the students. *Foundations* processes increase consistency.

Consistency can be difficult to achieve. Every staff member is so busy that taking the time to ensure that everyone is on the same page can seem impossible. When 50 or more staff members are expected to get together and make decisions, it might take three full staff meetings to resolve a simple issue such as whether hats should be allowed in the building. With *Foundations*, the decision-making process becomes much more efficient because the Foundations Team members represent all staff members at team meetings. This presentation, Team Processes, presents information on how to form and maintain a Foundations Team that is highly effective.

Figure 2a *The Foundations continuum of behavior support (A-10)*

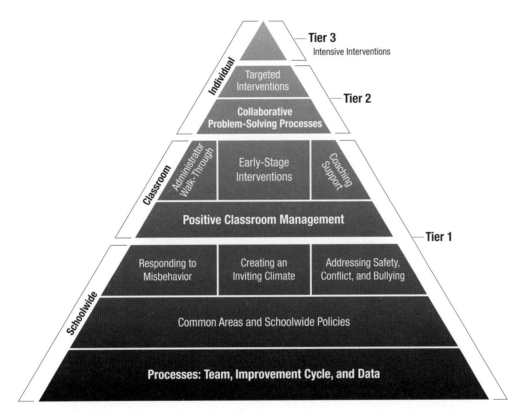

It's important to understand that the team will never develop final policies on its own. You want the staff to buy in to *Foundations*, and an element of that buy-in is that the entire staff is always involved in the improvement process. The team continually seeks staff opinions and recommendations so that everyone feels ownership over the work. The Improvement Cycle drives that process, and the team is responsible for maintaining the cycle. The team undertakes the following tasks:

- Collects, analyzes, and summarizes data from multiple sources and presents them to staff.

- Guides the staff in prioritizing areas for improvement—common areas, school policies, and specific issues such as bullying.

- Guides the development of revision proposals for the priorities.

- Ensures that all staff have a voice in the revision process and a vote in the adoption process.

- Monitors the implementation of adopted policies.

The team should also guide school improvement related to behavior (motivation, connectedness, safety, and discipline), maintain effective policies and procedures, and become the cultural historians of the effective policies and procedures—creating longitudinal progress that is sustained for years.

Task 1: Assemble the Foundations Team explains how to determine the optimal staff membership for the team and decide whether to include student, family, community, and social agency representatives. It also describes how each school group selects a representative to serve on the Foundations Team.

Task 2: Actively Engage the Staff discusses the importance of choosing a team name, summarizing and conveying to staff the purpose of the team, and making the team highly visible in the school.

Task 3: Establish Team Roles and Plan Effective Team Meetings describes how to identify team roles and responsibilities and establish a regular meeting schedule and ground rules for meetings. Using a team coach and participating in a partner school program are also discussed.

Task 4: Sustain an Effective Team suggests ways to ensure that the Foundations Team continues to be a leadership force in your school. The team should guide and maintain the culture of the school by assisting with the development of the School Improvement Plan, archiving all of the team's work, orienting new staff and new team members to the school culture, and effectively representing staff members so they view the *Foundations* process positively rather than feel encumbered by it. We also recommend a self-assessment exercise for team members. Finally, we list some issues that can negatively affect the Foundations implementation so you can avoid them or, if they are present in your school, take steps to reverse their effect.

Ongoing progress in *Foundations* depends on a fully functioning team that unifies and guides the staff in the continuous improvement of safety, climate, behavior, and discipline. All staff members should feel a vested interest in making the team work. The team will save staff time and improve consistency, which will improve the behavior and motivation of students. Better student behavior will improve everyone's senses of unity, collegiality, and efficacy in meeting the needs of students and families.

TASK 1

Assemble the Foundations Team

In this task, you will learn how to determine optimal staff membership for the team and decide whether to include student, family, community, and/or social agency representatives. The task also describes how groups will select their representatives to serve on the Foundations Team.

Establish goals.

As you prepare to assemble the Foundations Team, keep the following goals in mind:

- Every staff member should be represented by a specific team member. Teachers, specialists, paraprofessionals, cafeteria workers, custodians, bus drivers—staff in all categories need to be represented on the Foundations Team.

- Students, parents/families, the community, and social agencies should be represented, as appropriate.

- The Foundations Team should be large enough to ensure adequate representation for all staff but small enough that members can work efficiently together to accomplish tasks. Six to nine members are probably optimal for an effective Foundations Team.

- Each team member should have a designated backup person. When a team member cannot attend meetings, his or her backup person should attend and convey information between the staff member and the team.

Consider options for forming teams.

You may wish to use an existing team as the basis for your Foundations Team. If your school has already established a Disciplinary Committee or School Safety Team, for example, you can modify the team to ensure adequate representation of all staff members and nonstaff stakeholders. Or you may wish to establish a new team. Either way, the Foundations Team must be perceived as the preeminent behavioral team in the school, and the staff groups should be able to select their representatives.

Understand the principal's role.

The principal must be actively engaged with the Foundations Team and the *Foundations* process. Either the principal or an assistant principal may lead an improvement initiative on a campus and actively participate as a team member, but it should be just one person—that is, multiple administrators should not alternate attending meetings. If the assistant principal undertakes this role, the principal must actively support the effort and communicate to the entire staff the importance of the team's work. The principal must also help ensure that any agreed-upon policies and procedures are implemented with fidelity. The staff has to see that the principal is directly engaged in the project or the chance that some staff members will not follow through with implementing the improvements increases dramatically. In every example of a great *Safe & Civil Schools* implementation in a large urban school, the principal has actively and vocally supported all efforts.

Follow team membership recommendations.

The Foundations Team must include at least one building-based administrator (perhaps an assistant principal) and representatives for all certified and noncertified staff—teachers, paraprofessionals, specialists, custodians, cafeteria staff, and security. The team oversees processes related to disciplinary referrals and the implementation of school and district policies; administrators have the most information about these issues and must be present for any discussion.

Active Administrators

Here's an example of why it is so vital that administrators be an active part of the Foundations Team. Let's say that several staff members object to a particular procedure implemented in the school. Their representatives on the Foundations Team add this item to the agenda for a team meeting. When the item comes up for discussion, the administrator on the team states, "This procedure is actually defined by school board policy, and we cannot change it at the building level without violating board policy. I can get a copy of that policy for you to share with concerned staff. If they still have concerns after reading the policy, we can discuss how to determine the opinion of the rest of the staff. If there is enough concern and justification, we can ask the superintendent whether she thinks it is appropriate to go to the board to recommend a change. How can we share the policy and determine level of staff concern?" Team members set a process and timeline for these actions.

Now let's imagine what might happen with no administrator on the team. The item comes up for discussion at the team meeting, and team members end up spending three 30-minute meetings discussing the issue and developing recommendations to present at a staff meeting. During the presentation at the staff meeting, the administrator says, "This procedure is actually defined by school board policy, and we cannot change it at the building level without violating board policy. There is a chain of command for exploring such issues, and any concerns need to go through my office first." This situation not only risks undercutting the authority of the team, it may even embarrass the team members who were presenting the issue to the staff. It also makes the team feel like they have wasted 3 weeks' worth of work.

In both cases, the administrator needed to clarify board policy and define a process for addressing the concerns. The important point here is that when an administrator is present at team meetings, he or she can clarify the process right away in a manner that involves and empowers the team as a representative body for the entire staff.

Representation on the team must mirror the population of the staff as closely as possible. Because general education teachers make up the largest percentage of the staff, the team must include an adequate number of them. In a high school, representation of general education teachers may be organized by departments, grade levels, teachers with common planning periods, or professional learning communities, depending on how the lines of organization and communication work within the school. At least one special education teacher should represent the special education staff. Ensure that noncertified teaching staff (paraprofessionals) have at least one representative.

Once representation of teaching staff is mapped out, ensure that every member of the school staff is directly connected to a member of the team. For example, someone on the team must directly represent the custodial staff, even if that person is not a custodian. Someone must represent counseling staff, clerical staff, food service staff, and so on. To limit the team to nine members, some members will have to represent multiple groups. If possible, a representative of the Parent-Teacher Association (or a designee) should be on the team. Figure 2b on the next page shows examples of Foundations Team configurations for high school and K–8. Keep in mind that these are only examples and that each school should form the team based on lines of communication, influence, and affiliation.

Select team members.

First, form some logical groupings of staff, such as those shown in Figure 2b. For example, you might group teachers in grades 6–8 with clerical staff, teachers in grades 3–5 with counseling staff, and so on. When you form your groups, consider how staff naturally interact with each other. For example, in some schools, teachers of similar

Figure 2b *Sample Foundations Team member organization for high school and K–8*

Sample high school Foundations Team

Team member	Who member represents
Principal	Administrative team
9th-grade teacher	9th-grade teachers and clerical staff
10th-grade teacher	10th-grade teachers and paraprofessionals
11th-grade teacher	11th-grade staff, parent advisory groups, PTA, and counseling staff
12th-grade teacher	12th-grade staff, student council, and all other student groups
Special education teacher	Special education staff, psychologist, social worker, and mental health liaison
Custodian	Custodial and food service staff
Campus security officer	Campus security, nursing, and school volunteers

Sample K–8 Foundations Team

Team member	Who member represents
Principal	Administrative team
7th-grade teacher	6th-, 7th-, and 8th-grade teachers and clerical staff
3rd-grade teacher	3rd-, 4th-, and 5th-grade teachers and counseling staff
1st-grade teacher	Pre-K, kindergarten, and 1st- and 2nd-grade teachers; parent advisory groups; PTA; and school volunteers
Special education teacher	Special education staff, school psychologist, social worker, mental health liaison, and nurse
Custodian	All noncertified staff (paraprofessionals, custodial staff, and food service staff)

student age groups might spend time with each other. In other schools, staff might socialize by the floor or wing they work in, or by learning groups. Capitalize on the way staff have organized themselves to make it easier for their representative team member to communicate with them.

Next, have each group select someone to represent them on the Foundations Team. The representative will receive ongoing training in *Foundations* and MTSS and will be responsible for conveying that information to his or her constituents, so the group should select someone who is respected and influential—someone they can learn from. A staff member who has trouble with behavior management is not a good choice—he or she might reduce the effectiveness of the whole team and perhaps even create greater divisions among staff instead of serving as a unifying force.

Note that no parents or students are on the team, but they are represented by team members. Sometimes the team may need to discuss important internal staff business, such as staff morale or staff inconsistency in implementing a particular policy, but frank discussions about important business (which could be viewed as airing dirty laundry) are difficult when parents or students are present. Though we support actively involving students and parents in many specific MTSS activities (collecting and analyzing data, selecting priorities for improvement, and serving on task forces to develop new policies, for example), team members need the freedom to have frank, open, and even occasionally contentious discussions about internal staff issues.

Nonstaff representatives may serve on separate advisory panels or on an as-needed basis. Consider including students, parents/families, community representatives, and social agency representatives. Students, especially at the secondary level, can often contribute important information that the faculty might be unaware of.

Parent/community advisory panels and student advisory panels do not need to meet as often as the core Foundations Team, but they should be convened when their guidance would help shape or inform important policies. Alternatively, you can convene special task forces to address specific issues. For example, if morning arrival is chaotic and potentially unsafe, you might convene a task force that includes parents, district safety representatives, and even local police (who are aware of larger traffic issues) to develop a revision to morning arrival procedures that is acceptable to all interested parties. When the new procedures are fully operational and morning arrival is working well for both staff and parents, the task force can disband.

Clarify team members' terms.

Clearly specify how long team members are expected to serve. We suggest the following guidelines to ensure continuity.

- The administrator should be a permanent team member.

- Other team members might serve limited terms of 2 or 3 years to create stability, but no longer than 3 years to increase the level of staff participation. If you are forming your first team, ensure that all the members' terms don't expire at the same time—some members might serve for 1 year, some for 2, and some for 3.

- When team members are rotating, allow some overlap so that the departing members and the new members both attend team meetings for a time. Have the school groups select new team members in the spring so they can be mentored for a couple of months and be ready to take on full responsibilities in the fall.

- If possible, include people on the team who represent a range of roles in the school and a range of attitudes toward *Foundations*. Someone with a little skepticism might provide welcome balance to the very enthusiastic team members.

> ## ❧ FOUNDATIONS RECOMMENDATION ☙
>
> *Avoid rotating team membership between school years. Instead of selecting new members in August or September when the new school year is beginning, select them in the spring. Then the departing team member can mentor his or her replacement for a month or two so that the new member is ready to take on full responsibilities as soon as school starts in the fall.*

Orient new team members.

When staff members join the team, conduct at least one orientation session to ensure that they understand the Improvement Cycle and the current priorities for behavioral improvement. Also discuss past priorities for improvement to give new team members a sense of the direction in which school policies are moving.

Before the orientation session, have the new team members read and/or view the following. Review and discuss during the orientation session.

- Module A, Presentation 1, "Foundations: A Multi-Tiered System of Behavior Support"
- Module A, Presentation 3, "The Improvement Cycle"
- Module A, Presentation 4, "Data-Driven Processes" (at least the introduction)

Task 1 Action Steps & Evidence of Implementation

Action Steps	Evidence of Implementation
1. Decide whether your Foundations Team will be formed by modifying an existing team or by establishing a new team. 2. Determine the optimal staff membership for your team. Identify the number of team members and the groups that will be represented. 3. Decide whether (and how) to include student, family, community, and/or social agency representatives on your team. 4. Have groups select their representatives and form your Foundations Team. 5. Clarify the length of members' terms and how new team members will be selected and oriented to the team. 6. Give each team member a list of the people he or she represents and ensure that all staff members know who their representative is.	Foundations Process: Team Composition (see sample in Figure 2c on the next page).
7. Have team members view and/or read Tasks 3 and 4 of this presentation for information on how to make the team more effective. 8. Have team members start the *Foundations* process by reading and/or viewing the other presentations in Module A.	Foundations Process: Presentations/ Communications With Staff

Figure 2c   *Sample record of team composition and representation (A-16)*

Panther
R
I
D
E

Team composition and policy for selecting new members

PRIDE Team Member	Who Member Represents
Sheree Washington	Administrative team
Isabella Garcia	6th-, 7th-, and 8th-grade teachers and clerical staff
Tyson Little	3rd-, 4th-, and 5th-grade teachers and counseling staff
Jack Hughes	Pre-K, kindergarten, and 1st- and 2nd-grade teachers, parent advisory groups, PTA, and school volunteers
Than Huang	Special education staff, school psychologist, social worker, mental health liaison, and nurse
Wendy Franco	All noncertified staff (paraprofessionals, custodial staff, and food service staff)

Team members will serve no longer than two years, but may return to the team after a period of nonservice. Ms. Washington is a permanent member.

Volunteers for new team members will be considered at the April staff meeting. If too many staff volunteer for the team, Ms. Washington will select new team members from the volunteers. The new members will shadow their predecessors for the remainder of the year and will be ready to assume their roles on the team in the fall.

This sample can be printed from the Module A CD.

FOUNDATIONS ARCHIVE NOTEBOOK   p. 4

TASK 2

Actively engage the staff

For the Foundations Team to be effective, team members need a deep understanding of the Improvement Cycle. (The Improvement Cycle is explained in detail in Module A, Presentation 3.) The overall role of the team is to drive the Improvement Cycle. Team members must believe that collectively they can create a great school that inspires students (and staff) and even changes their lives.

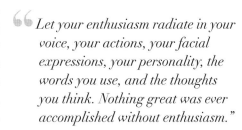

Let your enthusiasm radiate in your voice, your actions, your facial expressions, your personality, the words you use, and the thoughts you think. Nothing great was ever accomplished without enthusiasm."

RALPH WALDO EMERSON (1803–1882), American essayist and poet

Choose a team name.

Teams should brainstorm a unique team name—something fun and descriptive—as opposed to a name like Discipline Committee. The entire staff can be involved in picking a name. A good team name will help:

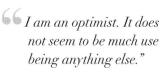

I am an optimist. It does not seem to be much use being anything else."

WINSTON CHURCHILL (1874–1965), British politician and prime minister

- Create a sense of team unity.
- Connect the team and the rest of the staff.
- Communicate that the purpose of the team is broader than a traditional view of discipline.

Staff can play up the team name by selecting a team logo, mascot, or colors to use on posters, in the school newsletter, and for school decorations. Acronyms based on the school Guidelines for Success (see Module C, Presentation 2), a catchy word or phrase, or the school mascot are popular choices for team names. Here are examples from real schools that have implemented *Foundations*:

- Foundations Team
- Responsibility Team
- FRED Team (Frequently Reviewing Educational Discipline)
- BERT not ERNIE (Behavioral Engineering Responsibility Team not Enforcing Rash Nasty Insensitive Expectations)
- PEP Team (Positive Effective Procedures)
- BISON Team (Behavior Improvement Schoolwide Opportunity Network)
- Panther PRIDE Team (Promoting Respect in a Diverse Environment)
- CARE Team (Committee for the Advancement of Respect and Education)

- LEAPS (Learning Effective Approaches for a Positive School)
- LASSO (Leading All Students to Successful Outcomes)
- CRUISE (Creating Respect and Understanding in a Safe Environment)
- ELITE Team (Engineering Lincoln's Independent Team of Excellence)
- TOPS Team (Team of Positive Skills)
- BASE Team (Bryan Adams Safe Environments)
- PRESS Team (Preparing the Restructuring of our Environment for Student Success)
- Solid Rock Team (Sense of Learning in Discipline, Respect for Classroom Kids)
- BET (Behavior Engineering Team)
- SCOPE Team (Safe Civil Orderly Productive Environment)
- Triple C Team (CCC: Campus Climate Committee)
- CASE Team (Civility and Safety for Everyone)
- HOPE Team (Help Organize a Positive Environment)

For consistency and clarity within the *Foundations* text and videos, we refer to the team as the Foundations Team.

Develop a summary of the team's purpose.

Figure 2d shows an adaptation of a statement that a *Foundations* school in Dallas, Texas, wrote to convey the purpose of the team to all staff. This is an example of a document your school may want to develop during the first year of implementation, once the team members have a thorough understanding of the Improvement Cycle and a good sense of school priorities. It's a great document to read to the team and the staff at the beginning of every school year (or more often) as a reminder of the team's purpose and responsibilities.

Make the team highly visible.

The team should be highly visible in the school. Some ideas for establishing and maintaining a positive presence are:

- Team presentation at a staff meeting at least once per month.
- Newsletter with behavior management tips and teaching tips (see Figure 2e on p. 50).
- Emails or memos that communicate recent team decisions or activities.
- Staff surveys or polls to get opinions and information about priorities, problems, and successes.

Figure 2d *Sample team purpose statement (A-17)*

THE **CASE** TEAM
Civil **A**nd **S**afe for **E**veryone

The purpose of the CASE Team is to promote a civil and safe learning environment by identifying problems of concern to the school community and developing solutions to those problems.

The CASE Team uses multiple sources of information to identify problems:

- Discipline referrals
- Surveys of students, staff, and parents
- Observations of common areas (cafeteria, hallways, parking lots, etc.)

The CASE Team incorporates the principles of STOIC when developing solutions:

Structure and organize environments for success.
Teach behavioral expectations to students.
Observe and monitor student behavior.
Interact positively with students.
Correct misbehavior fluently (be brief, calm, and consistent).

The CASE Team also monitors progress toward problem resolution and makes adjustments (restructuring and re-teaching, for example) to the solutions as needed.

The school district supports the CASE Team, and the team asks for faculty support as it begins the process of identifying problems of concern.

This sample can be printed from the Module A CD.

Use your team name to brand all your efforts—see Figure 2f on p. 51 for a wonderful example of branding. The CRUISE Team at Fletcher High School (Duval County Schools in Jacksonville, Florida) created a PowerPoint presentation for their fall inservice that cleverly plays on the team name. Staff members are crew members on the S. S. Fletcher of the BEACH Cruise Line, and the principal is the captain of the ship! (BEACH is the acronym for their Guidelines for Success.) The entire presentation is available to view on the Module A CD.

Figure 2e *Sample Foundations newsletter item*

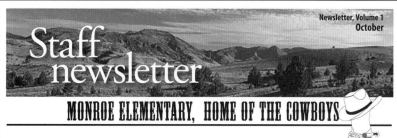

Newsletter, Volume 1
October

Staff
newsletter

MONROE ELEMENTARY, HOME OF THE COWBOYS

Tip of the Month
Foundations Team

When correcting students in common areas, be consistent, calm, and respectful.

- Get the student's attention and quietly say, "I need to speak to you, please."
- When other students are around, go to the misbehaving student and explain that you need to speak to him or her. "Step over here with me, please."
- When correcting a student, position yourself in a nonconfrontational stance. Have the student face out of the area so that you are looking toward the common area as you speak and can continue to supervisor other students. This positioning also keeps the misbehaving student from making eye contact with other students.

Summer School

We will be hosting summer school for the district. Summer school will be held Monday through Thursday, June 15 through July 17. Students will be served 20 instructional days, from 8:00 a.m. to 2:30 p.m. with a 30-minute lunch break. Free/reduced lunches and bus transportation will be available.

Attendance Challenge

We have just finished the fifth 6-week attendance period, and we fell just short of the district attendance goal of 97.7%. We had several days with extremely bad attendance. Early release days and the days before and after holidays were particularly problematic. Third grade and kindergarten tied for the win for this 6-week period; both av-

eraged 97.4% attendance. Way to go, kinder and third grade!

Grade	Week 1	Week 2	Week 3	Week 4	Week 5	Week 6	Week 7	Avg
PK	92.6	98.4	93	97.3	95.2	95.4	96.6	95.5
K	98.4	96.4	96	97.5	98.3	97.2	98	97.4
1st	94.7	98.1	95	97.9	95.8	97.4	96.5	98.5
2nd	97.7	95.4	95.7	98.5	98.7	97.8	96.9	97.2
3rd	97.4	98.2	94.4	98.6	98.2	98	96.9	97.4
4th	96.5	96.8	97.4	97	97	96.1	95.6	96.6
5th	94.4	96.2	92.3	97.7	98.6	98.4	97.7	96.5

If you are planning for a year, sow rice; if you are planning for a decade, plant trees; if you are planning for a lifetime, educate people.

—*Chinese Proverb*

Figure 2f *The CRUISE Team PowerPoint presentation (A-19); thanks to Duncan*
U. Fletcher High School and Duval County Public Schools in Florida

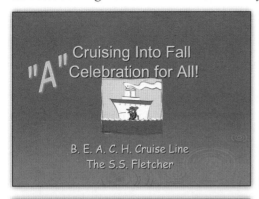

"A" Cruising Into Fall Celebration for All!

B. E. A. C. H. Cruise Line
The S.S. Fletcher

Guidelines For Success

B E INVOLVED
E NCOURAGE OTHERS
A CT RESPONSIBLY
C HALLENGE YOURSELF
H ONOR S[HIP] POLICIES

Welcome Aboard!
Crew Member Training

- Ship Captain: Helene Kirkpatrick
  - First Mates:
    - Ben Titus
    - Katrina McCray
    - Josie Johnson
    - Francine Parker
    - Chuck Scott
- Crew Members – Faculty and Support Staff

All Aboard. . .

- Passengers
  - Those students who come to class prepared, excited and willing with their destination in mind.
- Stowaways
  - Those students who attend regularly but who are less involved and are unsure of the destination. They are just "along for the ride."
- Shanghaied?
  - Those students who would rather be anywhere but here!

Crew Member Responsibilities

- Everybody needs to stay onboard for the duration, no matter how rough the seas.
- Even though you have received your passenger list, ALL passengers are your responsibility!
- You are not allowed to dislike any passenger on company time!
- When a passenger needs repeated direction, you must maintain a respectful attitude.
- Some passengers may have "excessive baggage" and will require more of your time and creativity.
- If a passenger should jump, fall or be pushed overboard, you must man a life boat.

B.E.A.C.H. Cruise Line Standards

- All performances "START ON TIME"
- All designated areas remain well organized to promote a safe, civil and productive environment.
- All passengers are greeted pleasantly throughout the day.
- All passenger identification must be verified at each "Port of Call"

Cruise Itinerary
Please Attend the Crew Member Training
Tuesday morning in room C-12.

- Foundations:
  - Start on time
  - Guidelines for Success
  - Common Area Lesson Plans
  - Staff Beliefs
- CHAMPS:
  - Day One!

Our "Islands of Adventure"

Work Force
GI
AP
SAT/ ACT
FCAT Again!
9/10 FCAT

These samples can be printed from the Module A CD.

"Ideas for Branding the Team Identity" below suggests more ways to incorporate the team name into school life and increase its visibility. You want to market the team as something that unifies the staff, saves staff time, and increases consistency so that the school can continue to improve.

Ideas for Branding the Team Identity

- Team name
- Logo
- Mascot
- Colors
- Community decorations
- Newspaper or newsletter
- Team rules or codes of conduct
- Team rewards
- Social or academic activities
- Celebrations
    - Birthdays
    - Accomplishments
    - Community diversity
- Team government
- Team recognition days
- Assemblies
- Displays of work, compliance, and accomplishment
- Bulletin boards
- Handbooks
- Alternate dress code and specialty T-shirts

Team Contests and Competitions

- Field trips
- Team song
- Team parties
- Team scrapbook
- Team name tags for special events
- Team calendar
- Team talent shows, spirit days, and dress-up days
- Team community projects
- Clean-up days
- Team participation at special events (school and community)
- Team rituals

Task 2 Action Steps & Evidence of Implementation

Action Steps	Evidence of Implementation
1. Choose a team name. If appropriate, involve the entire staff.	Foundations Process: Team Composition
2. Develop a one-page summary of the team purpose. This can be done over time, during the first year of implementation.	Foundations Archive: Mission Statement/Staff Beliefs/Team Purpose (see sample in Figure 2g).
3. Discuss a plan for how to be highly visible. At a minimum, the team should present to staff at least once per month.	Foundations Process: Planning Calendar, Presentations/ Communications With Staff

Figure 2g *Sample team logo and team purpose statement (A-18)*

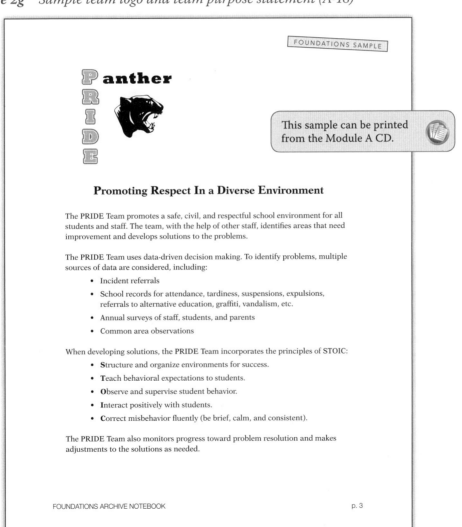

FOUNDATIONS SAMPLE

Panther
R
I
D
E

This sample can be printed from the Module A CD.

Promoting Respect In a Diverse Environment

The PRIDE Team promotes a safe, civil, and respectful school environment for all students and staff. The team, with the help of other staff, identifies areas that need improvement and develops solutions to the problems.

The PRIDE Team uses data-driven decision making. To identify problems, multiple sources of data are considered, including:

- Incident referrals
- School records for attendance, tardiness, suspensions, expulsions, referrals to alternative education, graffiti, vandalism, etc.
- Annual surveys of staff, students, and parents
- Common area observations

When developing solutions, the PRIDE Team incorporates the principles of STOIC:

- **S**tructure and organize environments for success.
- **T**each behavioral expectations to students.
- **O**bserve and supervise student behavior.
- **I**nteract positively with students.
- **C**orrect misbehavior fluently (be brief, calm, and consistent).

The PRIDE Team also monitors progress toward problem resolution and makes adjustments to the solutions as needed.

FOUNDATIONS ARCHIVE NOTEBOOK   p. 3

TASK 3

Establish team roles and plan effective team meetings

In Task 3, we describe how to structure the team so everyone can work efficiently and effectively. You'll identify team roles and responsibilities, establish a regular meeting schedule and ground rules for team meetings, and consider using a team coach and participating in a partner school program.

Assign team roles and responsibilities.

Assigning specific roles and responsibilities to team members will increase team efficiency and capitalize on the specific strengths of individual team members. It will also help ensure that tasks get done in a timely fashion.

Team members should get together and discuss the roles and responsibilities available. The administrator should be the team chair or cochair, but staff can fill other positions by volunteering for the roles they feel most qualified for. For example, a person who enjoys and is skilled at data analysis should volunteer for (or be encouraged to volunteer for) the Data/Evaluation Coordinator. A detail-oriented person who can multitask would be a good fit for Recorder. In some cases, the administrator might want to assign roles, but usually positions are filled through an informal voluntary process.

Listed below are roles and responsibilities that have worked well in *Foundations* schools; consider including some or all of them in your team. Note that there are probably more roles suggested than you have team members. Plan to combine some roles—for example, Keeper of the List and Staff Liaison or Materials Manager and Family Engagement Coordinator.

- *Chair:* Manages agendas and keeps people and discussions on task during meetings. Consider assigning cochairs—the administrator and one of the staff representatives.

- *Recorder:* Takes minutes during meetings, monitors tasks, and keeps records of all team activities (may be combined with Keeper of the List).

- *Data/Evaluation Coordinator:* Manages data collection, data analysis, and data presentations to staff.

- *Materials Manager:* Maintains the Foundations Archive, manages resources for use by team members, copies materials for meetings, etc.

- *Keeper of the List:* Maintains a reminder file of topics for future meetings (may be combined with Recorder).

- *Staff Liaison:* Ensures that the entire staff is consistently informed about and involved in team activities. Also periodically monitors staff members' perceptions of the team and the *Foundations* process.

- *Equity and Student Liaison:* Analyzes data for inequities and discrepancies between groups of students and serves as an advocate for students. For example, survey results may reveal that Black/African American students experience more bullying than Asian students. The Equity and Student Liaison should lead exploration of this issue, perhaps convening a focus group of students to talk about it.

- *Family Engagement Coordinator:* Oversees programs and incentives that encourage positive family interactions with school staff and family participation in students' school experiences. (This role is probably not necessary if the school has a Family Engagement Team that is as influential as the Foundations Team in the MTSS processes.)

- *MTSS Coordinator:* Ensures the seamless connection between universal prevention and Tier 2 and Tier 3 individual interventions. For example, this person ensures that teachers get the assistance they request in a timely manner and that problem-solving processes for individual students are effective and efficient. Consider the special education representative for this role.

Why Keeper of the List Is an Important Role

Let's say team members are discussing Guidelines for Success, and Kathy brings up a problem in the cafeteria. Out of respect for Kathy, team members begin to discuss the cafeteria issue even though they are not finished with Guidelines for Success. Valuable meeting time that was earmarked for Guidelines for Success is lost, along with the momentum and focus of the discussion. A better way to show respect for team members is for a cochair to say, "Kathy, that's a great idea for the cafeteria. Ben, you're Keeper of the List—would you please add Kathy's ideas about the cafeteria to the List and we'll talk about them another time. Now let's get back to Guidelines for Success."

Develop a team meeting schedule.

The team must meet on a regular basis to maintain the cycle of reviewing data, selecting priorities, and revising the policies and procedures that you want the staff to adopt and implement. If the team stops meeting (or meets but is not efficient), the process of continuous improvement grinds to a halt.

A regular meeting schedule gives team members a sense of the commitment required of them. It also facilitates more productive use of the team's time because members can anticipate the meetings and prepare accordingly. The team should meet often enough and long enough to get things done and maintain improvement momentum, but not so much that team members burn out. We recommend a minimum of 4 hours per quarter.

Schedule options include:

- Meet weekly for 30 to 45 minutes (best for the first year of implementation, when the team is gaining momentum).
- Meet twice a month for 1 hour (next best for the first year of implementation, when the team is gaining momentum).
- Meet once a month for a half day. Consider this schedule once *Foundations* is well established. Teachers' classes need to be covered, and the team needs to be able to outline tasks for the next month.
- Meet once a quarter for a full day. Very experienced teams can consider this option. Teachers' classes need to be covered, and the team needs to be able to outline 9 or 10 weeks' worth of business.

We recommend the more frequent meeting options for new teams.

Develop team meeting ground rules.

Rules for how team meetings should run can improve the team's ability to function smoothly and effectively. Rules will also increase the team's ability to lead the entire staff and help the team avoid becoming just another committee.

Following are examples of ground rules:

- An established minimum number of members must be present.
- Meetings will start and end on time.
- No side conversations during the meeting.
- All team discussions and disagreements will be respectful.
- Before speaking, team members will paraphrase what the speaker before them said.
- A cochair will serve as the on-task and on-time nag. Everyone should feel free to ask this person to nag them about staying on time and on task.

- Minutes will be kept for all meetings and will be distributed to the team and all staff.
- Meeting minutes will identify specific tasks to be accomplished with responsible staff and timelines. The Recorder should highlight assigned tasks so they really stand out.
- The ground rules will be clarified and communicated to all team members.
- Meetings will follow an agreed-upon agenda.

Figure 2h on pp. 58–59 shows a suggested agenda and minutes form you can use to keep meetings organized and moving. Three versions are available on the Module A CD (Form A-03a, b, c)—one for 30- to 40-minute meetings, one for 1-hour meetings, and one for 3-hour meetings. Note the suggested durations for each portion of the agenda to help keep the meeting to the allotted time. These forms are provided as fillable PDFs so the Recorder can take minutes right on the form.

Ensure that all team members agree on the ground rules and on an agenda format (use our suggested form or create your own).

Consider using a team coach (optional).

Consider discussing as a team whether to use a team coach. This might be an agenda item for one of the early team meetings. An objective set of eyes and ears to observe your school can be invaluable. A coach can meet with and help team members and also keep the staff informed and motivated. He or she can offer fresh ideas and access to new outside resources. A full- or part-time building-based Behavior Support Coordinator may serve in this role.

One *Foundations* school in Washington—Kenroy Elementary—was experiencing problems with communication and trust among staff members. An outside coach suggested arranging an inservice day with a professional to work on communication skills and building trust. The school took the coach's advice and participated in a very productive inservice. The staff created and agreed on the following Professional Code of Conduct:

- Be able to disagree without being disagreeable.
- Agree to not take questions as criticism.
- Agree to seek clarification on small issues. (If it bothers you, check it out.)
- Agree to accept final decisions.
- Value questions from other staff.

Where do you find a coach? Some district, state, or regional service centers have behavior support experts available for inservice training and observation of classrooms and common areas. Another option is to hire an independent consultant through an organization such as *Safe & Civil Schools*.

Foundations Team Meeting: Agenda and Minutes
Designed for a 60-minute meeting (p. 1 of 2)

Meeting Date and Time: _____

Members in Attendance: _____ _____ _____

_____ _____ _____ _____

_____ _____ _____ _____

Agenda and Reminder about this meeting was sent out a week before. Date reminder was sent: _____

☐ **Start the meeting ON TIME.** Time Started: _____

☐ **Review tasks from last meeting.** Report status of current tasks and discuss tasks that still need to be done. (10 min.)

_____

_____

_____

_____

_____

_____

_____

☐ **Review potential next tasks and decisions to address.** (5 min.)

_____

_____

_____

_____

_____

☐ **Team discusses what needs to occur to make the next tasks and decisions happen.** (30 min.)

_____

_____

_____

_____

_____

_____

_____

_____

_____

_____

_____

 This form can be printed from the Module A CD.

Foundations Team Meeting: Agenda and Minutes
Designed for a 60-minute meeting (p. 2 of 2)

Write down who is going to do what and when he or she will do it.

Who	Does What	When
1)		
2)		
3)		
4)		
5)		
6)		
7)		

☐ **Review** who is going to do what and when he or she will do it. (5 min.)

☐ **Ask if any other items need to be addressed** or need to be on the agenda for the next meeting. (3 min.)

☐ **Document** how the information discussed will be shared with the entire faculty. (5 min.)

_____

_____

_____

☐ **Debrief** how the team did with regards to following its ground rules. (3 min.)

☐ **Remind** people when the next meeting is.

Next meeting is _____ at _____ in _____
              (date)   (time)   (location)

☐ Meeting adjourned at **scheduled time.** Meeting adjourned: _____

Consider forming a partnership with another school (optional).

A coach can also help schools work with a partner school—that is, establish a relationship with another school that is working on similar issues. Foundations Team members can visit the partner school to see, for example, how it is addressing cafeteria or playground issues and how its team is communicating the Guidelines for Success to staff and students.

Larger districts may group schools into cohorts, with each cohort concentrating on different aspects of *Foundations* at different times. While one school is working on tardy issues, its partner school may be working on the cafeteria. Each school can visit the other to get ideas for working on a problem area when the time comes to address it.

Another benefit of the partner school concept is that schools come to understand that they are not alone—other schools have similar problems! Whether the issue is staff who are resistant to change or students who continue to text in class, knowing that other schools struggle with the same issues can be reassuring and motivating. *Foundations* schools have reported that the partner school program has been quite beneficial.

Task 3 Action Steps & Evidence of Implementation

Action Steps	Evidence of Implementation
1. Identify and assign team roles and responsibilities.	Foundations Process: Team Composition (see sample documentation in Figure 2i)
2. Decide on a regular meeting schedule.	Foundations Process: Planning Calendar
3. Develop ground rules for team meetings.	Foundations Process: Team Composition (see sample documentation in Figure 2j)
4. Decide whether and how to use a team coach. 5. Decide whether to participate in a partner school program.	The ideas and help you'll receive from these sources will probably be reflected in documents in the Foundations Process: Current Priorities, Presentations/ Communications With Staff, and Meeting Minutes.

Figure 2i *Sample documentation of team roles*

FOUNDATIONS SAMPLE

Panther PRIDE

Team Roles

PRIDE Team Member	Role
Sheree Washington	Cochair
Isabella Garcia	Data/Evaluation Coordinator
Tyson Little	Recorder, Keeper of the List
Jack Hughes	Staff Liaison, Cochair
Than Huang	Equity and Student Liaison
Wendy Franco	Materials Manager

FOUNDATIONS ARCHIVE NOTEBOOK p. 5

Panther
PRIDE

PRIDE Team Meeting Rules

- The Recorder will prepare an agenda with specific discussion items.
- Meetings will start and end on time.
- No side conversations during the meeting.
- All team discussions and disagreements will be respectful.
- Before speaking, team members will paraphrase what the speaker before them said.
- A cochair will serve as the "on-task and on-time nag."
- Meeting minutes will identify specific tasks to be accomplished with responsible staff and timelines.
- The ground rules will be clarified and communicated to all team members.

FOUNDATIONS ARCHIVE NOTEBOOK   p. 6

This sample can be printed from the Module A CD.

TASK 4

Sustain an effective team

In this task, we discuss ways to ensure that the Foundations Team continues to be a leadership force in your school. The team guides and maintains the culture of the school by assisting with development of the School Improvement Plan, archiving all of the team's work, orienting new staff and new team members to the school culture, and effectively representing staff members so that staff view the *Foundations* process positively rather than feel encumbered by it. We also recommend a self-assessment exercise for team members. Finally, we list some issues that can negatively affect the *Foundations* implementation so that you can avoid them or, if they are already present in your school, take steps to reverse their impact.

Guide and maintain the culture of the school.

The success of your Foundations Team will depend partially on your school culture (Are people open to the changes the team will propose? Do staff have a can-do rather than a can't-do attitude?), yet at the same time the team is responsible for guiding and maintaining your school culture over the long term. One definition of *culture* is "the set of shared attitudes, values, goals, and practices that characterizes an institution or organization" (Merriam-Webster Online Dictionary, n.d.). School climate generally refers to how people feel about aspects of the school: "I feel safe at school." "My teachers are really good." School culture is bigger than that. Culture is climate taken across time and includes the ideas and programs that develop over years.

In our many years of helping schools implement *Foundations*, we've seen schools develop great, truly transformative practices, only to have them all disappear when a new principal took over. The team needs to guard against such situations. One way is to ensure that your culture is documented. Later in this task, we explain how to organize your *Foundations* materials into notebooks so that new staff members can easily continue the programs and practices you worked so hard to develop and implement.

We are reminded of a cartoon that shows two teachers talking. The caption reads, "We had a great program last year, but she moved." Try not to let that cartoon represent your school by ensuring that your Foundations Team and your school culture are maintained and sustained over time. An important team job is to guide staff attitudes, values, goals, and daily practices so students and parents get consistent messages about the culture and climate of your school. To accomplish this, your team has to walk the walk, not just talk the talk.

I was presenting to a group of school superintendents, and I talked about how important it was to meet the needs of average students. One attendee came up to me afterward and told me about a program at his high school. He said that at the end of each semester, teachers nominated students for a graded, elective for-credit course called Leadership Club. The criterion for nomination was simply that a student have no known connection to the school—the student did not participate in any sports, clubs, or activities. Nominated students were asked whether they would like to take this class, taught by the school counselor. The students learned leadership, assertiveness, and communication skills and organized a school dance and a community service project. The superintendent said they didn't keep any formal data, but at least 90% of the students who took Leadership Club subsequently participated in school sports and clubs.

I was impressed with this idea, and I talked about it in other presentations. About 3 years later, a principal expressed interest in duplicating the program at her school, so I gave her the school contact information. When this principal contacted the school, she found that the superintendent, the principal, and counselor had all retired. When she asked about the Leadership Club, no one even knew what it was.

—R.S.

Self-assess your team-building skills.

Encourage team members to self-assess their effectiveness and set goals. Figure 2k on the next page shows a simple self-assessment tool called Are You an Effective Team Builder? It is available on the Module A CD (Form A-04). We suggest that, about four to seven months after you begin working on *Foundations*, all team members review this task (Task 4) and complete and discuss Are You an Effective Team Builder? The Keeper of the List can ensure that the team builder self-assessment is on the list of future agenda items.

Each team member should complete a separate form. This exercise is purely for personal growth, and forms do not need to be turned in. However, a team discussion of the results can be valuable. You might have each team member share at least one goal for personal improvement.

We suggest you conduct this exercise at least annually.

Figure 2k *Are You an Effective Team Builder? self-assessment tool (A-04)*

Are You an Effective Team Builder? (Self-Evaluation)

Directions: Rate yourself on a scale of 1–5, where 1 = rarely and 5 = always.

_____ I agree that I have the skills needed for my assigned role.

_____ I encourage team members by supporting their independence and autonomy as they carry out their assigned roles, solve problems, and deliver the team's message.

_____ I nurture and practice the spirit of teamwork across the school community.

_____ I insist on and practice open and honest communication.

_____ I follow through on my team role and the tasks that I take on.

_____ I respect personality differences and cultural diversity.

_____ I support and assist in providing quality professional development within the team and school community.

_____ I value constructive criticism.

_____ I believe that teaming—collaboration in general and our team specifically—will enhance our communal environment and the academic growth of our students.

_____ **Total Score**

Goals for personal improvement: _____

_____

_____

_____

_____

Scoring Rubric

A score of 35–45 means that you are aware of what it takes to be an effective team builder.

A score of 25–35 means that you are integrated into the team building process. As you learn and participate more, you will develop more foundational skills.

A score below 25 suggests you have room for growth! Team building is an evolutionary process, and you are beginning the journey.

 This form can be printed from the Module A CD.

Represent other staff members well and save them time.

Another function of the Foundations Team is to save time for the rest of the staff. This ties into sustaining the team because when staff recognize and value how the team implements an efficient improvement process without taking too much staff time, they will support the team in the long term. You want the staff to view the *Foundations* process positively rather than feel encumbered by it. Foundations Team members save time for the rest of the staff in several ways.

Team members seek input from staff and represent them at meetings, so other staff are not required to attend. Whenever the team is going to discuss an issue that affects staff members not on the team, the team member who represents that constituency should seek input from his or her constituents. You might post butcher paper in the staff room and ask staff to write ideas about the current issue on the paper. Or send an email to all staff inviting email feedback to representative team members. Staff should be asked what their priorities are and why—in other words, the specific problems behind their priorities.

Team members should even invite other concerned staff to the next team meeting. For example, whenever the team is going to discuss any aspect of the cafeteria, food service and custodial personnel should be invited to join the team meeting. If they cannot attend, their representative should bring their thoughts and opinions to the meeting.

Open-ended staff meetings with everyone in attendance tend to get bogged down. Decision making is difficult and debate is often monopolized by the most vocal and opinionated staff members. Poll staff members ahead of time and prepare pro and con arguments for solutions so that discussions during team meetings can be streamlined and productive.

Seemingly simple decisions can sometimes take a long time to talk through—for example, modifying the route that primary students take to the playground. Will students be visible to the supervisor at all times? Will they encounter groups of older students? Are there too many distractions along the way? If the discussion is limited to team members (with knowledge of staff opinions about the issue), other staff members' time is not affected.

Team members can develop testable interventions. The role of the team is to develop strategies to address particular problems or meet particular needs. In doing so, the team should generate hypotheses about which interventions might be effective and identify observable outcomes that can be used to determine whether an intervention is being effective. For example, to alleviate problems in the cafeteria, team members hypothesize that reducing the amount of time students stand in line might help. To determine whether the procedure works, they test it: Before the new strategies are implemented, they time how long it takes for a student to get from the end of the line (with the line at its longest) to the cashier. Then they do the same after the intervention is implemented and compare the times.

Guide the development of the School Improvement Plan.

The Foundations Team should be actively involved in helping the administrator develop the behavior portions of the School Improvement Plan (SIP). We have had the privilege of working with some large urban districts that require principals to maintain both an academic MTSS team and a behavior MTSS team each year. These two groups contribute to an academic component (instruction, curriculum, and assessment) and a behavior component (safety, climate, culture, and discipline) of the SIP. The Foundations Team should also be involved in monitoring the efficacy of the current SIP and determining the data that will be used to inform and develop next year's SIP.

Archive all work in progress and work completed by the team.

Part of the team's job is to maintain the cultural traditions of the school across staff changes. As you work through the *Foundations* process, you will accumulate many records of your work. It's important to archive all of these documents in organized binders that you— and future staff members—can easily refer to when necessary. For example, if a new principal enters the school, she should be able to find almost all the information she needs about school policies and proce-

Those who cannot remember the past are condemned to repeat it."

GEORGE SANTAYANA
(1863–1952), philosopher

dures in place, how students and staff are taught and review the expectations, and how Guidelines for Success are integrated into the school culture. The history of the improvement process should also be available. Records of strategies that *didn't* work and how staff worked to fix them are important, too.

We recommend that the Foundations Team maintain four notebooks or binders to record the cultural history of your school's policies and procedures and the work you do to arrive at those final policies and procedures. This archival work is probably best done by the team Recorder. With the Action Steps that follow each task, we reference one or more areas of the archives where you will probably file (and later reference) documents that relate to the steps. A sample archive (A-23) from a school that has implemented *Foundations* is available on the Module A CD.

Following are our suggestions for four archival binders and the sections in each one.

Foundations Process Notebook (working documents). Some sections—such as Meeting Minutes and Planning Calendar—can be cleared at the beginning of each new school year and started fresh.

- Team Composition
- Planning Calendar
- Meeting Minutes
- Data Summaries
- Current Priorities
- Safety
- Guidelines for Success
- Presentations/Communications With Staff
- Communications With Parents
- Students' Basic Needs
- Staff Beliefs
- Universal Screening
- 3-Level System for Responding to Misbehavior
- Attendance Initiatives
- Implementation Rubric and Summary and Implementation Checklists

Foundations Archive (final documents). When data show that policies and procedures are effective and the staff are ready to consider them final, they can be filed here.

- Mission Statement/Staff Beliefs/Team Purpose
- Long-Term Planning Calendar
- Guidelines for Success
- 3-Level System for Responding to Misbehavior
- Job Descriptions for Common Area Supervisors
- Schoolwide Policies
- Common Area Policies and Procedures
- Safety Policies
- Lesson Plans for Teaching Common Area and Schoolwide Policy Expectations
- Lesson Plans for Teaching Safety Expectations
- Lesson Plans for Teaching Guidelines for Success
- Lesson Plans for Teaching Expectations for Interacting With Adults
- Lesson Plans for Teaching Bullying Prevention
- New Student Orientation
- New Staff Orientation
- Student's Basic Needs
- Support Available to Staff
- Bullying Prevention
- Interventions for Individual Students
- Universal Screening
- Red Flags

Staff Handbook. This binder may be a work in progress as you develop the contents over time. An effective way to keep the handbook up to date is to have staff members bring their copies to staff meetings. At the meeting, hand out new and replacement pages, explain where they should be inserted, and have staff update their handbooks.

- Mission Statement
- Staff Beliefs
- Guidelines for Success and How to Incorporate Them Into Every School Environment
- Staff Roles and Responsibilities
- Information about MTSS and *Safe & Civil Schools* Philosophy
- Policies and Procedures in Place (these may be less detailed than those in the Foundations Archive, containing just what staff need to know)
- 3-Level System for Responding to Misbehavior
- Available Support
- Classroom Management Model
- Early-Stage Interventions

Student and Parent Handbook. This binder is less fluid than the Staff Handbook, but should be reviewed and updated annually.

- Mission Statement
- Staff Beliefs
- Guidelines for Success and What They Mean
- Policies and Procedures (for example, attendance, dress code, and discipline)

From this point forward in *Foundations*, the Action Steps at the end of each task offer suggestions for where to archive your work. For every improvement priority, document the data that led to the decision to prioritize the common area or schoolwide policy, the discussions and staff input that drove the revision, and the final policy.

Orient new staff and new team members.

At the beginning of the school year, team members should orient new staff and remind existing staff about important policies, procedures, and lessons. Conduct at least one orientation session to ensure that new team members understand:

- The *Foundations* process, team processes, and the Improvement Cycle (Module A, Presentations 1, 2, and 3)
- Current priorities for behavioral improvement that the Foundations Team is working on
- Past improvement priorities (to give a sense of the direction school policies are moving)

Orienting new staff is addressed in greater detail in Module C, Presentation 7.

Be aware of potential kisses of death for Foundations.

Unfortunately, some schools do not progress smoothly through the *Foundations* process. When we, the *Safe & Civil Schools* trainers, analyze why this happens, we find several common issues that affect implementation. We list these pitfalls and their symptoms below so you can avoid them or, if you recognize one happening in your school, take steps to reverse the trend. Laura Hamilton, one of the great *Foundations* trainers, created this list initially and refers to it as the Kisses of Death.

Kisses of Death to a *Foundations* Implementation

Active administrative support is lacking.

- Administrators on the team do not participate in team meetings.
- Administrators do not support, in words or actions, the implementation of approved policies, procedures, and Guidelines for Success.
- Administrators do not hold staff accountable for implementing approved policies, fulfilling their supervision responsibilities, completing office referrals, and so on.

The team does not meet regularly or is dysfunctional.

- Team members do not attend team meetings regularly.
- Team members do not behave professionally in team meetings and do not follow the team's adopted ground rules.
- Team members do not fulfill their team roles or other assigned responsibilities.
- Team members do not communicate effectively with the staff they represent.
- Team members do not serve as positive role models (for example, they do not enforce or follow the adopted policies or do not fulfill supervisory responsibilities).
- One or two team members carry all or most of the load.
- The team does not keep the Foundations Process Notebook up to date, resulting in lost momentum.

School staff is not kept actively engaged in *Foundations*.

- The school does not provide ongoing training in positive, proactive, and instructional discipline strategies.
- The team does not conduct scheduled reviews of Guidelines for Success, adopted policies, supervision requirements, and so on.
- The team does not provide regular updates on data related to the implementation of *Foundations* (office referral data, suspension data, survey results, data from follow-up observations, and so on).

The team does not systematically plan to ensure a smooth transition from year to year.

- The team does not keep the Foundations Archive and all additional pertinent information up to date and ready for distribution at the beginning of the school year (and during the year to new staff members).
- The team does not continually recruit and groom potential new Foundations Team members to replace current members who transfer, resign, or retire.
- The team does not sufficiently plan for significant changes that frequently occur in schools: changes in administration, changes in student population, and so on.

Other kisses of death include:

- The school does not devote enough attention to celebrating its successes in implementing *Foundations*.
- The school does not hold celebrations with students and staff.
- The school does not share successes with parents and the community.

Remember, your team needs to be the catalyst that ignites and fuels staff efforts to make your school a truly great place for all students. Winston Churchill said, "I am an optimist. It does not seem to be much use being anything else." So be an optimist about what you, the Foundations Team, can do for your entire staff and the students and community that you serve.

Task 4 Action Steps & Evidence of Implementation

Action Steps	Evidence of Implementation
1. Have team members complete the Are You an Effective Team Builder? self-assessment tool (Form A-04 on the CD).	Foundations Process: Meeting Minutes
2. Guide the development of the behavior portion of the School Improvement Plan and monitor progress.	Foundations Process: Presentations/ Communications With Staff
3. Sustain the culture of the school by recording all of the team's work and keeping it in organized binders.	Foundations Process Notebook, Foundations Archive, Staff Handbook, and Student and Parent Handbook

The Improvement Cycle

DOCUMENTS*

- Foundations Continuum of Behavior Support (A-10)
- Improvement Cycle (A-12a)
- Sample Voting Rubric, Version 1 of 4 (A-13)
- Sample decision-making process and revision policy communicated to staff (A-21)
- Evaluation flowchart (A-14)
- Samples of Foundations Archives (A-23)
- Sample evidence that new policies and procedures have been evaluated and results conveyed to staff (A-22)

* All documents listed are available on the CD. Other documents that are not shown in this presentation are also available on the CD (see Appendix C for a complete list).

INTRODUCTION

Foundations is a process driven by a set of beliefs and supported by the research literature. The process supports effective behavioral practices within a Multi-Tiered System of Support (MTSS) or Response to Intervention (RTI) framework. It is the base of behavioral support at the schoolwide, classroom, and individual student levels.

Figure 3a *The Foundations Continuum of Behavior Support (A-10)*

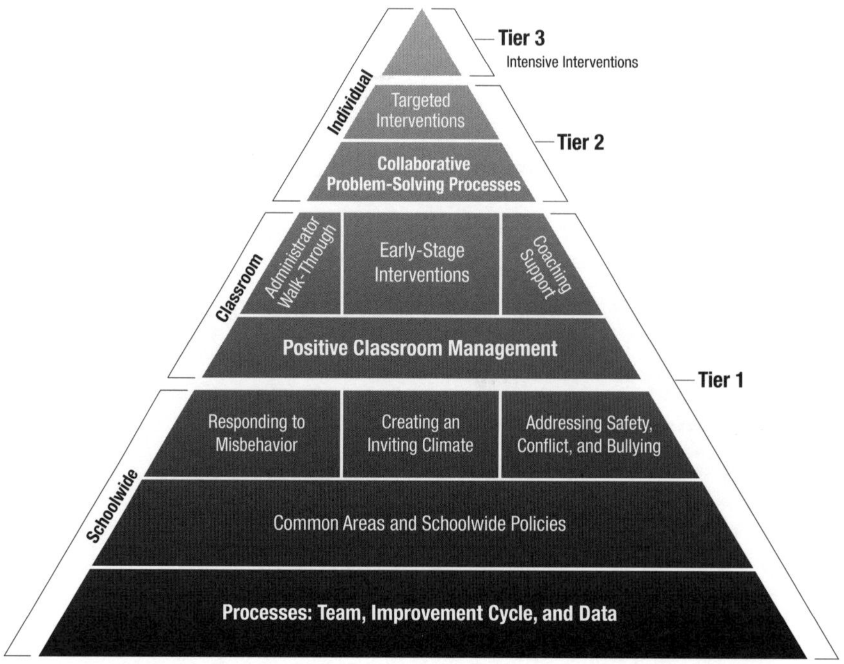

Central to the *Foundations* process is the Improvement Cycle—an ongoing, integrated sequence of activities driven by the Foundations Team. The five steps of the Improvement Cycle are **Review**, **Prioritize**, **Revise**, **Adopt**, and **Implement**. The Improvement Cycle is illustrated in Figure 3b.

Why is continuous improvement important? Let's use healthcare as an analogy. If you have to go to a hospital, you certainly don't want to go to one whose staff decided 10 years ago that they are so good they have no reason to improve. You also don't want to go to a hospital whose staff decided 10 years ago that they are so bad there is no hope of improving. You want a hospital that is continuously striving to provide better care for its patients because that's where you will most likely recover from your illness. Likewise, schools should continuously strive to improve their climate, safety, academic outcomes, and student behavior so that students have the best possible chance of success.

Figure 3b *Improvement Cycle (A-12a)*

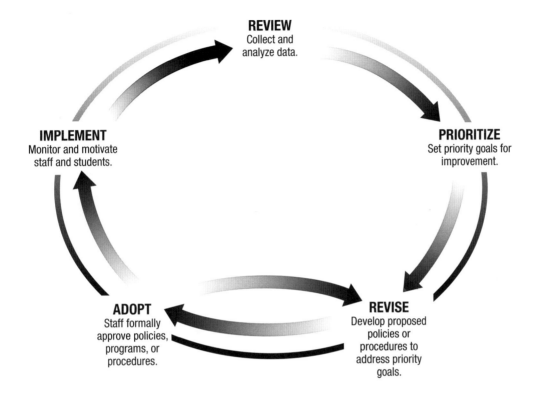

REVIEW
Collect and
analyze data.

PRIORITIZE
Set priority goals for
improvement.

IMPLEMENT
Monitor and motivate
staff and students.

ADOPT
Staff formally
approve policies,
programs, or
procedures.

REVISE
Develop proposed
policies or
procedures to
address priority
goals.

The Foundations Team's primary responsibility is to establish and maintain a continuous improvement process to make your school a better place for all students and staff. The entire staff are encouraged to provide feedback and opinions, and their participation through all phases of the cycle is crucial. One of the major responsibilities of the team is to save time for the staff while unifying the staff around the tasks of identifying priorities, then developing and implementing policies and procedures to address those priorities.

Students, parents and families, community members, and social agencies are also included in the process, as appropriate. For example, if an elementary school is concerned about morning arrival procedures, a task force of staff, students, and parents should be involved in developing new procedures. A high school concerned about racial division among students should include staff, students, and parents in a task force to generate an action plan.

This presentation provides information about effectively using the Improvement Cycle and guiding the entire staff in using the Improvement Cycle.

Note: Tasks 1 and 2 present overviews of the **Review** and **Prioritize** steps. See Module A, Presentation 4, "Data-Driven Processes" for detailed information about using and analyzing individual data sources, using multiple data sources to identify school improvement priorities, conducting surveys, and observing common areas.

The Data/Evaluation Coordinator is typically the lead team member for reviews. He or she should carefully read or view Module A, Presentation 4 as well as recommend others who should read or view particular sections of that presentation.

Task 1: Understand the Review and Prioritize Steps covers reviewing data from multiple sources about climate, discipline, and safety and using the data to guide staff in selecting a manageable number of common areas or schoolwide policies to work on.

Task 2: Understand the Revise Step explains how to develop comprehensive proposals for revising current policies and procedures to address the prioritized problems or concerns.

Task 3: Understand the Adopt Step describes how staff will vote to adopt or reject the proposal and how to proceed from either outcome.

Task 4: Understand the Implement Step covers the launch, evaluation, and maintenance of the new policies and procedures.

The Foundations Team's job is to maintain the Improvement Cycle. If the work of the team ever stalls or members think they have finished improving their school, it is time to review data to set another priority. Oliver Wendell Holmes said, "The great thing in this world is not so much where we stand as in what direction we are moving." The Improvement Cycle should guide your movement forward to make your school a better place for all students.

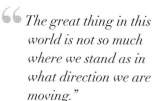

The great thing in this world is not so much where we stand as in what direction we are moving.

OLIVER WENDELL HOLMES, SR. (1809–1894), American physician and poet

TASK 1

Understand the Review and Prioritize steps

Task 1 explains how to review data from multiple sources about climate, discipline, and safety and use that data to guide staff in selecting a manageable number of common areas or schoolwide policies to work on.

Understand the Review step.

During the **Review** portion of the Improvement Cycle, the Foundations Team collects and analyzes data from multiple sources. The **Review** step should take place more or less quarterly. The data analysis informs decision making and can clarify objectives and goals for modifying student behavior. It also helps the team determine priorities—the policies or procedures to be revised first.

"While teaching will forever be in part an art, its foundations can and should rest on the sciences of human behavior" (Gordon, DeStefano, & Shipman, 1985, p. 63). Collecting and analyzing data is part of the objective, scientific side of behavior management. To evaluate your school's behavior management and discipline practices, ask and answer the following questions:

- What practices are working well and should be protected and celebrated?
- What practices are working adequately but could be improved?
- What practices are not working and need to be substantially modified or eliminated?

Also review multiple data sources to monitor improvement efforts that you have implemented. Consider whether changes to school practices are making things better, making things worse, or having no effect at all.

You will use data to answer the above questions. Consequently, the first step of the Improvement Cycle, and the first big task for the Foundations Team, is data collection and review. Some sources of data that can be used to answer the questions are:

- Surveys of staff members, students, and possibly parents.
- Observations of common areas.

- Summaries of student incident referrals (e.g., office referrals, detention).
- Summaries of other existing records (e.g., attendance, tardiness, suspensions, expulsions, referrals to alternative education, graffiti, vandalism). For example, data from the custodial staff on the amount of graffiti on campus can be valuable in assessing gang activity.

Note: See Module A, Presentation 4, "Data-Driven Processes" for detailed information about collecting and analyzing data and using multiple data sources to determine improvement priorities.

You'll decide which data sources to use based on the specific purpose of the review. If the review is part of planning for improvement priorities, we recommend using all or most available data sources. The first quarterly review of the school year often fulfills this purpose.

Another purpose of a review is to assess whether the identified priorities are still valid and evaluate whether changes have been effective. We recommend that schools review data for those purposes at least quarterly throughout the school year. Use incident referral data and other existing school records, and include any new observation and survey data as well.

&o FOUNDATIONS RECOMMENDATION ca

Review data quarterly to clarify your objectives and goals for modifying student behavior, determine priorities, and evaluate whether your revised policies and procedures are effective.

Note: Schools that have already begun the *Foundations* process should have decided on their improvement priorities for the new school year during the previous spring. Staff training for the new practices and any accompanying physical improvements to the building takes place before students begin classes. In these cases, the fall quarterly review can serve to monitor and evaluate the changes implemented when classes began as well as to identify new areas for improvement and areas that can be celebrated.

Information gained from reviewing data from previous years can also help staff identify and prepare for predictable spikes in misbehavior. Incident referral reports might show an increase in misbehavior before winter holidays and Halloween. Pinpointing the types of behaviors to expect during these times can help staff take steps to prevent them. For example, if data show that attendance has been a problem during the last few weeks of school, perhaps a schoolwide reward-based incentive program during that time period will motivate students to attend.

The sample calendar below illustrates how you might schedule the quarterly reviews. The team Keeper of the List might set up calendar reminders of tasks for the team to consider.

SAMPLE QUARTERLY REVIEW CALENDAR PLAN

School Year 1

•••••••••••••••••••••••••••••••••• *September 1* ••••••••••••••••••••••••••••

Classes begin. Wait about 30 days for staff and students to settle in before beginning the first review.

Consider collecting information from the staff about what went well and concerns they had about the start of the new year. Distribute a brief questionnaire or discuss at a staff meeting.

•••••••••••••••••••••••••• *October (end of first 9 weeks)* ••••••••••••••••••

Begin the first quarterly review:

- Schedule staff, student, and parent surveys for late October, November, or early December.

- Summarize and analyze first-quarter incident referral reports.

- Summarize and analyze other first-quarter records, such as attendance, tardiness, suspensions, expulsions, referrals to alternative education, graffiti, and vandalism.

- Conduct and analyze common area observations.

•••••••••••••••••••••••••••••••••• *November* ••••••••••••••••••••••••••••

Continue the first quarterly review:

- Administer and analyze staff, student, and parent surveys.

- Present analyses of incident referral data, other data, survey results, and observations to the Foundations Team. The team decides what to share with the entire staff. *Note:* A form for summarizing multiple data sources is available on the Module A CD and is explained in Module A, Presentation 4.

- Work with staff (or with staff input gained through team members' efforts) to identify school improvement priorities and begin working on those priorities.

·················· *January (at or near the end of the second quarter)* ··················

Begin the second quarterly review:

- Summarize and analyze second-quarter incident referral and other data reports.

- (Optional) Conduct and analyze observations of common areas in which improvements have been implemented.

- Present data analyses to the Foundations Team. The team decides what to share with the entire staff.

- Work with staff or with staff input to confirm or change improvement priorities; that is, decide whether you should add, modify, or eliminate one or more priorities.

·················· *March (near the end of the third quarter)* ··················

Begin the third quarterly review.

- Summarize and analyze third-quarter incident referral and other data reports.

- (Optional) Conduct and analyze observations of common areas in which improvements have been implemented.

- Present data analyses to the Foundations Team. The team decides what to share with the entire staff.

- Work with staff or with staff input to confirm or change improvement priorities; that is, decide whether you should add, modify, or eliminate one or more priorities.

·················· *May (near the end of the fourth quarter)* ··················

Begin the fourth quarterly review:

- Summarize and analyze fourth-quarter incident referral and other data reports.

- (Optional) Conduct and analyze observations of common areas in which improvements have been implemented.

- Present data analyses to the Foundations Team. The team decides what to share with the entire staff.

- Work with staff or with staff input to confirm or change improvement priorities. Focus on policies and procedures that can be implemented at the beginning of the next school year.

Determine team membership for the following year. New team members can begin working with the existing team to set summer tasks and new-year start-up procedures.

- Tasks for the summer might include revising procedures and designing lessons for a common area or important policy.

- In preparation for the new school year, outline tasks and assign staff members to orient all new staff to the school's policies and procedures.

School Year 2

•••••••••••••••••••••••••••••   *October*   ••••••••••••••••••••••••••••••

Conduct the first quarterly review:

- (Optional) Schedule staff, student, and parent surveys for late October, November, or early December. (Surveys may be administered annually, or, if cost is a concern, every two years.)

- Summarize and analyze first-quarter incident referrals and other data and compare with last year's data.

- Conduct and analyze common area observations and compare with last year's data.

•••••••••••••••••••••••••••••   *November*   ••••••••••••••••••••••••••••

Continue the first quarterly review:

- (Optional) Administer and analyze staff, student, and parent surveys. Compare with last year's data.

- Present incident referral, other existing data, survey, and observation analyses to the Foundations Team. The team decides what to share with the entire staff.

- Work with staff (or with staff input gained through team members' efforts) to confirm or change current improvement priorities and identify new priorities. Also identify areas that have improved from last year and celebrate the successes.

Conduct January, March, and May reviews as described for School Year 1.

Plan to continue this cycle of reviewing, analyzing, and reporting data.

Note: In subsequent years, the May quarterly review will include the Foundations Implementation Rubric; the rubric is a way to quickly assess the implementation status of previously addressed priorities. It's included on the CD and in Appendix A.

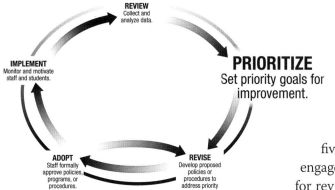

REVIEW
Collect and
analyze data.

IMPLEMENT
Monitor and motivate
staff and students.

PRIORITIZE
Set priority goals for
improvement.

ADOPT
Staff formally
approve policies,
programs, or
procedures.

REVISE
Develop proposed
policies or
procedures to
address priority
goals.

Understand the Prioritize step.

Use the information collected during the **Review** step to determine your improvement priorities—that is, what to work on first. An efficient way to begin is to summarize the review data, identify five or six potential priorities, and then engage the staff in developing a hierarchy for revisions. See "Engaging Staff in the Prioritize Step" (A-31) on the CD for suggestions on how to do this. Throughout the year, after each review, use the **Prioritize** step to evaluate whether the current priorities are correct or whether any changes are necessary. A balanced approach is needed when identifying how many improvements staff will work on at one time. Too many priorities may be confusing and cause staff to burn out; too few priorities may be frustrating and give staff the perception that no progress is being made.

Note that legitimate safety concerns should always be top priorities. If even a few students or staff members perceive a safety issue, at the very least the safety concern should be investigated with additional observation, interviews, or focus groups to determine whether it should become an immediate priority. If necessary, consider an administrative mandate about making safety the top priority.

When safety concerns are specific to one or more common areas, consider beginning the *Foundations* process with Module B, *Managing Behavior in Common Areas and With Schoolwide Policies.* When safety concerns relate to a general lack of safety or emergency procedures, consider beginning the *Foundations* process with Module E, Presentation 2, "Attributes of Safe and Unsafe Schools."

After addressing safety, select one improvement priority that is most likely to motivate staff to continue working with the new policies and procedures and to be receptive of new ideas. How do you know what that priority might be? Think of the behavior (student-to-staff disrespect, inappropriate dress, tardy to class), general location (out-of-control hallway or playground behavior), or grade level (the ninth-grade class is especially immature) that causes the most frustration among staff members. If you can reduce the frequency or intensity (or both) of that one problem, you'll go a long way toward increasing staff morale and job satisfaction. We call this technique *pain reduction.*

By reducing the staff's pain, you'll buy a lot of political capital for a relatively small investment of time. Once staff see improvement that positively affects them personally every day, it will be easier to appeal to their altruism—you can begin to talk about improvements that will help students not only behave better, but also learn and grow into responsible adults.

     &   FOUNDATIONS RECOMMENDATION   **&**

Legitimate safety concerns should always be top priorities. If even a few students or staff members perceive a safety issue, the safety concern should at the very least be investigated. After addressing safety, select the improvement priority most likely to motivate staff to continue working with the new policies and procedures and to be receptive of more new ideas. If you can reduce the frequency or intensity (or both) of that one problem, you'll go a long way toward increasing staff morale and job satisfaction. We call this technique pain reduction.

Additional factors to consider when determining which and how many common areas and schoolwide policies to work on are:

- Other curricular and staff development commitments
- District mandates
- Known upcoming changes in staff (particularly administration)

Former British prime minister Benjamin Disraeli (1804–1881) said, "The secret of success is constancy of purpose." In other words, choose your priorities, commit to them wholeheartedly, and work hard, and you will see improvements take shape.

Track the data used for prioritizing.

Ensure that you carefully archive all the data that led to your decisions about priorities so that you can use those same data sources to assess progress. For example, if survey and observation data led the team to identify the playground as a priority, archive the observation forms and survey responses as pre-intervention data. (Note the *exact* survey questions and percentage-who-agree data.)

After implementation, conduct observations and surveys again so your postintervention data will be directly comparable with the pre-intervention data. (Because you probably won't give the entire survey again during the same year, you might give a paper-and-pencil survey of just the playground items.) You'll be able to accurately determine the progress of your playground intervention by collecting and archiving the data systematically.

Here's an example of tracking specific data for pre- and postintervention comparison. Let's say that in student surveys conducted in the fall, about 48% of Asian students agreed with Item 5, "I feel safe in the hallways." Other racial groups agreed with this item at much higher percentages.

The school began investigating the reason for the discrepancy by convening a focus group of Asian students and their parents. The students and their parents brainstormed explanations for why so few Asian students agreed that they felt safe in the hallways and discussed possible solutions to the problem. The students expressed concern that any change in policy or procedures that specifically highlighted the issue could make the problem worse. They also reported that problems did not occur when adults were present in the hallways.

On the basis of this information, the staff adopted a plan to increase hallway supervision—with particular attention paid to intervening with *all* aggressive behavior, including peer-group horseplay, regardless of the target individual or group—and reduce the passing period time.

To evaluate the effectiveness of the new procedures, the school repeated some survey items in January, including Item 5, "I feel safe in the hallways." The responses to that specific question showed that 77% of Asian students agreed with the statement—an increase of 29% over the fall data (see Figure 3c opposite).

Figure 3d on p. 86 shows how Knik Elementary School in Wasilla, Alaska, compared responses to specific survey items over a 3-year period. The team at Knik found through data analysis that respect was a major concern. Consequently, they emphasized respect in all their improvement efforts.

The graph illustrates the great strides Knik made in improving school climate and culture. Initially, 44% of students agreed that students treat other students respectfully in the hallways. Three years later, 95% agreed. Initially, only 20% of students agreed that students treat other students respectfully on the playground. Three years later, 83% agreed. And initially, 49% of students agreed that it is easy to make friends at Knik. Three years later, 85% agreed.

If the team had not reviewed data and set priorities for improvement based on the data, Knik would probably still have the level of student-to-student disrespect reflected in the initial survey, making the school experience unpleasant for many students.

Knik Elementary's staff surveys also indicated a great improvement in how the school functions. After 3 years of implementing *Foundations*, the staff expressed 100% agreement with the following statements:

Figure 3c *(a) Fall and (b) winter student survey data (filtered for Asian, Black, Hispanic, and White students)*

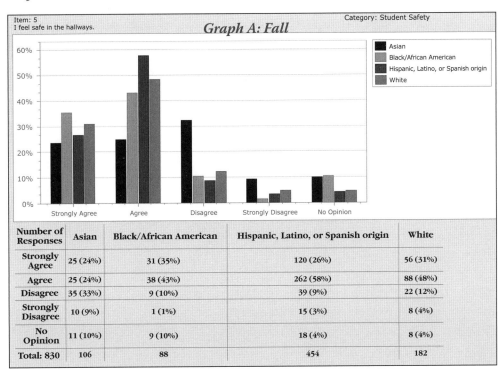

Number of Responses	Asian	Black/African American	Hispanic, Latino, or Spanish origin	White
Strongly Agree	25 (24%)	31 (35%)	120 (26%)	56 (31%)
Agree	25 (24%)	38 (43%)	262 (58%)	88 (48%)
Disagree	35 (33%)	9 (10%)	39 (9%)	22 (12%)
Strongly Disagree	10 (9%)	1 (1%)	15 (3%)	8 (4%)
No Opinion	11 (10%)	9 (10%)	18 (4%)	8 (4%)
Total: 830	106	88	454	182

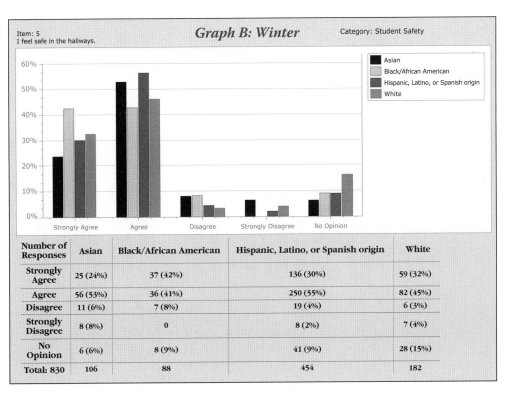

Number of Responses	Asian	Black/African American	Hispanic, Latino, or Spanish origin	White
Strongly Agree	25 (24%)	37 (42%)	136 (30%)	59 (32%)
Agree	56 (53%)	36 (41%)	250 (55%)	82 (45%)
Disagree	11 (6%)	7 (8%)	19 (4%)	6 (3%)
Strongly Disagree	8 (8%)	0	8 (2%)	7 (4%)
No Opinion	6 (6%)	8 (9%)	41 (9%)	28 (15%)
Total: 830	106	88	454	182

- The school has a consistent approach to behavior management and discipline.

- The school has adequate systems for identifying and helping students who are at risk for falling through the cracks (academically or behaviorally).

- I receive sufficient support when I have to deal with difficult students and discipline problems.

- I have a clear understanding of when and how I am expected to monitor student behavior.

- I have a clear understanding of when and how I am expected to motivate and encourage students to do their best.

Initially, staff agreement was not 100%, but the team and staff used these statements to target areas that needed improvement. In just 3 years, they achieved this remarkable result.

Be sure that you archive summaries of all the data you collect and analyze as you work through the **Review** and **Prioritize** steps.

Figure 3d   *Specific student responses to survey items compared year to year; thanks to Knik Elementary School in Wasilla, Alaska*

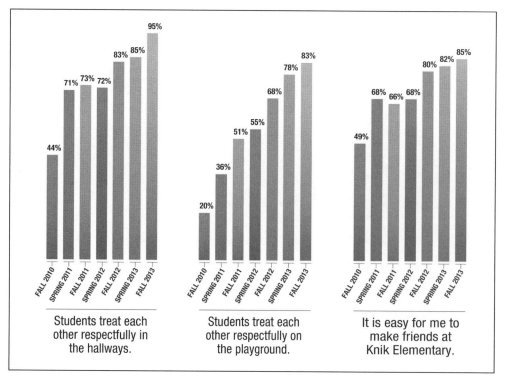

Determine a proposed improvement priority sequence for implementation.

Construct a long-term plan (3 years) for how and when you will implement the improvement priorities that you've identified. The following 3-year sequence is what we recommend if you are just beginning the *Foundations* process. Modify this plan if your data indicate that your school would benefit by working first on safety issues, such as emergency preparedness (Module E). Also plan to review and modify this suggested sequence each year. For example, if the team does not succeed in improving the targeted common area during the first year, it would be prudent to continue working on that area until data show that it has sufficiently improved and doesn't need to be a priority. This may mean that work on other suggested Year 2 priorities is delayed until Year 3.

ஐ FOUNDATIONS RECOMMENDATION ☞

Unless the data strongly indicate otherwise, follow the suggested Foundations *sequence for implementing improvements. During more than 20 years of experience, we've found that this sequence works well for most schools. Many schools experience significant schoolwide improvements in behavior as a result of working on just Guidelines for Success and one common area.*

SAMPLE IMPROVEMENT PRIORITY SEQUENCE

Year 1

- Develop Guidelines for Success (see Module C, Presentation 2). This task is almost always a productive starting point with or without any of the other suggested improvement efforts. Use information from the initial annual review to help identify guidelines that are meaningful for your school.

- Work on improving one or more common areas or schoolwide policies (see Module B). Target specific common areas based on the review data. Dramatically improved common areas often help a staff realize how much can be accomplished by working together.

Year 2

- Continue with Year 1 priorities. Expand common area improvement efforts to include more common areas (see Module B).

- Work on improving discipline procedures—specifically, determine the misbehaviors that should be handled with low-level staff corrections and those that warrant administrative involvement. This task includes establishing a 3-level system for responding to, documenting, and monitoring misbehavior (see Module D).

- Work on improving behavioral support for staff members who deal with severe and chronic student misbehavior and for students who exhibit such misbehavior. This task should include guidance for identifying students who need individual support (for example, use universal screening and red flags raised by data, such as chronic absenteeism). Also examine how staff members collaborate to make sure that staff and student needs are being met—for example, when and how should the counselor, administrator, social worker, psychologist, or behavior specialist become involved? (see Module F).

- Provide staff with additional training in classroom management and organization.

- Focus on improving school climate and student connectedness to school.

Year 3

- Continue with priorities from Years 1 and 2, as needed. Expand your efforts to all common areas and school policies as much as possible.

- Expand work on positive climate (see Module C).

- Begin work on conflict resolution and bullying prevention (see Module E).

- Work on improving behavioral support for students, including problem-solving processes, early-stage intervention strategies, and implementation of Tier 2 and Tier 3 behavior support plans (see Module F).

Task 1 Action Steps & Evidence of Implementation

Action Steps	Evidence of Implementation
1. Determine which data sources the team will collect, analyze, and review. (Module A, Presentation 4 provides more detail about this step.)	Foundations Process: Data Summaries
2. Guide the staff in setting priorities.	Foundations Process: Current Priorities
3. Set up a schedule for quarterly reviews during the school year.	Foundations Process: Planning Calendar

TASK 2

Understand the Revise step

In the **Revise** step, the Foundations Team (or another designated group of staff members) develop proposals for revising the priorities that were identified during the **Review** and **Prioritize** steps. Revisions generally consist of adding, modifying, or eliminating policies or procedures, always with the goal of improving safety, civility, and productivity.

We suggest you use STOIC as a framework for developing revisions of policies and procedures. STOIC can help ensure that the revision is comprehensive.

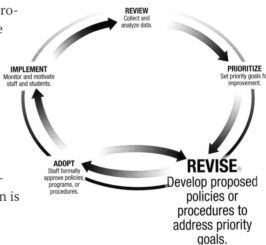

- **Structure**—Can we modify structural elements of the setting?
- **Teach**—Can we modify how we teach behavioral expectations to students?
- **Observe, Interact positively, Correct fluently**—Can we modify the supervisory elements of the common area or schoolwide policy?

We suggest two options for working through the **Revise** step. The basic approach—the one that most schools use—is the Foundations Team Approach. But some schools, usually those small enough that all staff can and should be directly involved in policy revisions, may choose the Whole Staff Approach. Decide in advance which approach will likely work best for your school. We explain the Whole Staff Approach first, then the Foundations Team Approach with a variation.

Whole Staff Approach

In the Whole Staff Approach, multiple task forces simultaneously guide the development and implementation of revision proposals for multiple improvement priorities. This approach is most effective when you have the luxury of a whole day when all staff members can work together.

For example, seven task forces might be formed to work on seven identified priorities:

- Guidelines for Success
- Staff Beliefs
- Playground
- Hallways and restrooms
- Cafeteria
- Arrival and dismissal issues
- Assemblies

The entire staff is included—every staff member is on one of the task forces. Each task force includes one or more Foundations Team members, allowing the team to easily monitor progress on all priorities.

Here's an example of how one high school structured their revision work. The entire faculty formed six task forces that each focused on a prioritized common area or schoolwide policy. They had already identified the improvement priorities: dress code, tardiness, disrespect, absenteeism, cafeteria, and electronics policy. All the task forces came together for a day of work during the summer, before school started. They followed this schedule:

Hour 1:	Each task force had 10 minutes to seek input from the entire staff.
Hour 2:	Each task force worked for an hour to develop a preliminary proposal.
Hour 3:	Each task force had 10 minutes to present to the staff and get more input.
Hours 4 & 5:	Each task force worked for 2 hours to revise their proposals based on staff input. They used STOIC as a framework.
Hour 6:	Each task force shared their revised proposal, and the entire staff voted on whether to adopt it.

If the proposal was adopted, the staff planned to begin the school year with the new policy or procedure in place. If the proposal was not adopted, the staff would begin the school year with the old policy or procedure and continue work on revising it. In the case of this high school, four of the six proposals were adopted, so the school accomplished a huge amount of work in a single day.

The task forces in this high school chose to continue work on their respective priorities, so they revised (as needed) and followed all the steps necessary to implement the new policies and procedures. However, another option is to have the Foundations Team take over all the improvement priorities, work on any necessary revisions, and manage the implementation steps. For this option, the staff should vote on the order in which the new policies and procedures are implemented.

The advantages of the Whole School Approach are:

- More staff might buy in to the improvement process, which translates to more staff follow-through.

- The rate of revision (and improvement) will be relatively fast.

Disadvantages are:

- Greater potential for staff burnout. Staff may already serve on several committees and don't want another commitment.

- Increased possibility of poor implementation. The entire staff might not have time to fully learn about the improvement process (they should read or view all of Module B), or staff may feel pressure or competition from other task forces and rush through the implementation.

At the secondary level, this approach can be strengthened by using prep periods for task force meetings. Staff who have first-period prep can work on one priority, staff who have second-period prep can work on another, and so on. Scheduling meeting times is easier with this plan.

*E*xample From the Field

I saw the power of the Whole Staff Approach during a *Foundations* meeting at an elementary school in the Pacific Northwest. A representative of the playground task force was presenting to the staff and recommended that playground supervisors (staff rotated playground duties) circulate throughout the entire playground to provide more supervision. The supervisors tended to remain in a covered area on rainy days. Many people became angry at the recommendation: "I'm not getting paid enough to ruin my shoes!" "I shouldn't have to . . ."

When the playground discussion ended, a representative of the hallways task force got up to present her task force recommendations. She had been critical of the playground recommendations just a few moments earlier. When she got to the front of the room, I could almost read her thoughts from her body language and facial expression: *I've been arguing against change and others' suggestions for years. Now I'm in the position of trying to sell the new policies that the hallways task force wants. Maybe I should have given the playground policies a chance . . .*

Involving more people in the process can foster respect and understanding and can create greater buy-in for policy changes and improvements.   —R.S.

Foundations Team Approach

In the Foundations Team Approach, the Foundations Team guides the development and implementation of the revision proposals for each improvement priority, one at a time. Ad hoc members (staff, student, and parents) might be used for some or all of the priorities. For example, representatives from the cafeteria may join the team to work on cafeteria priorities.

The advantage of this approach is that revision proposals might be more carefully and systematically developed and implemented. The Foundations Team has deeper knowledge and training in the improvement process.

Disadvantages are:

- The rate of priority revision will be slower than with the Whole Staff Approach.

- The staff might tire of hearing from the same people (the Foundations Team) over and over.

At the secondary level, this approach can be strengthened by using prep periods to communicate with staff. Team members who have first-period prep can communicate with and get feedback from staff who also have first-period prep, staff who have second-period prep can communicate with and get feedback from staff who also have second-period prep, and so on.

You can use a variation of the Foundations Team Approach to benefit from the strengths and knowledge of your staff. This variation can also help unify the staff by capitalizing on any existing school politics. Every building is susceptible to politics—cliques, beliefs, age groups, and a myriad of other factors can divide a staff into factions. Keep school politics in mind when considering the following variation.

Special Task Force Variation

This variation is especially useful when some staff members have strong opinions about certain issues or when some staff can provide needed expertise for a particular problem. For example, if students from a minority culture are having problems, staff members who have experience and knowledge of that culture might be able to evaluate the issue better than Foundations Team members can. Those staff members, along with one or two Foundations Team members, can form a special task force to work through the **Revise**, **Adopt**, and **Implement** steps for polices and procedures that relate to their area of expertise.

When staff members' opinions about how to revise a policy or procedure are divided, you can form a special task force to work on the **Revise** step. Invite staff members to volunteer for a position on the task force. The task force can include a couple of Foundations Team members and six nonteam staff members—three from each side of the issue. Task force members hash out their political divisions and forge a proposal to present to the entire staff in the next step of the Improvement Cycle, the **Adopt** step. If the proposal is adopted, the task force also oversees the implementation of the policy or procedure.

You might even form a few (one to three) special task forces to concurrently guide development and implementation of revision proposals for the top priorities. For example, form three task forces made up of Foundations Team members and other staff to work on the top three priorities, which might be (for example) Guidelines for Success, halls/restrooms, and disciplinary referral procedures.

The advantage of this variation is that it involves more faculty (promoting more buy-in), but not everyone all the time, which can burn people out. It's a good middle-ground approach.

A disadvantage of this variation is that once the initial task forces complete their work, improvement progress might stall. One way to reduce this possibility is to have the Foundations Team take over the responsibility for monitoring and maintaining the improvements after the task force has implemented the proposal.

Revision Process

Once you determine your school's approach to the **Revise step**, be sure to document it (see Figure 3e on p. 95). Following are important considerations for any approach and variation that you choose for working through the revision process.

- The objective for the Foundations Team or any task force is to develop *proposals* for staff consideration; the team or task force does not determine final policies and procedures.

- The Foundations Team or task force should meet as many times as necessary.

- The Foundations Team or task force should solicit staff opinions and recommendations, as needed, during proposal development. Below are some effective ways to gain staff guidance without taking too much staff time and energy:

  - Hold a 10-minute brainstorming session during a faculty meeting (no evaluating allowed). We recommend that discussions related to the improvement process that involve the entire staff should never take more than 10 minutes. If a discussion is so lively or contentious that it reaches the 10-minute limit, the task force needs to revisit the topic during a task force meeting. Then, at a later date, they can hold another 10-minute discussion with the entire staff. They can extend an open invitation to staff to attend the longer task force meeting, where the issues can be discussed in more detail.

  - Have staff members brainstorm on butcher paper posted in the staff room. Write the issue or question on the paper (or use a notebook) so all staff can respond in writing.

  - Write options for a particular issue on butcher paper and hang the paper in the staff room. Staff members can vote by writing their initials next to the suggestions they prefer.

⁎   FOUNDATIONS RECOMMENDATION   ⁏

Discussions related to the improvement process that involve the entire staff should never take more than 10 minutes of staff meeting time.

The Foundations Team or task force should review the applicable *Foundations* policy and procedure suggestions and best practice recommendations.

- Guidelines for Success—see Module C, Presentation 2
- Defining staff beliefs—see Module F, Presentation 3
- Improving common areas—see Module B
- Improving safety, discipline, and support procedures—see Modules D, E, and F

Task 2 Action Steps & Evidence of Implementation

Action Steps	Evidence of Implementation

Team members should work with the staff to:
 	
a. Make a decision about which approach (or approaches) to use for developing revision proposals.
 	
    • Whole Staff Approach
    • Foundations Team Approach
    • Special Task Force Variation
 	
b. Ensure that the Revise step proceeds appropriately and effectively.
	Foundations Process: Meeting Minutes, Current Priorities (see sample documentation in Figure 3e below)

Figure 3e *Sample documentation of decisions on development and implementation of improvement proposals*

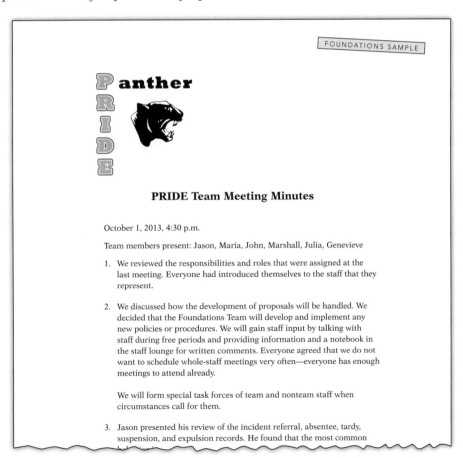

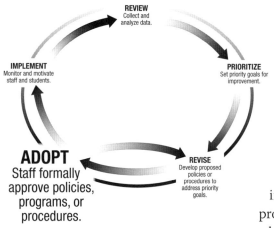

REVIEW
Collect and analyze data.

PRIORITIZE
Set priority goals for improvement.

IMPLEMENT
Monitor and motivate staff and students.

ADOPT
Staff formally approve policies, programs, or procedures.

REVISE
Develop proposed policies or procedures to address priority goals.

TASK 3

Understand the Adopt step

In the **Adopt** step, the Foundations Team or task force presents a revision proposal for a specific priority to the entire staff, and the entire staff formally accept (adopt) or reject the proposed change. This process should take place during a meeting (we'll call it a *decision meeting*) with all staff in attendance. For large staffs, the decision process may need to occur during prep-period, grade-level, or department meetings.

Improvement Cycle Flow

It's important to understand that the Improvement Cycle does not always flow in a continuous clockwise motion, as the graphic might suggest—it's quite a bit more fluid than that. Two (or more) improvement priorities can be at different points in the cycle. For example, the Foundations Team might be reviewing data about the dress code policy and at the same time be implementing new bus loading procedures. More than one task force can concurrently revise cafeteria entry and disciplinary referral procedures while the Foundations Team reviews playground observation data and implements a new restroom-pass procedure. The **Revise** and **Adopt** steps in particular often form their own cycle because a priority may be revised and presented for adoption two or three times before staff finally approve it.

We suggest the following procedures for the decision meeting to ensure that the entire staff is involved:

1. Confirm the date when the proposed policy will be presented during a staff decision meeting.

2. Share the proposed policy with the staff before the faculty meeting by email or by putting print copies into mailboxes. Determine who will be responsible for this task and when.

3. Decide which team members will prepare a 5-minute presentation about the proposal and coordinate the voting.

4. The staff discusses the proposal. (*Important:* Limit discussion to 10 minutes.)

5. Confirm the selected voting procedure and the criteria necessary for staff adoption of the policy. Make copies of ballots, if necessary.

6. The staff vote to adopt or reject the proposal.

We recommend that you use a system for reaching consensus on the adoption or rejection of proposals. Some voting systems to consider are the Five Levels of Satisfaction Voting System and the Thumbs Up Voting System.

Five Levels of Satisfaction Voting System. Staff members show their support or lack of support for a proposal by rating it on a 5-point scale, indicated with their fingers publicly during staff meetings.

5 fingers = I support the proposal wholeheartedly and am willing to help with it.
4 fingers = I support the proposal wholeheartedly.
3 fingers = The proposal is fine; I neither like it nor dislike it.
2 fingers = I am uncomfortable with the proposal, but will go along if over 90% of the staff accepts it. I will not be a passive or active obstructionist.
1 finger = I cannot live with the proposal and am willing to help the task force develop an alternative.

Important: Anyone voting 1 has to agree to help find an alternative to the proposal.

Figure 3f on the next page shows a voting rubric that can be displayed or distributed to staff so everyone understands how to vote. Four versions are available for printing on the CD (A-13). You might use the rubric as a ballot—hand out copies and have each voter circle a number. Collect the ballots and tabulate the results.

Establish your adoption criteria ahead of time. We suggest that the proposal be rejected if just one person votes 1 or if 10% or more of the staff vote 2.

Thumbs-Up Voting System. Staff members show their support or lack of support for a proposal by rating it on a 3-point scale, indicated with their thumbs.

Thumb up =   I fully support the proposal.
Thumb sideways = I only partially support the proposal, but am willing to implement it.
Thumb down =   I cannot support the proposal. It will not be good for students.

Important: Anyone voting Thumb down has to agree to help find an alternative to the proposal.

Adoption criteria: The proposal is rejected if even one person votes Thumb down.

Figure 3f *Sample voting rubric, version 1 of 4 (A-13)*

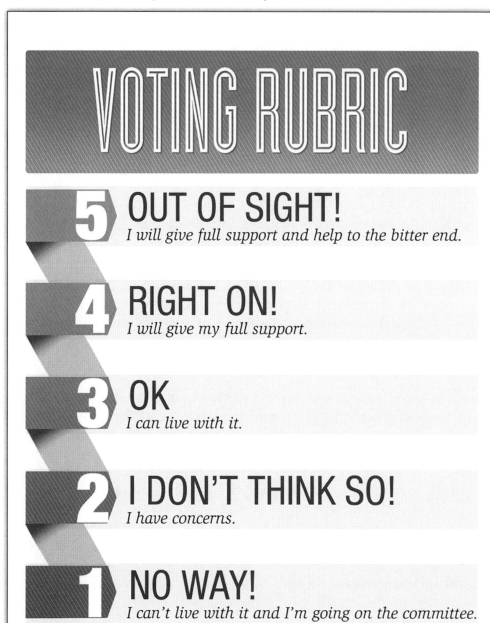

VOTING RUBRIC

5 OUT OF SIGHT!
I will give full support and help to the bitter end.

4 RIGHT ON!
I will give my full support.

3 OK
I can live with it.

2 I DON'T THINK SO!
I have concerns.

1 NO WAY!
I can't live with it and I'm going on the committee.

This sample can be printed from the Module A CD.

Adoption or rejection

If staff vote to adopt the proposal, the task force for that proposal—and the Foundations Team, if it's separate from the task force—works on its implementation (see Task 4).

If staff reject the proposal, the task force for that proposal works on developing an alternative proposal based on staff feedback, then presents the alternative proposal to the staff for a vote. After two additional attempts to revise the proposal (a total of three voting cycles), the issue should go to the principal, who will develop the final policy. Reasons for limiting the number of revisions and giving the principal the ultimate responsibility for the revision include:

- The team should not be stuck endlessly on any issue—neither the team nor the staff has time to waste.

- Divisive issues are often best resolved by a principal who has the courage to just say, "This is what we are going to do, and here's why."

View any divisive policy or procedure as an experiment. Set criteria to assess the concerns of those who disagree with the new policy or procedure, and assess those criteria after implementation. If the "losing" staff in the initial debate are correct in their concern (based on the criteria), the policy or procedure should be revised. The next experiment might include the policy or procedure that the "losing" staff recommended initially.

Figure 3g on the next page shows an example of a school's decision-making process and adoption guidelines.

Task 3 Action Steps & Evidence of Implementation

Action Steps	Evidence of Implementation
Team members should work with the staff to: • Identify the discussion and voting process that will be used to adopt or reject improvement proposals. • Ensure that the Adopt step is used appropriately and effectively.	Foundations Process: Meeting Minutes, Current Priorities
• Establish a procedure to limit the number of revisions and pass the responsibility to the principal when necessary.	Foundations Process: Meeting Minutes

Figure 3g *Sample decision-making process and revision policy communicated to staff (A-21)*

Memorandum
To: All staff
From: Foundations Team
Date: November 12

Subject: Decision-making process and revision policy for improvement priorities

1. To reach decisions regarding improvement priorities for our school, we will hold decision meetings that all staff should attend. All staff will receive a copy of the proposal a day or two before the meeting. Watch the posted schedule on the website for meeting times. During the meeting, you will have the opportunity to discuss the proposal and vote. We'll use the voting procedure illustrated below:

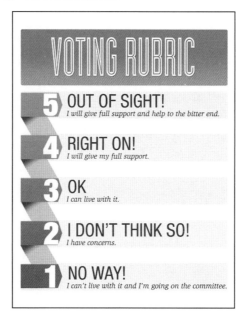

2. If the proposed revision to a policy or procedure is rejected, the Foundations Team (or special task force) will work on developing an alternative, based on staff input and concerns, and the proposal will be voted on again.

    After three voting cycles without a successful vote to adopt, the issue will go to the principal, who will develop the final policy.

 This sample can be printed from the Module A CD.

TASK 4

Understand the Implement step

In the **Implement** step, the Foundations Team or the task force that developed the proposal (or both) ensures that the adopted policies and procedures are launched, evaluated for effectiveness, and maintained over time.

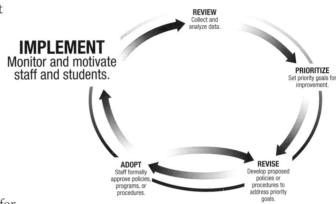

Launch the new policies and procedures.

We recommend the following steps for launching newly adopted policies and procedures.

STEP 1. Document the newly adopted policies and procedures in writing.

Keep *detailed descriptions* of all adopted policies and procedures in your Foundations Process Notebook. When you have data about their efficacy and are ready to consider them *final* policies and procedures, file written documentation in your Foundations Archive. See examples at the end of this task.

Keep *summaries* of final policies and procedures that will be implemented by all staff members in the Staff Handbook.

For example, if your school has adopted and finalized a new policy for managing and supervising the in-school suspension (ISS) program, place the documented details of the policies in the Foundations Archive binder. Give staff members who are responsible for the ISS program copies of the new policy, but don't include it in the Staff Handbook.

On the other hand, include expectations for staff supervision of the hallways in the Foundations Archive *and* in the Staff Handbook because all staff are responsible to some extent for hallway supervision.

Suggestions for organizing your Foundations Archive, Staff Handbook, and other records are in Module A, Presentation 2, Task 4.

STEP 2. Celebrate the adoption of new policies and procedures with staff (and students and parents, as appropriate).

A celebration is a great way to recognize the hard work and collaborative efforts of those involved in developing and implementing the improvements and to overtly acknowledge the importance of the new policies and procedures. The celebration can be as simple or elaborate as you like.

STEP 3. Make newly adopted policies and procedures visible (as appropriate) to enhance student and staff awareness of them and to validate their importance.

Students can create posters of procedure steps to hang in appropriate areas of the school. Some schools hold graphic arts contests—students design Guidelines for Success posters, and the winning poster is displayed prominently in many locations in the school.

STEP 4. Provide staff members (and students and parents, as appropriate) with all necessary information and training on newly adopted policies and procedures.

This action is important to ensure that all affected people know what they are supposed to do, how to do it (if necessary), why (as appropriate), and when they will start being held responsible for the new policies and procedures.

STEP 5. Introduce the new policies and procedures with a critical mass of implementation energy to focus attention on and generate enthusiasm for them.

For example, let's say a new set of procedures for how students are to enter, line up, and leave the cafeteria has been adopted. You can't just expect students to display the new behavior expectations and staff to enforce and supervise the new rules without training. The task force (or Foundations Team) should plan a training period something like the following.

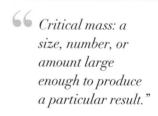 *Critical mass: a size, number, or amount large enough to produce a particular result."*

Monday (One week before the planned start date):

> Task force gives staff members a memo to share with students. The memo says that new cafeteria procedures will go into effect next week, and students will learn the procedures in class this week.

Tuesday (during a faculty meeting):

- The principal publicly thanks task force members and reminds staff members about the new procedures.

- The task force gives staff members plans for three 5-minute student lessons on the new procedures, scheduled as follows:

    > Lesson 1—Teach in all first-period classes on Wednesday
    > Lesson 2—Teach in all second-period classes on Thursday
    > Lesson 3—Teach in all third-period classes on Friday

Thursday: The task force meets with cafeteria staff and supervisors to train them on the new procedures.

Monday (start date):

- The principal makes a morning announcement to remind everyone about the new procedures.

- The principal, assistant principal, and two task force members are in the cafeteria during lunch to support students and supervisors and to take care of any necessary last-minute adjustments.

STEP 6. Support staff members (and students and parents, as appropriate) in the early implementation of new policies and procedures.

Continuing the above example of new cafeteria procedures:

Tuesday–Friday (week of the start date): Two task force members are in the cafeteria during lunch to support students and supervisors, answer questions, and monitor the implementation of the new policies.

Evaluate the new policies and procedures.

We recommend that the Foundations Team (or task force) review and evaluate the impact of recently adopted policies and procedures 4 to 6 weeks after implementation. The flowchart in Figure 3h on the next page illustrates this process. You should conduct additional common area observations and collect office referral data, then compare the pre- and postimplementation data.

If the new policies and procedures are having a positive impact on the school, provide positive feedback to staff, students, and parents.

Figure 3h   *Evaluation flowchart (A-14)*

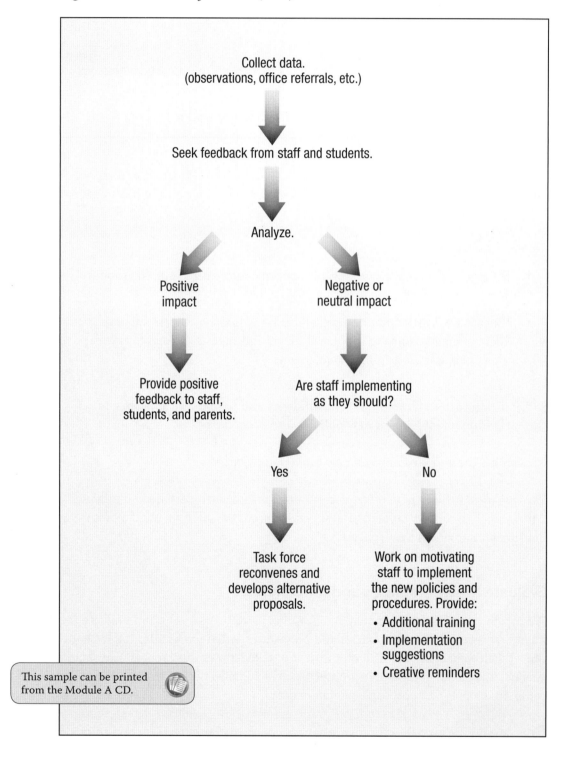

Collect data.
(observations, office referrals, etc.)

Seek feedback from staff and students.

Analyze.

Positive
impact

Negative or
neutral impact

Provide positive
feedback to staff,
students, and parents.

Are staff implementing
as they should?

Yes

No

Task force
reconvenes and
develops alternative
proposals.

Work on motivating
staff to implement
the new policies and
procedures. Provide:

• Additional training
• Implementation
  suggestions
• Creative reminders

This sample can be printed
from the Module A CD.

If the new policies and procedures are having a negative (or neutral) impact, determine whether staff implementation is the problem.

- If staff are implementing as they should, the task force should reconvene and develop alternative proposals for staff consideration.

- If staff are *not* implementing as intended, the task force or Foundations Team (or both) should work on motivating the staff to implement the new policies and procedures. The task force might provide:

  - Additional training
  - Implementation suggestions (see Figure 3j at the end of this presentation)
  - Creative reminders

If necessary, the principal should discuss the importance of follow-through privately with reluctant staff members.

Maintain the new policies and procedures.

The following actions can help you maintain adopted policies and procedures over time. Presentation 5 of this module offers many more suggestions for developing staff buy-in to the *Foundations* process.

Identify creative ways to incorporate the policies and procedures into the school culture. You might hold a brief celebration before a staff meeting, have a parent group prepare a staff lunch, or have the principal publicly thank the task force for their effort.

Develop an annual calendar of implementation activities that includes a timeline and the name of the person responsible. Include, for example, when to re-teach expectations, remind faculty of their roles, or honor food service staff.

Provide staff members with ongoing implementation ideas and reminders:

- Include teaching or behavior management tips in the staff newsletter or in memos from the Foundations Team.
- Keep the Foundations Team visible—use a creative logo on reports and memos and announce team activities, for example.
- Check in with your constituents often and ask how things are going.
- Celebrate accomplishments.
- Contribute to staff meetings with updates on team activities and with fun events such as skits.

Solicit staff ideas on ways to facilitate the implementation:

- Ask staff members (particularly well-respected staff members) to review and report on implementation ideas.
- Conduct staff surveys or give brief questionnaires on specific topics.
- Include a 5-minute brainstorming session on the staff meeting agenda.
- Poll your constituents about issues of concern.
- Provide a place in the staff room where staff can write down ideas and concerns for the team.

Ask for administrative support:

- If some staff are resistant, ask the administrator to make a statement about his or her and the school's commitment to improving the school through *Foundations*.

- Report successes and accomplishments to the school board and central office and invite feedback. For example, the superintendent might visit and congratulate the staff on their progress.

- Use staff incentives. For example, the administrator can recognize staff members who are implementing *Foundations* concepts well by writing notes to the staff members; the notes are also entered into a drawing for a weekly prize.

Have staff acknowledge the good work of other staff. For example, staff members can nominate other staff members for weekly drawings for small prizes.

Conclusion

The Foundations Team's main job is to maintain the Improvement Cycle. Every year, you will review meaningful data to identify a manageable number of improvement priorities, and you'll develop revision proposals for each priority. You will take the proposal through the adoption process and, once it has been adopted, implement the policy or procedure and review it for efficacy. You may have different priorities at different stages of the Improvement Cycle at one time. You might be working on launching new arrival procedures while you are in the beginning stages of developing a new dress code policy. Every semester you should be working on one, two, or three (or more if possible) priorities, because every semester your data review should tell you that your school could be better. If you, the Foundations Team, ever think you are done or forget what your job is, review data to identify some priorities and keep the Improvement Cycle moving constantly.

Task 4 Action Steps & Evidence of Implementation

Action Steps	Evidence of Implementation
Team members work with the staff to: • Ensure that all newly adopted policies and procedures are launched effectively. • Ensure that any new policies and procedures are evaluated for effectiveness (including quality of staff implementation) a reasonable time after they have been introduced. • Ensure that effective policies and procedures are maintained over time.	Foundations Process: Planning Calendar, Meeting Minutes, Current Priorities Foundations Archive: Schoolwide Policies, Common Area Policies and Procedures, Safety Policies, Lesson Plans Staff Handbook: Policies and Procedures, Staff Roles and Responsibilities Student and Parent Handbook: Policies and Procedures (See examples of documentation in Figures 3i and 3j on the pages that follow.)

Figure 3i *Samples of Foundations Archives (selected pages) (A-23); thanks to Tioga Middle School and Fresno Unified School District in California*

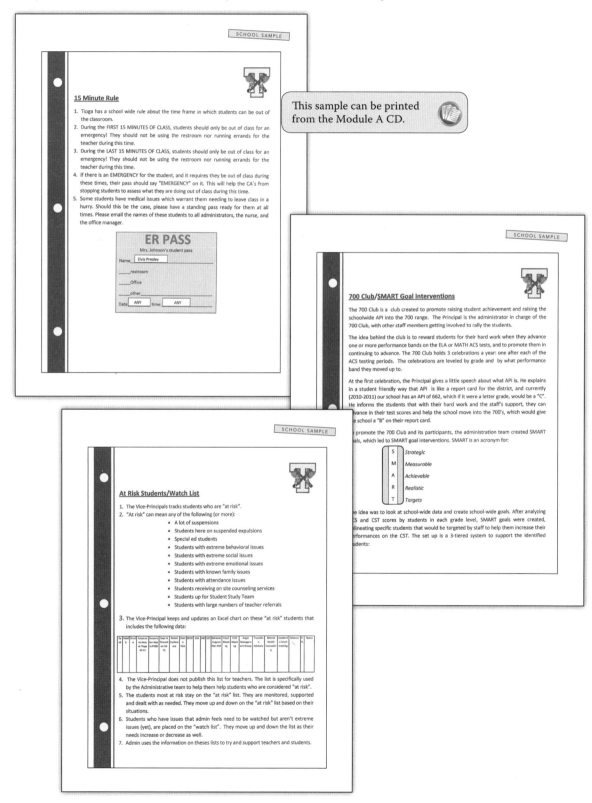

Building Community Relationships

At Tioga, we believe that it is important to not only support our community, but encourage our community to support our students/school. We have staff that is involved in making these community connections and establishing relationships with businesses. We arrange for these businesses to come and visit our school so they can see the wonderful things taking place here. Currently (2010-2011 school year), we have business relationships with:

EECU: Supports Tioga with a donation of $3,500 each year for materials and supplies, plus they also purchased our MicroSociety checks, withdrawal slips and deposit slips for our Micro ventures. EECU also partners with our Micro bank and Micro credit union for advice and training as needed. They also come out in the spring and set up a mock environment called "Wise Up" where students learn how to set up a checking account, accrue life expenses, and pay the expenses accordingly.

Jamba Juice: sells smoothies on our campus once a week. We get 20% of the total sales, which we use for materials and supplies for the Micro cafe and various emergencies as they arise.

Aetna: sends volunteers as they are available and they donate supplies as they are able (for our MicroSociety warehouse). They also donated our glass display cabinet in room 35.

Cafeteria Procedures

1. The morning routine is set up so that:
   a. Students arriving on the a.m. bus who want breakfast enter the cafeteria at the east doors as they enter school. They are directed to walk in the first kitchen door, secure their breakfast, and exit the second kitchen door.
   b. Students are directed to sit at the next available seat in the row. They are not allowed to sit anywhere they'd like. The row must be filled up before a new row can be started at the tables.
   c. When students are done eating, they may dismiss themselves. They must clear their eating area of all trash and dump the trash in the trash cans by the east doors as they leave the cafeteria.
   d. No food is allowed to be taken outside.

The lunch-time routine is set up so that:
   a. Classes are released on a rotating schedule so that there is no overly large cluster of kids coming to lunch at once.
   b. The Vice-Principal creates the schedule and emails it to the teachers 4 different times throughout the year (at the beginning of each quarter) and the schedule lets each teacher know when to dismiss their students (5 min. early, 3 min early, etc.)
   c. All students are directed to walk down the main hallway to lunch, escorted by their teacher. We have an extra 3 min. built into our lunch schedule to accommodate teachers doing this. Teachers are expected to remain with their class until the actual lunch bell rings.
   d. Each teacher is also told (by the schedule) which door to the cafeteria they are to walk their students to (east doors, line 1 and 2, or hallways doors, line 1 and 2).
   e. Students follow the same instructions for sitting at tables as the morning routine.
   f. The school social worker is on the microphone during lunch (up on the stage) to direct, or redirect, students as needed, reminding students to keep talking to a minimum so they can eat lunch and go outside to have social time/fresh air/exercise.
   g. Students also follow the same dismissal procedures as the morning routine.

CST Tutorials

1. By the assigned due date, teachers must make phone calls to ALL of the student's parents/guardian (use listed phone numbers until you reach somebody) to inform them of the afterschool tutorial (day, time, teacher expectation, etc.) and to let them know their student must get a permission slip signed in order for their student to be afterschool with you. Do not consider leaving a message an appropriate contact. This will log in as two hours of "prep" work for this task.
2. YOUR contract will TOTAL a maximum of 35 hours X $30 per hour = $1,050.
3. You are to enroll 25-30 students in your tutorial with the assumption that 20 students minimum will be in daily attendance.
4. By the assigned deadline, please submit to the Principal your lesson plans for the afterschool tutorials you will be teaching for the upcoming week. The lesson plan should include the STANDARD(s) you are targeting, a lesson objective, and the activities included. Please log in one hour of prep for this task each week you run your tutorial.
5. An Afterschool Program staff person will be putting in your box or delivering to you an attendance sheet for the students who have signed up to participate in your afterschool tutorial. This MUST be completed each day you host a tutorial session. This is for auditing purposes since our tutorial contracts are funded by SCE/LEP monies and we get attendance via our Afterschool Program.
6. Our After School Program Coordinator will designate an Afterschool program staff member to pick up the attendance sheets from you on a weekly basis.
7. Because we get credit for students in your tutorial sessions by the Afterschool Program, snacks will be delivered to your room each day you host a tutorial session. Please inform the ASP Coordinator (as well as the admin in charge) of the days of the week you will be implementing your tutorial program (preferably TUES. and THURS. from 2:30-3:30).
8. If you are absent on a day where you normally have tutorial, and will not make it in for tutorial, please notify the office first thing in the morning so they may announce it to the students in a timely manner; this gives students an opportunity to notify parents of the change in their schedule as well.
9. If a student needs to take the 3:45 bus after attending your tutorial, you must let the ASP Coordinator know so that bus passes can be brought to you. Student without this pass will NOT be allowed on the 3:45 bus!
10. Please inform students that PERFECT attendance and PERFECT behavior will earn them a trip to Santa Cruz Beach Boardwalk during the last week of school. This is your "carrot" to keep them coming and staying on task. If a student has an excused absence (out ill from school all day due to fever/vomiting/etc., their absence from tutorial is excused).
11. This will be funded through our Afterschool program.
12. If a student drops due to any reason (behavior, lack of interest, family issues, etc.) PLEASE inform me immediately and we will target another student to fill the vacancy.

Figure 3j *Sample evidence that new policies and procedure have been evaluated and results conveyed to staff (A-22)*

MONROE ELEMENTARY, HOME OF THE COWBOYS

Memorandum
To: All staff
From: Foundations Team
Date: December 15, 2013

Subject: Evaluation of new cafeteria policies

The new procedures for lining up in the cafeteria and supervising students were implemented on November 5. On December 12, Jamal and Teresa observed both lunch periods. The average score for the cafeteria was 87%, a great improvement over the 65% score from September 20. The cafeteria staff also commented that they see a big improvement in overall behavior and noise level. Congratulations to everyone involved!

We all take turns supervising lunch, and we've done a good job of correcting consistently and referring to the posted expectations. We can improve the cafeteria (and students' general sense of school as a positive, safe place) even more by providing more positive interactions. Let's try to keep these suggestions in mind:

- Recognize students who are following the expectations and praise them specifically.

- Provide noncontingent attention—ask individual students how they are, initiate brief conversations, welcome students by name to the cafeteria, etc.

- For every correction you give to a student, try to praise or give noncontingent attention to that student at least three times.

- Remember to keep scanning and circulating as you interact with students.

Thanks, everyone. Let's keep up the good work!

This sample can be printed from the Module A CD.

Data-Driven Processes

> **NOTE:** This presentation contains more detail than most of the other presentations. After reading or viewing the presentation, use the text as a reference as you work on the **Review** and **Prioritize** steps of the Improvement Cycle.
>
> This entire presentation is essential material for the Data/Evaluation Coordinator, and we are primarily addressing this person in the following text. He or she will be responsible for recommending data sources, reviewing data, compiling results, and presenting summaries to the Foundations Team.
>
> Other team members can review the entire presentation, but they will find certain tasks most useful. For example, the administrator will use Task 4 to coordinate retrieval of incident referral data with the Data/Evaluation Coordinator. The Staff Liaison and Family Engagement Coordinator should read Task 2 in order to recommend when and how to give staff, student, and parent surveys. Everyone who is involved in conducting common area observations will find valuable information in Task 3.
>
> Remember, it is the team's responsibility to convey the importance of collecting data to staff, to summarize and analyze the data, and to make the data accessible to administrators and staff.

DOCUMENTS*

- Data Summary Form (A-05)
- Data review summary (A-24)
- Documentation of improvement priority sequence (A-25)
- Sample survey (A-26)
- Sample letter about surveys to parents (A-27)
- Sample letter to parents about survey results (A-28)
- Common Area Observation form (A-06)
- Sample documentation of data shared with staff (A-29)
- Behavior Incident Referral Form (A-07 and A-08)

* All documents listed are available on the CD. Other documents that are not shown in this presentation are also available on the CD (see Appendix C for a complete list).

INTRODUCTION

During the **Review** step of the Improvement Cycle, the Foundations Team collects and analyzes data from multiple sources. These data allow schools to make informed, objective decisions based on solid information about their behavior management practices and improvement priorities. During the decision-making process, you'll ask questions such as:

- What policies and procedures are working well and should be celebrated and protected?

- What is working adequately but could be improved?

- What is not working and should be substantially modified or eliminated?

- Have newly implemented policies and procedures resulted in positive, negative, or no change?

If the data sources you are currently using do not help you answer these questions, consider changing or adding methods of data collection. You'll get some ideas for improving your data collection processes in this presentation.

Data help schools avoid ineffective but all-too-common decision making based on:

- Subjective feeling

- Instinct or overreaction to a single piece of information, such as one parent complaint

- Custom or tradition—the "we've always done it this way" mentality

- Power, influence, and politics—in some schools, a few very vocal staff members drive policy implementation, regardless of what the staff as a whole think is correct

The sources of data that schools might use include:

- Surveys of staff members, students, and possibly parents

- Observations of the school's common areas

- Incident referrals—that is, documentation of student misbehavior, such as office referrals and detention assignments

- Existing school records for attendance, tardiness, suspensions, expulsions, referrals to alternative education, graffiti, and vandalism

To get the most out of this presentation, we suggest you follow these steps:

1. View the entire video presentation or read the entire printed presentation.

2. Decide which data sources your school will use.

   For the first quarterly review of the school year, use all (or most) of the available data sources. If staff, students, and parents complete surveys in early or mid-fall, include these data and compare them with results from previous surveys (if available). You can also ask staff how the new year is going for them so far—which policies and procedures are working well and which aren't?

   For subsequent reviews, use incident referral data and other existing school records. Include any new observation data as well.

   Note: In previous versions of *Foundations*, we referred to *annual* reviews and *periodic* reviews. In this version, we refer to all the reviews as *quarterly* to clarify the recommended minimum frequency of Foundations Team reviews. During each quarterly review, the team should examine current trends and a year-to-date comparison with previous years. Although the team may review data on a quarterly basis, the school administrator (and optionally the Foundations Data/Evaluation Coordinator) should review incident data, particularly office discipline referrals, at least monthly for problematic trends or patterns.

   Of course, if your school year is not divided into quarters, or if it runs on an atypical schedule, create a schedule that corresponds roughly to our sample quarterly review calendar plan (detailed in Module A, Presentation 3, Task 1).

   ---

3. Design a plan for using the data sources. The Data/Evaluation Coordinator on the Foundations Team can be primarily responsible, but if several data sources are used, some of the responsibilities for collecting, analyzing, and reporting results might be assigned to other team or staff members.

4. All staff who are closely involved in collecting and analyzing the data should view the relevant tasks in this presentation a second time and work through the corresponding Action Steps.

5. Determine how to involve the entire staff in the **Review** process. At a minimum, all staff members should be informed why, when, and how any **Review** activities will take place. Analyses and conclusions based on the **Review** activities should also be shared with the staff quarterly.

This presentation has five tasks:

Task 1: Use Multiple Data Sources to Identify Improvement Priorities explains how to compile all your pertinent data results onto a form, use the form to help decide what you should work on first, and determine a proposed improvement priority sequence.

Task 2: Use Survey Data to Make Decisions describes the advantages and limitations of using survey data and presents several examples of the useful information that can be gleaned from surveys.

Task 3: Use Common Area Observation Data to Make Decisions discusses how to schedule common area observations and compile and interpret the results.

Task 4: Use Incident Referral Data to Make Decisions explains how to analyze and interpret your school records and presents examples of how the data can lead to decisions about improvement priorities.

Task 5: Use Other Existing Sources to Make Decisions introduces the concept of 90% Thresholds as a guideline for making decisions and presents examples of other useful data sources, such as suspension data and focus groups.

TASK 1

Use multiple data sources to identify improvement priorities

In this task, you learn how to compile all pertinent data results onto the Data Summary Form. The form makes it easier to identify safety issues, student behaviors, school locations, staff practices, and family and student perceptions that need improvement. It facilitates data-based decision making about what to work on first to improve your school's behavior management practices. We present this information in Task 1 so you understand the goal you are working toward while you study Tasks 2, 3, and 4.

Identify data sources and use them to identify school strengths and areas that need improvement.

Identify all the data sources available for analysis; they may include surveys, incident referral data, common area observations, attendance and tardiness rates, suspensions, expulsions, referrals to special education, and vandalism and graffiti reports (we discuss these sources in more detail in later tasks). Then, for each separate data source, identify possible conclusions about school strengths and weaknesses (that is, areas that can be celebrated and those that need improvement).

Figure 4a shows an example of the Data Summary Form (Form A-05 on the Module A CD). Some common issues are listed in the Category column in alphabetical order. You may add rows to the table to accommodate issues that are specific to your school. In the example, "Location—Blacktop: wall-ball area" was added to the default categories.

Note: The categories on the Data Summary Form correspond to categories in the *Safe & Civil Schools* Climate & Safety Surveys report discussed in Task 2.

If data indicate that particular issues may be problematic, write them in the Possible Problems row or add a row. Examples of possible problems include serious issues such as drug, alcohol, or tobacco use; personal property theft or damage; school property theft or damage; student sexual contact; weapons; students hurting other students; and threats or violence toward staff. Also include less severe but still highly problematic behaviors such as classroom disruptions, tardiness, noncompliance, and so on.

In Figure 4a on the next page, the Data/Evaluation Coordinator has indicated with brief notes the issues that data indicate are problematic. Viewing all of the potential indicators in one place, side by side, facilitates the identification of problems that need to be prioritized.

Figure 4a *Example of completed Data Summary Form (A-05)*

Data Summary Form (p. 1 of 4)

Data/Evaluation Coordinator: _____ Date of review: _____

Category	Student Surveys	Staff Surveys	Parent Surveys	Incident Referrals	Common Area Observations	Other Data Sources*
Arrival						
Bullying						
Bus and transport to and from school					loading area score = 45%	2 suspensions
Dismissal						
Harassment						
Location—all						
Location—cafeteria	loud, pushing & shoving	language, disrespectful behavior			score = 39% student lang. a problem	1 serious injury

*Other data sources include average daily attendance, tardiness, suspensions, expulsions, referrals to alternative education placements, referrals to SPED, number of students referred to SPED who did not qualify, vandalism, graffiti, illegal activity, injury reports, feedback from staff, social-emotional support (counselors, school social workers and psychologists, focus groups, red flags, summaries of universal screening.)

Data Summary Form (p. 2 of 4)

Category	Student Surveys	Staff Surveys	Parent Surveys	Incident Referrals	Common Area Observations	Other Data Sources*
Location—classroom						
Location—courtyard and commons area					Student language a problem	
Location—hallways						
Location—locker rooms and gym						
Location—parking lot						
Location—playground Blacktop: wall-ball area						5 incidents of vandalism, graffiti
Location—restrooms						
Parent and family perceptions of school						

Data Summary Form (p. 3 of 4)

Category	Student Surveys	Staff Surveys	Parent Surveys	Incident Referrals	Common Area Observations	Other Data Sources*
Possible problems	Recent transfers feel locals discriminate against them; Student language		Concerned about conflict b/w locals & newcomers	3 in September		Absences 20% lower compared with last year. Tardies also lower
Respectful interactions						
Rules, expectations, and procedures						
Rules, expectations, and procedures—classroom						
Rules, expectations, and procedures—schoolwide	Low % agree	Low % agree			Not emphasized when staff corrects	
Staff interactions and perceptions						
Staff interactions and perceptions—discipline policies		some concern about consistency				
Staff interactions and perceptions—expectations						

Data Summary Form (p. 4 of 4)

Category	Student Surveys	Staff Surveys	Parent Surveys	Incident Referrals	Common Area Observations	Other Data Sources*
Staff interactions and perceptions—staff-staff interactions						
Staff-student interactions						
Student safety						
Student/parent comfort communicating with staff						
Students' feelings about school	Low		Low			
Student-student interactions						
Other:						
Other:						

You (the Data/Evaluation Coordinator) can use this form as you present a summary of your data analyses to the Foundations Team. The form makes it possible to communicate simply and visually to other team members what the data suggest. You can augment the relatively concise results displayed on the form with your own more detailed reports. The team can then decide how to summarize the information and present it to the staff as you all begin the process of setting priorities.

You might use a separate copy of the form to record school strengths and improvements for presentation to the team.

Generate overall conclusions based on all of the data sources together.

First, compare all the data summaries and identify any strong positive trends that are evident across several data sources. Report these strengths to staff, students, and parents as causes for celebration. Existing opportunities such as staff meetings, school announcements, school assemblies, parent newsletters, and website postings can all be used to communicate the positive news. Results from some data sources, such as observations, incident referrals, and suspensions, will be appropriate for staff only. Results can be shared with students if the staff decide that students would benefit from the knowledge—if they would be motivated or feel pride in their school, for example, or if it would help rally energy to improve some aspect of the school, such as attendance or school pride.

Second, identify any strong negative trends evident across several data sources—you will want to give these issues serious consideration as top improvement priorities. For example, if surveys, incident reports, and vandalism and graffiti records indicate that hallways are problematic, improving behavior, supervision, and safety in the hallways should be one of your priorities. Report on the identified improvement priorities at the same time you report strengths and successes so staff, students, and parents hear what they can be proud of as well as what needs to be improved.

In the example in Figure 4a, strong positive trends are evident in attendance and tardiness (see Other Data Sources in the Respectful interactions row). Several data sources indicate that the cafeteria needs improvement. Surveys and observations also suggest that schoolwide expectations can be improved, a task that ties into a cafeteria improvement priority. This school serves many families who have recently moved to the area to work in a new industry; the Data/Evaluation Coordinator has written "concerned about conflict between locals and newcomers" in the Possible Problems row. The staff might discuss how they can alleviate this perceived problem in conjunction with boosting students' positive feelings about school. The Data Summary Form allows the team to get a sense of how various possible problems compare and then quickly identify two or three tangible potential improvement priorities. See the important note below and "Pain Reduction" on p. 120 for additional information on prioritizing issues.

IMPORTANT: Legitimate safety concerns should always be top priorities. If even a few students or staff members perceive a safety issue, at the very least the safety concern should be investigated with additional observation, interviews, or focus groups to determine whether it should become an immediate priority. If necessary, consider an administrative mandate about making safety the top priority.

When safety concerns are specific to one or more common areas, consider beginning the *Foundations* process with Module B, *Managing Behavior in Common Areas and With Schoolwide Policies*.

When safety concerns relate to a general lack of safety or emergency procedures, consider beginning the *Foundations* process with Module E, Presentation 2, "Attributes of Safe and Unsafe Schools."

Third, identify any trends within or across data sources that do not make sense or are contradictory, and try to find an explanation. Following are three typical reasons for conflicting or inconsistent data:

- **The data from one or more of the sources are based on a data collection anomaly.** For example, a common area observation was inadvertently conducted on a day when students were unusually stimulated or distracted.

- **Specific survey responses are based on insufficient information or experience from the respondents.** For example, if student surveys and observations suggest a problem in the cafeteria but staff surveys do not, the discrepancy might be because most staff don't spend time in the cafeteria and don't have first-hand knowledge of the situation. If this is the case, staff perceptions of the cafeteria should be given relatively little weight when determining improvement priorities.

- **Specific survey responses are based on perceptions tinted with rose-colored glasses.** If surveys indicate few problems but observations and incident referrals suggest problems, give less credence to the survey results.

Pain Reduction

After addressing safety, select an improvement priority that is most likely to motivate staff to continue working with the new policies and procedures and to be receptive to new ideas. How do you know what that priority might be? Think of the behavior (student-to-staff disrespect, inappropriate dress, tardy to class), general location (out-of-control hallway or playground behavior), or grade level (the ninth-grade class is especially immature) that causes the most frustration among staff members. If you can reduce the frequency or intensity (or both) of that one problem, you'll go a long way toward increasing staff morale and job satisfaction. We call this technique *pain reduction*. By reducing the staff's pain, you'll buy a lot of political capital for the relatively small investment of time. Once the staff have seen improvement that positively affects them personally every day, it's easier to appeal to their altruism—you can begin to talk about improvements that will help students not only behave better, but also learn and grow into responsible adults.

Determine a proposed improvement priority sequence.

Construct a long-term plan (3 or more years) for how and when you will implement the improvement priorities that you've identified. The 3-year sequence that we recommend is outlined below and is presented in more detail in Module A, Presentation 3, Task 1. If you've ascertained that your school should work on safety issues first, modify the plan to include safety as the top priority.

> ## ✦ FOUNDATIONS RECOMMENDATION ✦
>
> *Unless the data strongly indicate otherwise, follow the suggested* Foundations *sequence for implementing improvements. During over 30 years of experience, we've found that this sequence works well for most schools. Many schools experience significant schoolwide improvements in behavior as a result of working on just Guidelines for Success and one common area.*

SAMPLE IMPROVEMENT PRIORITY SEQUENCE

Year 1

- Develop Guidelines for Success (Module C, Presentation 2).

- Work on improving one or more common areas or schoolwide policies (Module B).

Year 2

- Continue with Year 1 priorities.

- Expand improvement efforts to include additional common areas and schoolwide policies (Module B).

- Work on improving discipline procedures, specifically all aspects of staff response to misbehavior (Module D).

- Work on improving behavioral support for staff members who deal with severe and chronic student misbehavior and for students who exhibit such misbehavior (Module F).

- Provide staff with additional training in classroom management and organization (Module F).

- Focus on improving school climate and student connectedness to school (Module C).

Year 3

- Continue with priorities from Years 1 and 2, as needed.

- Work on safety, conflict resolution, and bullying prevention (Module E).

- Work on improving behavioral support for students, including problem-solving processes, early-intervention strategies, and implementation of Tier 2 and Tier 3 behavior support plans (Module F).

Schools that have already gone through the initial steps of *Foundations* and are now implementing a continuous Improvement Cycle should use the results from multiple data sources to set priorities for the next quarter or semester. For example, the school should not work on disciplinary incident referrals (the content of Module D) unless one or more data sources indicate that they are problematic.

Improvement Cycle Flow

It's important to understand that the Improvement Cycle does not always flow in a continuous clockwise motion, as the graphic (p. 75) might suggest—it's quite a bit more fluid than that. Two (or more) improvement priorities can be at different points of the cycle; for example, the Foundations Team might review data about the dress code policy and at the same time implement new bus loading procedures. More than one task force can be revising cafeteria entry and disciplinary referral procedures concurrently while the Foundations Team is reviewing playground observation data and implementing a new restroom pass procedure. The **Revise** and **Adopt** steps in particular often form their own cycle because a priority may be revised and presented for adoption two or three times before staff finally approve it.

Involve the entire staff in determining the improvement priority sequence.

Present the proposed sequence of improvement priorities to the entire staff during a staff meeting or inservice. Include all supporting data and other rationale in the presentation. It's important to get staff input before beginning work on any improvements because the staff should have a sense of shared ownership in the process of defining priorities.

If the staff does not agree with the proposed sequence, develop one or more alternative sequences based on staff recommendations and suggestions (see the **Revise** step in the Improvement Cycle). Continue this process until the staff agrees on a sequence.

Once staff agree on a proposed sequence, proceed with the **Revise**, **Adopt**, and **Implement** steps of the Improvement Cycle for each priority. Remember that different priorities can proceed at different rates.

Task 1 Action Steps & Evidence of Implementation

Action Steps	Evidence of Implementation
1. Decide on the data sources you will use and establish timelines and actions for collecting and reviewing those data.	Foundations Process: Planning Calendar
2. Identify conclusions about school strengths and areas that need improvement from each individual data source used in the review. Complete a Data Summary Form (Form A-05).	Foundations Process: Data Summaries
3. Generate overall conclusions based on consideration of all the data sources together. • Report areas of strength (evident across multiple data sources) to staff, students, and parents as causes for celebration. • Consider any negative trends (evident across multiple data sources) as possible improvement priorities. • Strongly consider safety as a top improvement priority if there are any safety-related concerns. • Explain any trends that do not make sense or are contradictory across data sources.	Foundations Process: Presentations/ Communications With Staff, Communications With Parents, Current Priorities (see example of documentation in Figure 4b).
4. With staff (or with staff input gained through team members' efforts), determine a proposed improvement priority sequence. Unless the data strongly indicate otherwise, follow the suggested *Foundations* improvement priority sequence.	Foundations Process: Current Priorities (see example of documentation in Figure 4c).
5. Present the proposed improvement priority sequence to the entire staff. • If the staff agrees with the sequence, proceed with the Revise, Adopt, and Implement steps of the Improvement Cycle. • If the staff does not agree with the sequence, develop and present an alternative sequence that reflects staff input and feedback. (Continue this process until the staff agrees on a sequence.)	Foundations Archive: Presentations/ Communications With Staff, Current Priorities

Figure 4b   Sample data review summary (A-24)

Jefferson Elementary School
Home of the Wildcats!

RESPECT Team Report
First quarterly data review summary
October 3

Strengths and successes:
Attendance has improved. We are averaging 96% average daily attendance so far this year compared with 92% at this time last year. In addition, only 12% of our students are chronically absent compared with 21% last year. Congratulations to all!

Areas that need improvement:
Several data sources indicate that the cafeteria is in need of attention. Student and staff surveys indicate concern with this setting. Some of the surveys included comments that the cafeteria is too loud, students push and shove each other in line, and there is bad language and disrespectful behavior toward other students as well as staff. The cafeteria observation scores average 39%, which is quite low, and the observers also reported bad language, disrespect, and generally high noise level. We had one incident this year of a student tripping another, resulting in a sprained wrist.

Surveys and observations suggest that the use of schoolwide expectations can be improved. Observations of the cafeteria, hallways, and bus loading zone indicate that staff often do not refer to the expectations when correcting students. Surveys also suggest that the expectations for behavior in common areas have not been taught or emphasized enough.

Tardiness continues to be a problem, but less so than last year at this time.

We have a possible problem that we've named "Locals/Newcomers Conflict." Surveys tell us that transfer students feel that the students who have grown up here discriminate against them. We've had three incidents of fighting that have originated from this type of conflict.

The data also indicate some concern among staff about the consistency of the enforcement of discipline policies, and they indicate low school pride (e.g., students think that school is unimportant) among students. The wall-ball area of the blacktop has been the target of vandalism and graffiti five times this fall.

This sample can be printed from the Module A CD.

Figure 4c   Sample documentation of improvement priority sequence (A-25)

Jefferson Elementary School
Home of the Wildcats!

RESPECT Team Report
Priority Sequence
Adopted November 1

Year 1

- **Guidelines for Success:** The Foundations Team will begin work on this task immediately.
- **Cafeteria:** Improve cafeteria climate, policies, and procedures. A special task force has been formed for this purpose; it includes cafeteria supervisory staff.
- **Common area expectations:** For all common areas, the Foundations Team will work on a plan to teach and reinforce expectations more clearly and emphatically than we have in the past. This new emphasis on expectations relates to the cafeteria improvement priority above; we will ensure that all other common areas are addressed as well. Plans will include the display of large expectations posters in all common areas, lesson plans, and a schoolwide reinforcement system such as The Principal's 200 Club.

Year 2

- Continue with Year 1 priorities. Depending on data from the fall 2014 review, consider prioritizing improvements to hallway or playground.
- Work on improving discipline procedures—specifically, what misbehaviors should be handled with low-level staff corrections and what behaviors warrant administrative involvement. Work on establishing a 3-level system for responding to, documenting, and monitoring misbehavior.
- Implement universal screening (SSBD) to identify students who need Tier 2 and Tier 3 support.
- Work on improving behavioral support for staff members who deal with severe and chronic student misbehavior and for students who exhibit such misbehavior. Determine a procedure for staff members to collaborate to make sure that staff and student needs are being met (for example, when and how should the counselor, administrator, social worker, psychologist, or behavior specialist become involved?).
- Provide staff with additional training in classroom management and organization.

Year 3

- Continue with priorities from Years 1 and 2, as needed.
- Work on improving behavioral support for students.

This sample can be printed from the Module A CD.

TASK 2

Use survey data to make decisions

Staff members, students, and parents can provide valuable information about school settings, situations, policies, and procedures through surveys.

Advantages of surveys include:

- Surveys are a relatively easy way to get information from many people.

- Surveys are confidential—people who are uncomfortable talking about school issues might feel comfortable answering questions and writing about issues anonymously.

- Online surveys have negated the tedious, time-consuming manual scoring, compiling, and reporting needed for paper and pencil surveys.

- Online surveys are available 24/7, scoring is automatic, and reports are created and available almost immediately online.

- Some online surveys, such as *Safe & Civil Schools* Climate & Safety Surveys, provide reports that allow you to filter responses and analyze trends by grade, race/ethnicity, and gender.

Some limitations of surveys are:

- They measure people's perceptions, not objective facts.

- Results must be considered cautiously to avoid inaccurate conclusions. For example, most staff are not in the cafeteria as much as students are, so staff opinions about safety in the cafeteria should not carry as much weight as student opinions and interviews or focus group data from staff who are in the cafeteria dailiy.

- They can be time consuming and logistically challenging to administer, especially for a large school. Each student needs to have some time on a computer. Schools need to plan for parents who don't have computer access at home; for example, school computers need to be made available during back-to-school nights or parent-teacher conferences.

- Most online surveys are not free—they must be purchased. Free surveys typically do not have the depth or analytical capabilities of the *Safe & Civil Schools* Climate & Safety Surveys. Many of the examples in this task are taken from Climate & Safety survey data.

Make some initial decisions about administering surveys.

Decide who will take the surveys, what surveys to use, and when and how to administer them.

Who will take the surveys?

Staff. We recommend that you survey all staff members, even if you cannot survey students and parents. Both certified and noncertified teachers and other staff should participate, including itinerant and part-time staff.

Students. Decide which grade levels should participate. This decision may depend on the complexity of the survey questions. For Climate & Safety Surveys, we recommend that students in Grades 3 and above take surveys. Students in kindergarten and Grades 1 and 2 will probably have difficulty understanding the questions, so the results will be unreliable. However, administrators may ask teachers of the primary grades, especially Grade 2, to decide whether to administer surveys to their students.

Another question is whether to administer surveys to all students or to a random sample of students from each grade. Surveying all students increases the reliability of the results, but it also increases the time needed for the survey. If online surveys are conducted as part of class visits to a school's computer lab, it is probably easier and less time consuming to have all students complete the survey rather than try to manage a random sampling of students.

Parents. Surveying parents and guardians can be difficult logistically, but it can be beneficial from a public relations standpoint. Most parents really appreciate being asked for their opinions about their children's school experiences. Parents' experiences with the school might be limited, however, so the value of the information may be questionable.

What surveys will we use?

Many online surveys are available. You will want a reliable, valid survey. Unless someone on your staff is an expert at creating surveys, you should choose surveys that are already available commercially.

The validated *Safe & Civil Schools* Climate & Safety Surveys are available from Pacific Northwest Publishing at pacificnwpublish.com/products/Climate-&-Safety-Surveys. These surveys were written specifically to accompany the *Foundations* program and have provided valuable information to schools for more than 20 years.

If your school is required to take a state survey, you will get some good data from responses to that survey. For example, California offers comprehensive survey services. See California Healthy Kids Survey, California School Climate Survey, and California School Parent Survey at chks.wested.org. Another option is a private company, such as PRIDE Surveys at www.pridesurveys.com. At SurveyMonkey (www.surveymonkey.com/mp/education-surveys), you can create your own survey questions or use provided templates.

If you are interested in what makes a survey reliable and valid, check out the information at www.statpac.com/surveys/index.htm.

Although the surveys mentioned above are more extensive, a simple survey for staff and students, like the one illustrated in Figure 4d, asks respondents to agree or disagree with five basic statements about each of the major locations in the school. You can adapt the survey in any way necessary to make it directly applicable to your school. For example, high schools will probably need to say courtyard or commons instead of playgrounds. If your school has breezeways instead of hallways, substitute breezeways.

You can administer a simple survey like this online through a site such as Survey-Monkey, or you might have students and staff take it on paper. If you choose the pencil-and-paper method, someone will have to compile the results and create meaningful summaries. Microsoft Excel is a good program to use for that task.

You can ask for simple yes/no responses—survey-takers check a box if they agree with the statement and leave the box blank if they disagree. Or you might instruct survey-takers to rank their level of agreement on a 5-point scale, such as:

> 1 = I strongly agree
> 2 = I agree
> 3 = I disagree
> 4 = I strongly disagree
> 5 = No opinion

When will we administer the surveys?

We recommend administering surveys in mid-fall or midwinter. Avoid the honeymoon period early in the school year when everyone is still settling into the school routine. Too late in the school year is also not ideal because students (and staff) are typically looking forward to summer break, not thinking about current issues. Don't schedule surveys too close to any schoolwide testing periods either, because students and staff might be anxious and tense.

ဆ FOUNDATIONS RECOMMENDATION ಞ

Mid-fall or midwinter is the best time to administer surveys.

Figure 4d *Sample survey for staff and students (A-26)*

Place a check (✓) in the box if the statement is true.	On school grounds before school	In the classroom	On the playground	In the halls	In the cafeteria	On school grounds after school	On the bus	Walking to and from school
1. Students feel safe.								
2. Students treat other students respectfully.								
3. Students are taught how to behave responsibly.								
4. Students treat staff respectfully.								
5. Students treat students respectfully.								

We recommend that you survey the staff and students every year. If this schedule is not practical for your school, survey the staff every year and the students every other year. Feedback from parents is also useful, so try to survey parents whenever you survey students.

How will we administer the surveys?

The more consistent the administration of the surveys, the more reliable the results. Ideally, all survey-takers receive the same instructions for answering the questions and complete the surveys on the same date at approximately the same time. Of course, this scenario is a little unrealistic, but you can strive toward the ideal. Have the online surveys available for a finite period of time, perhaps a week or two, and make sure everyone knows the deadline.

An example of an instruction that should be given consistently concerns the No Opinion response option. (Other surveys may have a Not Applicable or similar response.) If survey takers have no experience with or knowledge of an issue posed in a question, instruct them to answer No Opinion rather than indicate whether the issue is problematic. For example, cafeteria staff might not be able to answer the question "Students have been taught the rules and expectations for behavior in the locker room and gym," so rather than guess or assume that the statement is true, they should answer No Opinion.

Another important consideration is the availability of computers with Internet access. Staff and parents may be able to use their personal computers (although you can't assume they have computers with Internet access), but students will need access to school computers to complete online surveys.

- **Staff.** Certified teachers might complete the survey during a staff meeting or an inservice. Arrange for use of the computer lab during that period. There's no reason why staff can't use their personal computers as well; they would just require log-in instructions, such as the survey URL and password.

  For other professional and classified staff members, have computers that they can easily access available in the school. Most surveys take 10 to 15 minutes at the most to complete, so all staff should be able to arrange a time to take the survey. Ensure as much privacy as possible for staff members.

- **Students.** Schedule each class for a half hour or so in the computer lab. Depending on the size of the school, it might take a day or many days for all students to complete the surveys. One or two members of the Foundations Team might need to manage the scheduling to account for all students. The logistics will vary from school to school depending on where and when students can access computers and the number of computers available.

- **Parents.** A good way to encourage as many parents as possible to take surveys is to schedule the surveys to coincide with a PTA meeting or parent-teacher conferences. Have computers available with the survey site already loaded so parents can just sit down and take them. Of course, the survey results will reflect only the opinions of parents who were motivated to attend the PTA meeting, so the data might be skewed.

  Another option is to send letters home that tell parents how and when to access the surveys online. The letters should inform parents that computers are available at school and the public library if they do not have Internet access at home. Figure 4e shows an example of such a letter. (A template is available on the Module A CD.) With this option, you may get fewer responses from parents who do not have home Internet access, so the data might be skewed.

Interpret survey results.

The examples of data analysis that follow are taken from *Safe & Civil Schools* Climate & Safety Surveys, but **the concepts can be applied to data and reports available from other surveys.** If your school is already taking other surveys, such as state surveys, you can easily assimilate that information into *Foundations*.

Figure 4e   *Sample letter inviting parents to complete survey (A-27)*

Pine Mountain
Middle School

Parents/Guardians of Pine Mountain Middle School Students—We Need Your Opinions!

Our school is committed to providing a safe and encouraging place for your child. You can help us continue to make improvements to our school by completing a short online survey.

Students in grades 3–12 and all staff at every school in the district are participating in the *Safe & Civil Schools* Climate and Safety Survey. We want to know what *you* think, too. All responses are anonymous. The resulting data will allow us to see if the three groups—parents/guardians, students, and staff—agree or disagree about important issues. We will be able to identify what we are doing well and what we need to work on, such as safety in a particular location of the school, students' understanding of the expectations for behavior, or communication with families.

Examples of questions include:

- Are staff members supportive of students?
- Are families informed about the rules and expectations for student behavior?
- Are student cliques a problem at this school?

It's Quick and Easy!

- The survey should take less than 10 minutes to complete.
- It's available online, 24 hours a day, for two weeks—Oct. 15 through Oct. 29.
- You can complete it on any computer with Internet access—at home, work, the public library, or our school. We will have computers available in the front office and in the school library.
- Just one parent or guardian from each household should take it.
- You can choose to read the survey in English or Spanish.

Here's How to Take the Survey

- Go online to **www.NotARealURL/PineSchool** (use Internet Explorer or Safari browser)
- Enter the User ID: PineMSXX
- Enter the Password: parent
- Be sure to complete every page of the survey until you reach the final page that says "Survey Complete." Then click Close.

The survey is available from **Monday, Oct. 15,** through **Monday,**

> This sample can be printed from the Module A CD.

Thank you! If you have any questions about the survey, please feel free to call the school office.

The TRENDS Survey online reports allow you to view results for individual questions and for broad categories of issues, including the following:

- Bullying
- Bus and transport to and from school
- Harassment
- Location (separately by cafeteria, classroom, hallways, playground, etc.)
- Parent/family perceptions of school

- Possible problems
- Respectful interactions
- Rules, expectations, and procedures (for classrooms and schoolwide)
- Staff interactions and perceptions
- Staff-student interactions
- Student safety
- Student and parent comfort communicating with staff
- Students' feelings about school
- Student-student interactions

You can also view results grouped by gender, grade, and race/ethnicity; compare the staff, student, and parent responses; and compare data from different years. Figure 4f on the next page shows the Climate & Safety Surveys reports home page and an example of a standard report.

Following are typical questions you should try to answer as you look at your data set:

- Are there any safety concerns that need to be addressed?
- What concerns are most urgent for staff?
- What are the biggest strengths and weaknesses in the school as perceived by parents?
- What category of concern is most significant to students?
- What locations are students concerned about? What subgroup of students is most concerned?
- What are the biggest discrepancies in perceptions among staff, students, and parents?

We suggest you follow these steps to analyze your survey reports.

STEP 1. Analyze the responses from each major group (staff, students, and parents) separately.

STEP 2. Identify specific items or categories (or both) that indicate cause for concern based on the responses of one or more of the subgroups.

Compare the responses of the various subgroups to determine whether items (or categories) of concern represent a problem for all or just some members of the major group. For example:

- A Student Report by Race/Ethnicity indicates that 53% of Black/African American students agree with the statement "Staff members treat students fairly," while 74% of Hispanic students and 81% of White students agree with the statement.

- A Student Report by Gender indicates that 66% of girls agree with the statement "I feel safe in the hallways," while 94% of boys agree with the statement.

Figure 4f Safe & Civil Schools *Climate & Safety Surveys Reports home page and an example of a report*

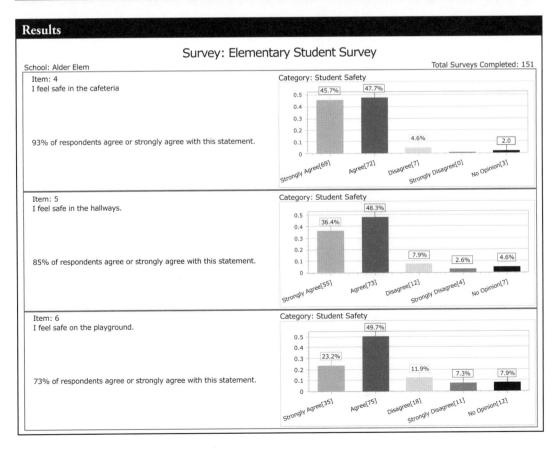

STEP 3. Compare the responses of the major groups with each other and identify locations or issues to target as improvement priorities. For example:

- A Category Summaries Report indicates that 98% of staff responded positively to items in the category Parent/Family Perceptions of School, while only 58% of parents responded positively. The school might decide to prioritize making the school more welcoming toward families and communicating more effectively with families.

- A Possible Problems Rank Order Report indicates large discrepancies between staff, student, and parent responses to the question "Is drug/alcohol/tobacco use by students a problem at this school?" The school should conduct focus groups and in-depth analyses of the drug/alcohol/tobacco issues to understand the actual extent of the problem.

Figure 4g shows an example of a report that compares staff and student responses. The columns Staff % Agree and Student % Agree indicate the percentages of staff and students who answered "I agree" or "I strongly agree" with the corresponding statement.

Figure 4g Safe & Civil Schools *Climate & Safety Surveys Rank Order Report (partial) from an urban high school, sorted by Student % Agree*

Item	Question	Category	Staff % Agree	Student % Agree	Staff-Student Discrepancy
14	Students treat each other respectfully in the hallways. [Staff]	Student-Student Interactions	50.0	48.4	1.6
28	If students have a problem they can't solve on their own they know they can go to a staff member (e.g., teacher, counselor, or principal) for help. [Staff]	Staff-Student Interactions	91.7	48.4	43.3
13	Students treat each other respectfully in the cafeteria. [Staff]	Student-Student Interactions	66.7	51.6	15.1
21	Staff members are kind to students. [Staff]	Staff-Student Interactions	91.7	51.6	40.1
19	Students treat each other respectfully in their classrooms. [Staff]	Student-Student Interactions	58.3	54.8	3.5
24	Staff members treat students fairly. [Staff]	Staff-Student Interactions	91.7	54.8	36.8
42	Students are proud to be part of this school. [Staff]	Students' Feelings About School	8.3	54.8	46.5
17	Students treat each other respectfully in the bus loading/unloading areas. [Staff]	Student-Student Interactions	66.7	58.1	8.6
20	Students treat staff members respectfully. [Staff]	Staff-Student Interactions	58.3	58.1	0.3
27	Staff members let students know when they do things right. [Staff]	Staff-Student Interactions	83.3	58.1	25.3
39	For most classes, teacher do a good job of making sure students know how they can get help if they fall behind. [Staff]	Rules, Expectations, and Procedures	100.0	58.1	41.9

Perhaps the most obvious discrepancy between staff and student responses in Figure 4g is Item 39, "For most classes, teachers do a good job of making sure students know how they can get help if they fall behind." All staff members agree with the statement, but only 58.1% of students agree. The large discrepancy points to an area that needs attention. This particular problem could be relatively easy to address by making teachers aware of the problem and having them regularly give information and encouragement to students about getting help when needed—specifically, when (prep period, before school, after school) and where the student can approach the teacher to request assistance.

Other issues are not so easily addressed. For most of the Staff-Student Interactions questions, there is quite a gap between staff and student responses. About half of the students do *not* think that they can talk to a staff member about a problem, that staff members are kind and treat students fairly, and that staff members let students know when they do things right, while between 83% and 92% of staff think the opposite is true. This discrepancy indicates that staff need to rethink how they interact with students and make an effort to establish a more respectful and positive schoolwide climate. Working on this issue will be more difficult and take longer than making sure students know how to get help.

The item in Figure 4g that is perhaps the most revealing is 42, "Students are proud to be part of this school." The percentage of students who agree with this statement is alarmingly low—54.8%—and indicates a real need to work on school pride and the importance of school. Staff beliefs about the students' sense of pride are truly worrisome—only 8.3% of staff think that students are proud to be part of the school. That one bit of information—that more than half of the students are proud of their school—can and should positively inform every subsequent interaction between staff and students. Just knowing that students care, even if they don't always show that they do, can inspire and motivate staff to continue striving to improve school climate and safety. School pride should be an improvement priority in this school. As a first step, the Foundations Team might convene a focus group of staff and students to talk about the responses to this survey item and what can be done to positively affect school pride.

Figure 4h on the next page is another example of staff-student comparison data. Some people assume that elementary students are unable to thoughtfully answer survey questions, but this example shows a range of student responses—from 10.1% to 47.2%—indicating that students are really thinking about the questions, not just giving the same answer to all questions.

Items 62–65 illustrate how staff view bullying and aggression problems quite differently than students do. It would be well worth analyzing the student responses to these items for trends by grade, gender, or race/ethnicity. If many third-grade girls, for example, agree that cliques and bullying are problems, a focus group of third-grade girls can help determine why and what actions staff can take to alleviate the bullying. If the girls are not very open to discussion in a focus group setting, a couple of adults (the counselor and a teacher, for example) might talk with several girls individually.

Figure 4h *Sample* Safe & Civil Schools *Climate & Safety Surveys data from a suburban elementary school (Possible Problems Rank Order Report)*

Item	Question	Staff % Mod/Ser	Student % Mod/Ser	Staff-Student Discrepancy
54	Does student misbehavior in classrooms (such as disruptions) make it difficult for students to learn at school [Staff]	20.5	42.7	22.1
55	Is inappropriate student language a problem at this school? [Staff]	8.8	47.2	38.4
56	Is inappropriate student dress a problem at this school? [Staff]	5.9		
57	Is inappropriate sexual contact between students a problem at this school? [Staff]	0		
58	Does this school have a problem with students having weapons? [Staff]	0	12.9	12.9
59	Is drug/alcohol/tobacco use by students a problem at this school? [Staff]	0	10.1	12.9
60	Is theft or damage of personal property by students a problem at this school? [Staff]	0	20.2	12.9
61	Is theft or damage of school property by students a problem at this school? [Staff]	0		
62	Are student cliques (i.e, students excluding other students) a problem at this school? [Staff]	11.8	34.3	22.5
63	Does this school have a problem with students physically hurting (e.g., hitting, pushing, grabbing, kicking) other students? [Staff]	11.8	33.7	21.9
64	Does this school have a problem with students bullying other students? [Staff]	11.8	43.3	31.5
65	Does this school have a problem with students picking on (or teasing in a mean way) other students? [Staff]	23.6	42.1	18.6

Figure 4i *Sample Climate & Safety Surveys data from an urban high school (Custom Filter Report filtered for Black/African American, Hispanic, and White boys in grades 9 and 10)*

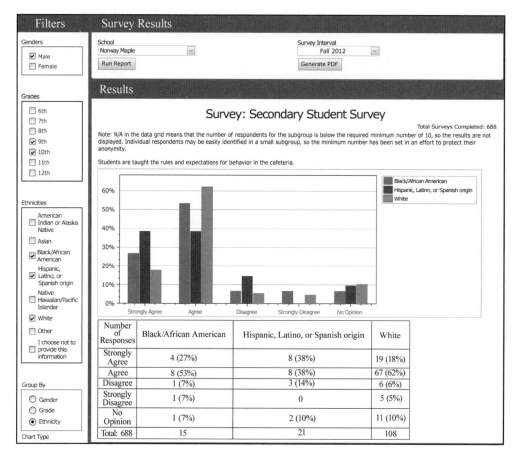

In *Safe & Civil Schools* Climate & Safety Surveys, you can filter student responses by grade, gender, race/ethnicity, and any combination of those subgroups. Figure 4i on the previous page shows an example of data filtered for Black/African American, Hispanic, and White boys in grades 9 and 10.

Survey data also allows you to track progress across years. Figure 4j below shows 3 years of survey data from an elementary school in Alaska. Charts and graphs that allow staff to visualize the progress they and students are achieving can be very satisfying and motivating. And if progress is not being made, it is easy to identify the areas that need more work.

Figure 4j   *Student survey data that show progress across 3 years; thanks to Knik Elementary School in Wasilla, Alaska*

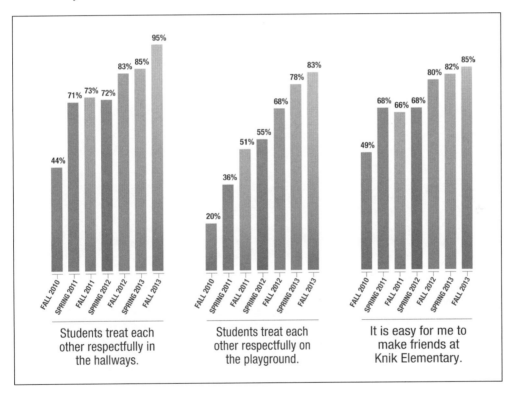

Report survey results to staff and others.

Survey reports for staff, students, and parents should be made available to staff. Print or create PDF files of some select reports and distribute to staff. Ensure that you maintain the confidentiality of individual staff members, students, and parents.

Give students and parents feedback if they have taken surveys. The feedback can be simple or detailed, as appropriate, but should share information about what was learned from the surveys—major positive findings, major concerns, and preliminary thoughts on priorities for improvement. Figure 4k shows a sample letter to parents about survey results.

If the data is not automatically archived online and available in subsequent years, be sure to archive the data and reports in the Foundations Archive so that they are available in the future. For instance, in the high school example above, the team would like to have that survey information available next year for comparison after they've implemented ways to improve school pride. They hope that a higher percentage of students and a *vastly* higher percentage of staff will report that students are proud to be part of the school.

Figure 4k   Sample letter to parents about survey results (A-28)

FOUNDATIONS SAMPLE

Pine Mountain Middle School

Dear families,

Thank you for taking the *Safe & Civil Schools* Climate & Safety Surveys a few weeks ago. We value your opinions. We want to tell you about some of the things we learned from your responses.

- Students are proud to attend Pine Mountain Middle School! Most students think that school is important, and they are glad to come to school most of the time.

- Pine Mountain is a safe school. Almost no one expressed concerns about safety.

- Most parents said they feel welcome at school and are comfortable discussing problems with the staff. We want everyone to feel this way! Please know that you are always welcome here to talk about your children.

- Bullying is a problem, despite our no-bullying policy. We are renewing our efforts to educate students about bullying and to enforce consequences for teasing, harassing, excluding others, and any other bullying-type behavior.

- We learned that we can probably do a better job teaching behavior expectations for some of our common areas. We are going to re-teach all expectations in the coming weeks.

Thanks again.

Sincerely,

Sheree Washington

Sheree Washington, Principal

This sample can be printed from the Module A CD.

Task 2 Action Steps & Evidence of Implementation

Action Steps	Evidence of Implementation
1. Develop and implement a plan (specifying timelines and individuals responsible) for purchasing and administering surveys and interpreting and reporting results annually or, at a minimum, every two years. • Identify who will be surveyed. • Identify the surveys that will be used. • Identify when the surveys will be administered. • Identify how the surveys will be administered. • Identify the process for interpreting the survey results, with improvement priorities in mind. • Identify how the survey results will be shared with students and parents (if appropriate). • Identify how the survey results will be reported to the staff.	Foundations Process: Planning Calendar, Data Summaries
2. Ensure that the survey results are archived on a secure server (ask the company that provided the surveys), or design and implement a plan for archiving the survey results.	Foundations Process: Data Summaries

TASK 3

Use common area observation data to make decisions

Members of the Foundations Team (and/or observers from outside the school) can collect common area observation data by spending time in each of the school's common areas and evaluating several variables using a predesigned observation form.

Some advantages of common area observations are:

- Common areas have a big impact on school climate.

- Observers may notice more and different potential improvements than would common area supervisors, who are busy with their duties and probably used to the status quo.

- Common area observation data provide information about subtle problems and issues that are not reflected in other data sources. For example, after observing three lunch shifts in the cafeteria, an observer might realize that the cumulative noise level has drained her emotionally and mentally. The cafeteria workers experience the noise every day—imagine what they feel like!

- Observations can create a unique opportunity for staff to reflect about current practices. Unless a time is purposely scheduled just for observation, staff are usually too busy to step back and objectively observe and think about school procedures and policies.

A limitation of common area observations is that results must be considered cautiously to avoid inaccurate conclusions. Observation days might not be representative, and observers might be unable to see past existing regularities.

Make some initial decisions about conducting common area observations.

Decide on the common areas to observe, the observation tools to use, and the person who will conduct the observations.

Which common areas will we observe?

Typical locations and events targeted for observation include:

- Arrival
- Hallways
- Restrooms

Module A: Foundations of Behavior Support—A Continuous Improvement Process

- Playground and courtyard
- Cafeteria
- Commons
- Assemblies
- Dismissal
- After-school programs

If incident referral data or anecdotal evidence suggests other problematic locations, you will want to observe them as well. Some contexts may involve multiple physical areas. For example, arrival includes where students walk onto campus, exit buses, enter the cafeteria (if breakfast is served), enter their classrooms, and all areas between. Similarly, high school or middle school lunchtime areas include where students leave their classrooms, walk to the cafeteria, socialize after lunch, walk back to their classrooms, and all the areas between.

What observation tools will we use?

A suggested observation tool (Common Area Observation, Form A-06) is provided on the Module A CD. Note that this form is organized into sections to make the observation systematic. The 3-point scale allows the observer to score the common area and compare the scores objectively with previous observations and with other common areas. Instructions for scoring are included on the form. Figure 4l on pp. 143–146 shows an example of a completed form.

Observers should review and receive training for the observation tool before they conduct an observation so they are clear about what to watch for. They should also be sure to get any information needed in advance of the observation, such as the time students are scheduled to be in the area and the number of supervising staff members who are scheduled to be present.

If you will be conducting common area observations for the first time in your school, you might want to have observers use a simpler form or just write down their observations. The observers will be viewing the common area for the first time through the eyes of a data collector and might need to get a general sense of how the area works before they can focus on the details that the observation form calls for. They might need to learn about the unique aspects of the physical layout of the common area. Then they will be more prepared to use the *Foundations* form for subsequent observations.

A short observation form might suggest the following broad categories of data:

- Are the behavioral expectations emphasized, both visibly (e.g., large posters) and by supervisors?
- Do any safety issues exist (e.g., unsupervised students, unsafe physical structure of the area, area open to the public, and so on)?

- Do staff and students behave respectfully toward others?
- Do supervisors correct misbehavior appropriately?
- Do students take part in activities appropriate for the setting?

Consider taking video of the common area during critical times and in key areas. However, your use of video will depend on district and school policy.

⁎   FOUNDATIONS RECOMMENDATION   ⁏

Observers should review and receive training for the observation tool before they conduct an observation so they are clear about what to watch for.

Who will conduct the observations?

We recommend that at least three people observe each targeted common area. They can observe together or at separate times, whatever is easier logistically. Sometimes arrangements must be made to cover the observers' other responsibilities. For example, if one or more elementary teachers are observing morning arrival, someone needs to take over their other morning responsibilities (picking up students at the bus or from breakfast, escorting students to class, staying with the class until 10 to 15 minutes after the bell rings) so they can observe the entire arrival period and have time to complete the observation form while their memory is fresh.

Option 1: Three members of the Foundations Team (or group responsible for data collection) observe in all common areas over the course of a day, then repeat the observation on a different day of the week.

An advantage of Option 1 is that the observers might be better able to objectively compare different common areas because they have first-hand knowledge of each area. If their day is dedicated to observation, observers can use any downtime to discuss and complete the observation forms. Also, compiling comparative data across common areas might be easier for three dedicated observers than for a larger group of observers (as in Option 3).

The disadvantage of this option is that you might have to arrange for substitutes to cover the observers' regular duties.

Option 2: This is the same as Option 1, but the observers include one or two outsiders. The outside people might be from a partner school, partner business, parent group, district office, or educational service center. These outsiders can bring a fresh perspective to the observation process. Ensure that they meet with the team after the observation to share their opinions and insights.

Figure 4l *Common Area Observation Form (A-06)*

This form is also used in Modules B and D.

Common Area Observation (p. 1 of 4)

Date: __10/3__   Setting: __Cafeteria__   Time in setting: __20 minutes__

Observer(s): __M. Figueroa, K. Washington, Z. Cho__

- Time students are scheduled to be in area: __11:30__   Approximate number of students present: __200__
- Number of assigned supervising staff present: __8__
- Number of staff with no supervisory responsibilities present: __2__
- Number of students present before supervisors are required to be present: __30__
- Number of minutes students are present without supervision: __3__
- Number of minutes students remain in the area after the bell rings: __5__

Answer key: 2 = Yes; 1 = Somewhat; 0 = No; N/A = Not Applicable

A. Rules, expectations, and procedures—schoolwide

1. The Guidelines for Success are prominently posted.   2   1   0   (N/A)
2. The common area expectations are prominently posted.   2   1   0   (N/A)
3. The student traffic flow is well organized. (Explain if any physical obstacles impede student movement—e.g., lockers, doors.)   (2)   1   0   N/A
4. The policy is implemented without the interference of any existing regularities—arrival or dismissal routines, classes released early or late, parent routines.   (2)   1   0   N/A

Maximum Points __4__   Score __4__   Percentage __100%__

B. Student safety

5. The scheduled supervisors are present in the area before students arrive.   2   (1)   0   N/A
6. The supervisors circulate throughout the area during the observation period.   2   (1)   0   N/A
7. The supervisors continuously scan the area during the observation period.   2   (1)   0   N/A
8. The area is free of obvious physical safety hazards.   (2)   1   0   N/A
9. The observation period is free of any incidents that involve the physical safety of students. (If no, explain.)   (2)   1   0   N/A

Maximum Points __10__   Score __7__   Percentage __70%__

C. Respectful interactions—staff-student

10. Staff members welcome students; they meet and greet them.   (2)   1   0   N/A
11. Staff members provide specific praise for students who meet expectations.   2   (1)   0   N/A
12. Staff members intentionally strive to provide 3:1 ratios of interactions.   (2)   1   0   N/A
13. Supervising staff members and students interact frequently.   (2)   1   0   N/A
14. Interactions between supervising staff members and students are generally positive.   2   (1)   0   N/A

Maximum Points __10__   Score __8__   Percentage __80%__

 This form can be printed from the Module A CD.

Common Area Observation (p. 2 of 4)

D. Correction (The following six questions should be answered only if you observe supervising staff members correcting student behavior. When multiple supervisors are present, observe each person separately, then rate the supervisors as a group.)

15. Staff behavior when correcting students is calm, respectful, and instructional.   ② 1 0 N/A
16. Student response to being corrected by supervising staff members is compliant and respectful.   ② 1 0 N/A
17. Staff members refer to Guidelines for Success and/or common area expectations when correcting behavior.   2 1 ⓪ N/A
18. Staff members respond to all misbehavior.   2 ① 0 N/A
19. Staff members correct misbehavior consistently from student to student.   2 ① 0 N/A
20. Staff members use a variety of appropriate consequences (e.g., time owed, positive practice, etc.).   2 ① 0 N/A

Maximum Points __12__   Score __7__   Percentage __58%__

E. Student behavior

21. Interactions between students are generally appropriate.   ② 1 0 N/A
22. Students use appropriate language (i.e., no obscenities).   ② 1 0 N/A
23. All students are dressed appropriately according to school expectations or dress code. (2 = 100%; 1 = 95%; 0 = <95%)   2 ① 0 N/A

Maximum Points __6__   Score __5__   Percentage __83%__

F. Productivity

24. All students are engaged in an activity appropriate to the setting. (2 = 100%; 1 = 95%; 0 = <95%)   2 ① 0 N/A
25. All students leave the setting at the designated time. (2 = 100%; 1 = 95%; 0 = <95%)   2 ① 0 N/A
26. The materials, equipment, and structure of the setting seem adequate for the intended purpose.   2 ① 0 N/A
27. You would feel comfortable if an outside visitor (e.g., the district superintendent) saw the setting.   2 ① 0 N/A

Maximum Points __8__   Score __4__   Percentage __50%__

 This form can be printed from the Module A CD.

Figure 4l (continued)

Common Area Observation (p. 3 of 4)

Directions: Transfer each category's Maximum Points, Scores, and Percentages to the Summary Table below. Low scores relative to maximum points (that is, low percentages) indicate possible problems. High percentages generally indicate a positive, well-functioning common area. When you compare these data with those from previous or subsequent observations, be sure to consider the relative Maximum Points.

Summary Table

Category	Maximum Points	Score	Percentage (Score/Max. Points X 100)
A. Rules, expectations, and procedures—schoolwide	4	4	100%
B. Student safety	10	7	70%
C. Respectful interactions—staff-student	10	8	80%
D. Correction	12	7	58%
E. Student behavior	6	5	83%
F. Productivity	8	4	50%
Total:	50	36	72%

Example:

In the example below, student safety should be considered first—you should always strive for 100% in the safety category. Then consider addressing student productivity (50%) and staff correction techniques (67%).

Category	Maximum Points	Score	Percentage (Score/Max. Points X 100)
A. Rules, expectations, and procedures—schoolwide	4	4	100%
B. Student safety	8	6	75%
C. Respectful interactions—staff-student	10	8	80%
D. Correction	12	8	67%
E. Student behavior	6	5	83%
F. Productivity	8	4	50%
Total:	48	35	73%

Presentation 4: Data-Driven Processes   **145**

Common Area Observation (p. 4 of 4)

Optional Student Behavior Checklist

2 = All students meet expectations
1 = Most students meet expectations
0 = Most students do not meet expectations
N/A = Expectation is not applicable for this policy

1. Students display appropriate pace and speed when moving.	2	(1)	0	N/A
2. Students stay in appropriate areas of the school.	(2)	1	0	N/A
3. Students arrive on time to designated location.	2	(1)	0	N/A
4. Students display designated voice levels.	2	1	0	(N/A)
5. Students travel appropriately up and down stairs.	2	1	0	(N/A)
6. Students maintain appropriate group size.	(2)	1	0	N/A
7. Students are respectful toward peers.	(2)	1	0	N/A
8. Students are respectful toward adults.	(2)	1	0	N/A
9. Students use lockers quietly and appropriately.	2	1	0	(N/A)
10. Students demonstrate expected line behaviors.	2	(1)	0	N/A
11. Students follow table expectations in the cafeteria.	2	(1)	0	N/A
12. Students play in appropriate areas of the playground.	2	1	0	(N/A)
13. List other expectations for the common area.				
a. Other: Clean up after yourself.	2	(1)	0	N/A
b. Other:	2	1	0	N/A
c. Other:	2	1	0	N/A
d. Other:	2	1	0	N/A
e. Other:	2	1	0	N/A

*Maximum Points __18__   Score __13__   Percentage __72%__

* Do not include questions that are N/A (not applicable). For example, if you answer N/A to questions 11 and 12, the maximum points possible for this category are 22. If you answer all questions with 0, 1, or 2, the maximum points possible are 26.

 This form can be printed from the Module A CD.

Option 3: Members of the Foundations Team enlist other staff members to form groups of three, and each group observes a different common area. For example, an eighth-grade teacher on the team may recruit teachers from other grades to assist in observing dismissal. An advantage of this observation option is that staff who are not team members get involved constructively in the **Review** step of the improvement process.

When will we conduct the observations?

We recommend that for each common area, you conduct at least two and optimally three observations on different days of the week—Monday, Wednesday, and Friday, for example. Schedule observations for typical days, not for days with special events. Avoid days right before a holiday, before major testing, or when assemblies are planned.

Early fall is a good time to conduct observations, and additional observations in spring can help you plan for the upcoming school year. You should also plan to conduct observations of specific areas after new procedures have been implemented for those areas.

How do we conduct the observations?

Observers should be familiar with the items on the form so they know what specifically to look for. During the observation period, observers should not try to fill out the form, but instead just watch and listen. After the observation, each observer fills out an individual form. If you wish to write comments or explanatory notes about any item on the form, use a separate piece of paper.

If possible, observe a whole period, but snapshots of different times on different days can yield useful information as well. For a complex period such as a high school lunch period, when students are relatively free to move around the school, observers could spend time in the cafeteria as well as related areas—adjacent hallways, the courtyard or commons—to evaluate how students and staff function in all contexts.

Here are some additional tips:

- Do not stand in a group; observers should stand well separated from one another.

- Don't carry a clipboard unless you normally do, so the students don't guess that they are being observed. Clipboards can change student behavior!

- When multiple supervisors are present, take the time to observe each person separately (see Section D on the Observation Form). However, rate the supervisors as a group so that individuals are not singled out.

Compile and interpret observation findings.

Follow these steps to compile your observation results.

STEP 1. All observers for a common area complete separate individual observation forms.

STEP 2. All observers for a common area work together to complete a single consensus Common Area Observation form.

STEP 3. Calculate the scores for each category from the consensus form.

Detailed instructions for the calculations are included with the Common Area Observation (Form A-06 on the Module A CD).

(Note that an optional Student Behavior Checklist is included with the Common Area Observation form. If you choose to use it, follow Steps 1 and 2 above, then calculate the score and percentage.)

To interpret the results, observers summarize their findings for each common area in terms of useful variables—that is, the categories from the observation forms. The Common Area Observation form includes items under the following categories:

- Rules, expectations, and procedures—schoolwide
- Student safety
- Respectful interactions
- Correction
- Student behavior
- Productivity

Low scores in relation to the maximum points (that is, low percentages) indicate possible problems. High scores generally indicate a positive, well-functioning common area. When you compare these data with previous or subsequent observations, be sure to consider the relative Maximum Points. The total percentage might be the most accurate overall measure with which to compare different settings.

In Figure 4m on the next page, correction (67%) and productivity (50%) are categories that should be considered for improvement in the cafeteria—*after* any student safety issues (70%) are addressed.

Report observation results to staff.

Provide staff with a summary report of the observation data as part of the first quarterly review and as part of your follow-up on any new procedures that have been implemented. Archive the common area observation data so they are available for comparisons with data collected in the future. Figure 4n shows samples of documentation that show data were shared with staff.

Figure 4m   *Example of an observation summary by category*

Setting: Cafeteria

Category	Maximum Possible Points	Score	Percentage (Score/Max Points)
Rules, expectations, and procedures—schoolwide	4	4	100%
Student safety	10	7	70%
Respectful interactions	10	8	80%
Correction	12	8	67%
Student behavior	6	5	83%
Productivity	8	4	50%
Total	48	35	73%

Task 3 Action Steps & Evidence of Implementation

Action Steps	Evidence of Implementation
1. Develop and implement a plan (specifying timelines and individuals responsible) for collecting, compiling, interpreting, and reporting common area observation data. • Identify which common areas will be observed. • Identify the observation tool that will be used. • Identify who will conduct the observations. • Identify when the observations will be conducted. • Identify how the observation findings will be compiled and analyzed. • Identify how the observation findings will be reported to the staff.	Foundations Process: Planning Calendar, Data Summaries
2. Design and implement a plan for archiving the common area observation findings.	Foundations Process: Data Summaries

Figure 4n   *Sample documentation that data were shared with staff (A-29)*

ADAMS ELEMENTARY
BULLDOGS

MEMORANDUM
FROM: Foundations Team
To: All staff
DATE: April 20
SUBJECT: Common Area Observations

We recently completed the third series of common area observations for the year. Thanks to Tyrone and Marcia for their great work!

As you know, our focus this year was on improving the safety and climate of the playground. The observation scores increased from 50% last fall to 95% in April, so the data show we have largely succeeded with this goal. Reports from playground supervisors are also positive. Congratulations to everyone!

The data show that the hallways and cafeteria have improved as well. Even though we did not specifically target these settings, it seems as though the lessons on expectations for appropriate behavior have carried over into other areas of the school.

At our next staff meeting, we'll discuss which common area to target for improvement next year. Please come prepared with some ideas and opinions!

	October	January	April
Cafeteria	85%	95%	98%
Hallways	81%	90%	90%
Playground	50%	87%	95%

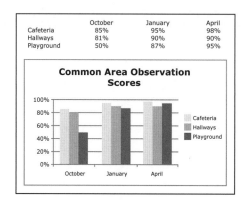

These samples can be printed from the Module A CD.

Figure 4n (continued)

Jefferson Elementary School
Home of the Wildcats!

RESPECT Team Report
Data Review Summary
October 15, 2013

Successes:

- Attendance has improved—congrats to all!
- Based on this fall's surveys, the misbehavior problems on the playground have improved dramatically. Last year only 61% of students agreed that students treated each other respectfully, and only 73% agreed that the playground was safe. This year, 89% of students agreed about respect and 91% agreed about safety.

Observations of Common Areas:

- The playground is much better!
- There are some safety concerns for the arrival and dismissal periods. Pickup and drop-off are chaotic, and the problems must be addressed. The Foundations Team proposes that arrival/dismissal be the next improvement priority.

Incident Referrals:

- Playground referrals are down by 58% compared with this time last year.
- Thursday has the most classroom-based referrals.
- Noncompliance is the most common incident leading to office referrals.
- Problems with bus loading (dismissal) leads to referrals for bullying, fighting, and horseplay.

TASK 4

Use incident referral data to make decisions

Use incident referral data to determine trends or patterns in student misbehavior. Evaluate documents such as office referrals, referrals to detention, and the like and examine variables such as location, day of week, time of day, and type of misbehavior. (We discuss variables in much more detail a little later.) The trends and patterns that you discern can be very useful in determining school improvement priorities.

All schools should be using a computerized data management system to store and analyze incident referral data. The system need not be fancy—even an Excel worksheet can be very useful if enough data are entered and the user has the basic skills necessary to create some charts.

Following are some examples of commercial data management systems.

- SWIS—School-Wide Information System (www.swis.org)
- AIMSweb Behavior (www.aimsweb.com/products/subscriptions/complete/order=now)
- PowerSchool (www.pearsonschoolsystems.com/products/powerschool)
- Review360 (r360.psiwaresolutions.com)

Note: The examples of incident referral data analysis in this section are taken from the TRENDS data management system (no longer available), but the concepts can be applied to almost any data system.

Incident referral data can be used to:

- Provide a reasonably objective indication of a school's current strengths and policies and procedures that are working well.
- Identify policies and procedures that are problematic and help with setting priorities for working on improvements.
- Assist in determining whether to target improvement efforts at the schoolwide, classroom, or individual student level.
- Conduct pre- and postmeasures of the effectiveness of new policies and procedures.
- Establish longitudinal measures of progress toward identified improvement goals.

When using and analyzing incident referral data, keep the following limitations in mind.

Incident referral information needs to be considered carefully to avoid inaccurate conclusions. For example, if there has been a change of administrator, the definition of *office referral* may also have changed, and so an increase or decrease in incident referrals may not indicate that behavior is improving or worsening. Or if you have reemphasized the enforcement of a particular policy, such as tardiness or dress code, incident numbers may increase for a time, making the problem look as though it is worsening when in fact it is just being enforced and reported more accurately. The increased number of incidents may be a necessary (and temporary) first step to improving the behavior, so it could be a good sign.

The usefulness of the data is reduced unless all incidents—not just office referrals—are included in the data collection. Sometimes administrators reduce the number of reported incidents simply by not counting all types of incidents or by telling staff to not send students to the office. Those administrators won't ever get a true picture of the school's problems, how and where improvements can be initiated, or the progress that students and staff are capable of.

As a school implements all aspects of Foundations, *fewer and fewer students are sent to the office for disciplinary actions.* This reduction of office referrals occurs because staff and students prevent misbehavior from occurring and staff become increasingly able to handle behavior problems that do occur earlier and in the setting in which the infraction takes place. As a result, the few students who continue to receive referrals are not useful gauges of schoolwide problems as much as they are a reflection of individual struggles, crises, and lack of social and behavioral skills. Incident data is then useful for assessing progress of individual behavior management plans, but surveys and observations may be better metrics for setting priorities for schoolwide climate and connectedness.

Include the following incidents in your data collection; ensure that you can disaggregate the categories that involve students being removed from instruction from categories that are notifications between staff and administration:

- Office referrals, including suspensions and expulsions
- Referrals to detention, the problem-solving room, and the like
- Incidents staff write to gain administrative input about a current or potential problem
- Incidents staff write to notify the administration about a current or potential problem

Note: Module D offers detailed information on how to organize and coordinate school discipline procedures.

Make some initial decisions about using incident referral information.

Address the following questions to ensure that you are collecting the necessary data during your incident referral process.

Do we need to create or revise an incident referral form? Do we need to review how our behavior data management system is working?

Figure 4o shows some sample behavior incident referral forms. (Forms you can print are available on the Module A CD.) A comprehensive form that all staff fill out for all referrals and higher level incidents (see above), along with a trained data entry person, helps ensure that good, consistent data are collected. (We discuss the use of referral forms in detail in Module D, Presentation 2.) Some data management systems allow all staff to access the system and enter incident records. One of the advantages of this type of system is that the data are always up to date (there's no backlog of referral forms to be entered).

❧ FOUNDATIONS RECOMMENDATION ❧

Schools should use a data management system that allows all staff to access the system and enter incident records. Alternatively, staff can use a comprehensive paper referral form, and administrators or office staff can enter information from the forms into a data system.

Who will be responsible for generating data summaries and reports?

A primary consideration when identifying this person or persons is the confidentiality of the information. Teachers should not have access to data about other teachers' number of referrals, which students they have written referrals for, and the like. An administrator or designee such as a school psychologist who already has a legitimate reason to know this information is a good choice to generate the data summaries and reports. The Foundation Team's Data/Evaluation Coordinator might also assist with data summaries and reports if the administrator has considered and resolved any confidentiality issues that might arise.

Which incident referrals (from how far back in time) will we include in the review?

Incident referral reports should be analyzed at least quarterly and should include data from the beginning of the school year. If possible, compare current reports with year-to-date reports from the previous year (as well as with previous reports from the current year) to spot trends—what is improving and what is getting worse.

Figure 40 *Sample behavior incident referral forms (A-07 and A-08)*

 These forms can be printed from the Module A CD.

Interpret incident referral data.

The person assigned to generate data summaries and reports should follow these procedures every time data are analyzed.

1. Identify the total number of incidents.

Over time, you will be able to compare the number with those from previous years to track your progress—is the number increasing or decreasing? Group incidents by their severity so you can track higher level incidents such as suspensions as well as lower level incidents. The data management system used in our examples groups incidents into four severity levels that you can report on separately or in combinations. Graph A in Figure 4p below shows examples of incident referral reports that compare year-to-date data for several years. Graph B on the next page shows Level 4 incidents. In this system, Level 4 consequences typically include expulsion, alternative placement, and police liaison referral.

Figure 4p *Incident referral reports that compare year-to-date data from school years 2009–10 through 2013–14. (Graph A) Year-to-date Level 3 incidents (office referrals); (Graph B) Year-to-date Level 4 incidents (expulsion, etc.).*

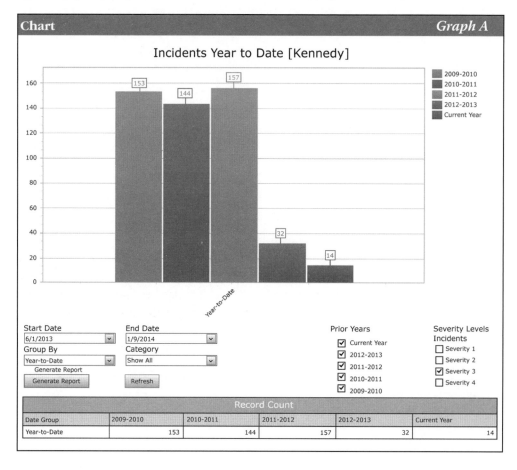

Figure 4p (continued)

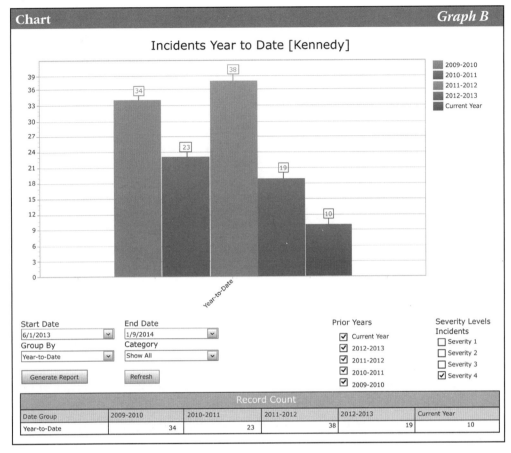

| Chart | Graph B |

Incidents Year to Date [Kennedy]

Legend:
- 2009-2010
- 2010-2011
- 2011-2012
- 2012-2013
- Current Year

Bar values: 34, 23, 38, 19, 10

Start Date: 6/1/2013
End Date: 1/9/2014
Group By: Year-to-Date
Category: Show All

[Generate Report]   [Refresh]

Prior Years
- ☑ Current Year
- ☑ 2012-2013
- ☑ 2011-2012
- ☑ 2010-2011
- ☑ 2009-2010

Severity Levels Incidents
- ☐ Severity 1
- ☐ Severity 2
- ☐ Severity 3
- ☑ Severity 4

Record Count

Date Group	2009-2010	2010-2011	2011-2012	2012-2013	Current Year
Year-to-Date	34	23	38	19	10

2. Identify the total number of students involved in the incidents.

If you find that a large number of referrals come from many different students, you might need to focus your improvement efforts at the schoolwide level. If you find that a small percentage of students are responsible for most of the referrals, you will probably want to focus on working with those individual students.

For example, let's say that data show that 69 students (about 20% of 350 total students) are responsible for all office referrals to date this year. The high percentage of students receiving office referrals indicates that staff should continue to work on universal prevention. If only 5% of students were receiving referrals, individualized approaches with those students would be warranted.

3. Examine information about each pertinent variable.

Your data management system should include several variables and allow you to sort and filter incident data based on one or more of the variables. Manipulating the data in this way can help you discern trends and patterns in your school.

Following are the main variables (the who, what, when, and where) that you will probably be most interested in.

Date. This variable allows you to track trends and patterns across time. How does the September referral rate compare with February's? Are there more incidents per day during December and in the last month of school? If so, for next year plan to conduct brief staff inservices in November and in the second-to-last month of school to brainstorm options for re-teaching expectations and increasing structure during these problematic periods.

Time of day. In many schools we've worked with, the data showed that most classroom-based referrals occurred in the afternoon. This information led the schools to prioritize helping teachers identify ways to increase the structure of afternoon instructional periods.

Day of week. Data sometimes show a spike in referrals on certain days of the week. For example, if more classroom-based incident referrals occur on Wednesday or Thursday than on Monday or Friday, it might indicate that students are being sent to the office based on teacher emotions more than student behavior.

Location of incident. If most incidents take place in the hallways, for example, addressing behavior in the hallways might be a high priority.

Type and severity of incident. If the data reveal that 40% of referrals are for insubordination, a schoolwide focus on following directions, accepting corrections, and interacting positively with adults could help students learn to comply. In addition, a brief inservice with staff on how to supervise and how to avoid power struggles could be useful.

Staff correction used. If a corrective consequence (detention, for example) is assigned repeatedly with no corresponding reduction in misbehavior, perhaps that consequence is ineffective for the student or students and staff should consider alternatives.

Reporting staff member. Administrators may want to analyze which teachers write the most incidents and why. A staff member might have a difficult and volatile mix of students and need additional support. Or a staff member might have an ineffective classroom management plan and benefit from coaching in how to implement more effective procedures.

Reports that display staff names should not be shared with staff. However, it might be useful to display a chart that shows the combined number of classroom removals of the 10% of staff who are the highest referrers (with no names) compared with the other 90% of staff.

Note: In this analysis, it is important to separate classroom referrals (in which students are removed from class due to classroom misbehavior) from other referrals, such as dress code or tardiness. In some schools, 10% of the staff may be responsible for 75% of the classroom referrals.

Student information. Data that include race/ethnicity, gender, grade level, and special education status can help you identify any issues that may require deeper analysis. For example, if one race/ethnicity has many more electronics policy violation referrals per capita than other groups, it would be useful to identify whether the behavior is indeed more frequent or whether staff is supervising and enforcing the policy with one group of students more than others. Another example is to analyze whether students of one race/ethnicity are more likely than other groups to get out-of-school suspension for first-time public displays of affection.

After you examine each variable separately, look for interactions between the variables—time of day and location, for example. The data should allow you to ask and answer the following types of questions:

- What are the trends by grade level, gender, and race/ethnicity? For example, what categories of offenses do Black/African American fifth-grade boys most frequently exhibit? (See Figure 4q on the next page.)

- Which students are receiving which consequences? Do staff give one race/ethnicity harsher consequences than a different race/ethnicity for the same offense?

- Have assigned consequences been enforced? Did students who were assigned detention actually serve detention?

- Which individual students need intervention support of greater intensity? Is the support working?

- Do teachers, administration, and support staff communicate adequately about behavior and discipline concerns?

- Is positive feedback being used sufficiently?

The report in Figure 4r on the next page shows dress code violations that resulted in in-school suspension by race/ethnicity. The racial norm score allows you to compare data for different race/ethnicity groups, taking into account the difference in group sizes. The racial norm formula equalizes the groups of students—essentially, if each racial group included the same number of students and accrued the same number of incidents, each group's racial norm score would be 1.

Figure 4q *Categories of incidents for fifth-grade boys by race/ethnicity*

Data

Behavior Analysis

Legend:
- Aggression
- Bullying
- Defiance/Refusal to Comply
- Dishonesty
- Disrespectful/Impolite Behavior
- Disruption of Learning
- Gang Involvement
- Property Damage
- School Rule Violations
- Substance Problems/Illegal Activities
- Tardy to School/Class
- Work Completion/Organization Issues

| Export to PDF | Export to Excel | Refresh Chart | Refresh Data | Chart Type: Side-by-Side | Start Date: 6/1/2012 | End Date: 5/31/2013 |

Applied Data Filters
Excluded Values:
Record Type: [COMMENDATION] [CONCERN]
Race: [Two or More[3%]] [Native Hawaiian/Pacific Islander[7%]] [None Specified[1%]]
Grade: [3] [1] [2] [4] [K] [PK]
Gender: [F]

| RecordType | Type | SubType | Location | Context | Activity | Severity | Gender | SchoolYear | Grade |

Record Count • Category ▲

Race ▲	Aggression	Bullying	Defiance/Refusal to Comply	Dishonesty	Disrespectful/Impolite Behavior	Disruption of Learning	Gang Involvment	Property Damage	School Rule Violations	Substance Problems/Illeg Activities
American Indian Alaska Native [21%]		1			2	1			1	
Asian [11%]	1	1	5	1	2	10		2	1	
Black/African American [19%]	2	1	31	1	1	2	1		1	
Hispanic/Latino [24%]	21	8	25	2	11	19	2	4	6	
White [14%]	8		1	2	3	1				
Grand Total	32	11	62	6	19	33	3	6	9	

Figure 4r *Dress code violations that resulted in in-school suspension by race/ethnicity, record count, and racial norm*

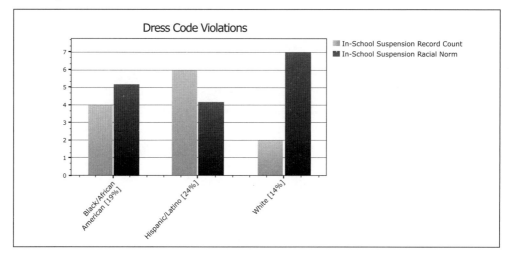

Dress Code Violations

Legend:
- In-School Suspension Record Count
- In-School Suspension Racial Norm

Report incident referral data to staff.

The person or persons in charge of generating summary reports should provide representative reports to all staff at least quarterly. You can then determine trends by quarter. Be sure to properly archive the data so that they are available for comparisons with data collected in the future.

Recommended Features in a Data Management System

Choosing a data management system is an important decision. An Internet search reveals many options. As you examine the possibilities, think about the following features that we think are valuable components of a robust behavioral data management system.

- The system can be customized to some extent so that locations, categories of behaviors, and corrective consequences match your school's unique needs.

- In addition to office referrals, the system tracks, charts, and reports positive feedback, behaviors of concern (such as internalizing problems), classroom problems, and information about moderate misbehavior sent to the administrator.

- It allows all staff members to enter detailed information about each incident directly into the system, reducing data entry requirements for office staff. It also creates feedback loops between staff members about specific incidents or issues.

- Staff can receive email notifications whenever a record for one of their students is entered into the system.

- The administrator and selected other staff members can view and work with behavioral records as soon as the records are entered into the system, making it possible to address misbehavior and concerns as soon after the incident as possible.

- A wide range of charts and reports are available. Schoolwide data can be broken down by grade, race/ethnicity, gender, location, and other factors. Data for individual students can be broken down by location, time of day, day of week, subject, and other factors.

(continued)

Recommended Features in a
Data Management System (*continued*)

It's also important that teachers have systems to track classroom behavior, both positive and negative. A schoolwide behavioral data management system might include a classroom component, or you might find a separate system or app that meets your needs. Teachers should be able to use the data to ask and answer questions such as:

- What are the misbehavior trends in my classroom by student, type of offense, type of activity (small group instruction, independent work, etc.), time of day, day of week, month, and so on?

- What is my ratio of positive interactions as compared with corrective interactions with students?

- Have I paid individual attention to every student over the course of the week?

- Does gender or race/ethnicity skew any patterns of positive or corrective attention to students?

- Which individual students need intervention support of greater intensity? How is the support working?

Task 4 Action Steps & Evidence of Implementation

Action Steps	Evidence of Implementation
1. Review your school's current practices regarding incident referrals (misbehaviors that are documented, information that is recorded on the referral form, etc.) Decide whether to use Module D at this time to improve current practices for correcting misbehavior. *Important:* A decision to revise current incident referral practices does not preclude using any currently collected data. The revision can occur at the same time as (or after) the current data have been summarized and analyzed.	Foundations Process: Meeting Minutes
2. Design and implement a plan for using incident referral information. • Create or revise your incident referral form and review the effectiveness of your behavior data management system. • Identify who will be responsible for generating the data summaries and reports. • Identify which incident referrals (from how far back in time) will be included in the summary. • Identify how the data will be summarized—which variables you will use and in what combinations. • Identify how the incident referral information will be reported to the staff. 3. Design and implement a plan for archiving the incident referral data (if your system does not automatically archive it).	Foundations Process: Meeting Minutes

TASK 5

Use other existing data sources to make decisions

In Task 5, we present examples of data sources, such as suspensions and focus groups, that you can use in the **Review** and **Prioritize** steps as you gather information and decide which areas of the school to work on. We begin by introducing the concept of 90% Thresholds as a guideline for making decisions.

Understand the concept of 90% thresholds.

You have a vision for improved student behavior, and *Foundations* provides the tools to implement your vision. Bridging the vision and the implementation of your improvement requires measurable objectives. Consider using the 90% Thresholds as guidelines:

- Every family helps children attend at least 90% of school days, on time and ready to learn.
- Every administrator ensures that at least 90% of school minutes (minus lunch) are instructional minutes.
- Every teacher uses at least 90% of instructional minutes for instructional activities.
- At least 90% of students are engaged during every instructional activity.
- Every student is engaged for at least 90% of instructional minutes.

Note that the 90% figure is *not* a goal—it is a general guideline that you can use to identify where to focus your staff development time and effort. If your data indicate more than 90% compliance, you can probably maintain universal procedures while extending and improving targeted and intensive procedures. But if data indicate less than 90% compliance, you need to focus on universal procedures.

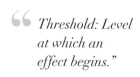 *Threshold: Level at which an effect begins."*

Let's look at each of these thresholds.

Every family helps children attend at least 90% of school days, on time and ready to learn.

Ten percent of a 180-day school year is 18 days—almost an entire month of school. If students miss 18 days or more, they will certainly learn less than if they had attended regularly. Early in the school year—20 days in, for example—target students who have already been absent 2 or more days. They are on the path to missing a month or more of the year. Average daily attendance data can be a smokescreen and make you complacent. For example, even if your overall average daily attendance is 95%, it is still possible that as many as 25% of your students are chronically absent. The excellent attendance of most students keeps the daily average high, even though a significant number of students have a problem with chronic absenteeism.

To encourage good attendance, you must establish a positive, inviting climate. Children cannot be punished into attending school. Simple reward programs can sometimes yield huge results.

For example, a kindergarten reading teacher in British Columbia had an attendance problem—of the 14 students in her group, two were regularly absent and several others were often absent. To try to improve attendance, she instituted a point system. When 12 of the 14 students were on time to class, the group earned a point toward a mystery reward. When the group earned 5 points, the students got to open a mystery envelope and learn what their reward was—extra recess time, coupons for a treat in the cafeteria, or a positive phone call home, for example. Within a few days of implementing this simple system, attendance improved drastically. The students *wanted* to attend school—they valued not only the positive rewards, but also the group camaraderie, the fun of earning points and tracking their accumulation, and the overall positive atmosphere of the class.

Every administrator ensures that at least 90% of school minutes (minus lunch) are instructional minutes.

Rising above this threshold can be difficult. In secondary schools with 50-minute periods and 5-minute passing periods, the passing periods by themselves account for close to 10% of school minutes. Ensuring that tardiness is kept to a minimum is key. Tardy students not only miss instruction, they often disrupt class when they enter late, affecting both the teacher's and the other students' focus on learning. Some teachers in schools where tardiness is a problem don't even bother to teach during the first five minutes of class, bringing instructional minutes way below the 90% threshold. Programs such as *Start on Time* (see Table 4a on the next page) have achieved a 96% reduction in tardiness at several schools we've worked with, and that low rate has been maintained over time. (One school, for example, reduced tardies from 820 down to between 20 to 40 per 6-period day.) By reducing tardiness, administrators protect instructional minutes for teachers.

Every teacher uses at least 90% of instructional minutes for instructional activities.

Rising above this threshold can also be difficult. Effective classroom management is the goal—transitions between activities should be efficient, housekeeping minutes should be kept to a minimum, and reinforcement activities should be simple and quick, yet effective. Charles Payne (2008) found in his Chicago Public Schools research that

Table 4a *Programs to manage instructional time*

START on Time!	On the Playground
START on Time! is a schoolwide program for reducing tardiness. In secondary schools, tardiness, especially related to hallways and restrooms, can affect the entire school day, not just first period.	For elementary schools, the *On the Playground* schoolwide program can help ease transitions to and from the playground so that instructional time is not lost as students adjust to the calmer atmosphere required in the classroom.

Both programs are available from Pacific Northwest Publishing, www.pacificnwpublish.com.

the better teachers—those who achieved the best academic gains—averaged 14% non-instructional classroom minutes. The group of teachers with the least academic gains averaged 29% noninstructional classroom minutes. Imagine—over a quarter of the time allotted for instruction was used for other activities. Those teachers (and their students) would benefit from coaching and training in classroom management.

At least 90% of students are engaged during every instructional activity.

This threshold requires a highly motivational and inspirational classroom management plan *and* great instruction. The corresponding goal is for all teachers to provide highly engaging lessons with all students participating. We discuss the classroom level of the multi-tiered system of behavior support in Module F.

Every student is engaged at least 90% of instructional minutes.

The goal is to have every student empowered with the skills to stay focused, persevere, and achieve mastery. Even if you are successful at exceeding the previous threshold—nine out of ten of your students are engaged—you might not be meeting this threshold. If your off-task students are often the same students, you need to work on behavior management practices to get those individual students above this threshold.

How do the 90% Thresholds relate to common areas and schoolwide policies? The overall goal that drives the threshold concept is for students to be at school and focused on instruction. Common areas and schoolwide policies that are not managed well and contribute to problems such as disrespect, excess noise, disorder, teasing, bullying, and harassment can hinder students' ability to focus on academic instruction. For example, students who are bullied may have very high absentee rates and may not meet the minimum 90% threshold. The more minutes students are engaged in active, meaningful, well-designed instruction, the more they learn, so ensure that misbehavior takes no time away from instruction.

Use other existing data sources to determine improvement priorities.

In previous tasks, we discussed the advantages of and procedures for using survey data, common area observation data, and incident referral data to make decisions. Other data that you routinely collect throughout the school year are also useful as you consider your improvement priorities. These data may include:

- Average daily attendance and absence rates
- Tardiness rates
- Suspensions, expulsions, and referrals to alternative education placements
- Referrals to special education
- Numbers of students referred to special education who did not qualify
- Instances of vandalism and graffiti
- Instances of other illegal activities
- Injury reports
- Feedback from staff
- Social-emotional support (information from counselors, social workers, and school psychologists)
- Focus groups
- Red flags
- Summaries of universal screening

Some of this information is confidential, so make sure that only approved staff have access to the details and do the work summarizing and analyzing this data. Also consider confidentiality when reporting the summaries to the staff. Ensure that the data are properly archived so they are available for future comparisons.

Average daily attendance and absence rates. Average daily attendance can act as a barometer of school safety, climate, and policy. If the rate is lower than 95% or if your school has quite a few students who exhibit chronic absenteeism (they miss more than 10% of school days), consider working on attendance as a schoolwide priority. Note that in Module C, Presentation 4, we include suggestions about attendance and tardiness policies and how to improve average daily attendance.

Also examine how many individual students are chronically absent (defined as missing 10% or more of school days). Students who are chronically absent should be flagged so the counselor (or another appropriate person) can work on an individual support plan for the students. If many students are flagged, working on chronic absenteeism should be a schoolwide priority. *Analyze quarterly and at year-end.*

Tardiness rates. Examine tardiness data and compare it with staff survey items relating to tardiness to determine whether tardiness is a problem you should focus on. In some secondary schools, tardiness is so severe that many teachers quit reporting all the tardies.

If surveys indicate that tardiness is frustrating for staff but the reported number of tardies is low, convene a staff focus group to explore the issue, including how to start collecting accurate data. If many students are tardy, consider a schoolwide focus (see Module C, Presentation 5 for more details). If a small number of students are chronically tardy, the counselor or another appropriate person should develop individual behavior support plans for those students. *Analyze quarterly and at year-end.*

Suspensions, expulsions, and referrals to alternative education placements. Research shows that exclusionary disciplinary practices are largely ineffective. At least quarterly, analyze whether your use of exclusionary procedures is static or trending up or down. Also analyze the data for patterns by variables such as gender, grade level, race/ethnicity, special education, and Section 504.

Note that Modules B and C discuss proactive and positive ways to change behavior to reduce the need for in- and out-of-school suspension, and Module D is about correcting students without escalating the misbehavior to suspendable offenses and creating alternative consequences for responding to severe misbehavior. *Analyze at least quarterly.*

Referrals to special education. Examine the number of students referred to special education for emotional and behavioral issues. Is the number increasing or decreasing? If the number is increasing, could it be an indication that staff need more assistance in dealing with troubled students—for example, how to avoid power struggles? *Analyze annually, typically at year-end.*

Number of students referred to special education who did not qualify. In other words, are all the referrals to special education really necessary? These data might reveal a need for more training for teachers in how to deal with misbehavior in the classroom. Teachers might be resorting to special education referral to solve behavior problems instead of working with the students through effective classroom management and intervention strategies. *Analyze annually.*

Instances of vandalism and graffiti. Vandalism and graffiti can be indicators of school pride and student connection to the school. Determine if the school or district maintenance staff are recording the number of incidents and amount of time spent repairing damage to the grounds and building. Especially viewed across years, a downward trend (less damage) might be a powerful indication that the school's efforts to improve safety and climate are effective. On the other hand, if the trend is upward, examine student survey data more closely and perhaps conduct student focus groups to investigate what might be happening with student connection to school. *Analyze annually, typically at year-end.*

Instances of other illegal activities. Increases in illegal activity might indicate that better supervision is needed. If supervision has just been improved, the increased number of incidents may be a temporary spike—which could be a good sign if the number begins trending down within a month or two. *Analyze annually, typically at year-end.*

Injury reports. The Foundations Team should review a summary of injury reports by location at least every 2 years. Urgent safety items need to be prioritized immediately. For example, if the data show an unreasonably high number of playground injuries, analyze the STOIC variables to determine whether, for example, recess is too long (students have too much unstructured time), supervision is inadequate, or students don't know the expectations for safe use of the equipment. *Analyze annually or every 2 years, typically at year-end.*

Feedback from staff. Analyze frequently throughout the year, especially at the beginning and end of the year. Ask staff what they want to work on and what problems they see. Sometimes numeric data can mask issues that are important to staff.

Social-emotional support (information from counselors, social workers, and school psychologists). Ask these staff members whether they are seeing any trends or patterns in the students they work with and whether they can identify any programs or strategies that might benefit all students as well as the high-needs students.

Focus groups. If any data from other sources are confusing or not interpretable, arrange a focus group to gather in-depth information. For example, a focus group of students might be able to clarify why many students responded negatively to a particular set of survey questions. Conduct focus groups as needed. We present more information about focus groups below.

Red flags. Red flags are data that indicate a student may be at risk for school failure or dropping out of school. Red flags can include grade retention, chronic absenteeism, failing two or more classes at the secondary level, and chronic discipline referrals. If many students are flagged and you cannot provide individual services for all of them, strive to identify and implement universal strategies to support *all* students. Proactive universal procedures can reduce the number of students who are flagged in the future.

Summaries of universal screening. If you are implementing universal screening processes for behavior and too many students are identified as at risk for internalizing or externalizing behaviors, analyze the identified students to determine universal strategies to support *all* students and to reduce the number of students who are identified as at risk in the future.

Use focus groups to dig deeper.

A focus group is a quick and effective strategy for gaining insights and information from students. Following are some suggestions for planning and conducting them.

Group Leaders

Have two adults lead the group. One staff member leads the discussion, and the other takes notes and observes the process. Select staff members who are respected by a broad cross section of students.

Consider whether the gender or ethnicity (or both) of the staff members is important for connecting with the students. For example, you would not have a male staff member talk with female students about concerns related to the bathroom.

Scheduling

Plan for each focus group to take no more than 30 minutes. If the students are younger, less than 30 minutes is appropriate.

If possible, arrange for the students to arrive 5–10 minutes before the scheduled start time so you can begin the focus group on time with everyone present.

The location should be a room with privacy and enough chairs for the students to sit in a circle.

Students

Select four to eight students who are representative of the specific target group— grade level, male students, Black/African American students, or entire student body, for example. Keep the following in mind as you form your student focus group:

- In general, select students who will be returning to your school next year.

- Avoid selecting only student "leaders." As much as possible, include representatives from all the subgroups of students in your school—low-, average-, and high-performing students; low-profile and popular students; athletes, artistic, and musical students; and at-risk students and student leaders.

- Try to balance the group based on gender and race.

- Ask the administrator or district office whether students need parental consent to participate in a focus group.

- Consider identifying one or two potential replacements in case a student is sick or refuses to participate at the last minute.

- In a large school or a school with many student groups (based on age, grade, ethnicity, and so on), you may need two or three focus groups to obtain a representative sampling of student opinions.

Running the Group

Develop a script for your introduction and prepared questions. Ask your team to help identify key questions to ask.

In your introduction, tell students that by participating in the focus group, they are helping the school become a better place for students and staff. Their opinions, concerns, and suggestions for addressing issues about common areas will be taken seriously and used to improve the school's policies and procedures. Also stress that their names will not be associated with specific comments; the notes from the meeting will be a composite of all student comments and suggestions.

Stay with your scripted questions when conducting the focus group.

Try to get every student involved in the focus group discussion. Avoid being defensive or judgmental about student comments.

Advise the students on how they might respond if other students ask about the group.

Here's an example of how information from focus groups helped solve a serious but cryptic problem in one high school. This high school's 550 students (65% White, 27% Black/African American) answered survey questions about school climate and safety. In response to questions about safety in the hallways, students as a group were positive. However, the Foundations Team analyzed the survey data further, by grade, gender, and race/ethnicity, and found that most Black/African American females in the ninth grade did not feel safe in the hallways.

To discover the reasons these students answered the survey as they did, the team conducted a focus group with some Black/African American ninth-grade girls. The students said that in certain hallways, male students groped the girls' buttocks every day.

To address the problem, the Foundations Team increased adult supervision in the identified hallways and planned and implemented schoolwide lessons on what constitutes sexual harassment and the consequences for such behavior. Without the schoolwide student survey data, the ability to analyze the survey results in depth, and the information gleaned from the focus group, this serious problem might have continued for weeks or months before adults became aware of it and took steps to stop it.

Task 5 Action Steps & Evidence of Implementation

Action Steps	Evidence of Implementation

1. Design and implement a plan for using information from other existing data sources.
 	
   • Identify which of the available sources might be useful.
   • Identify who will be responsible for summarizing information from the identified sources.
   • Keep confidentiality considerations in mind.
   • Identify whether and how the information from other sources will be reported to the staff.
   • Consider the 90% Threshold concept when analyzing data.
 	
2. Design and implement a plan for archiving information collected from other sources.
	Foundations Process: Meeting Minutes, Data Summaries

Developing Staff Engagement and Unity

INTRODUCTION

This presentation provides information about the importance of staff engagement and unity, and how to develop them in your school. We begin with a brief history of how *Foundations* schoolwide behavior support evolved.

In the early 1980s, I (Randy) was working on classroom management with all of the teachers at a local elementary school. These teachers were very receptive to the concepts that I was helping them with, and they accomplished a great deal by the middle of the year. They asked if they could extend this work into the playground, hallways, and so on, and I agreed to give it a try. So, during the spring, we worked on all the common areas and Guidelines for Success.

Toward the end of that spring, a colleague who works with schools in central Washington contacted me. When I told her about my work at the elementary school, she asked if I would be willing to do the same with some schools in the Wenatchee, Washington, area. We set up a 4-day training for 25 or 30 schools. Most schools sent just one or two people to the training, usually a principal or a counselor, but one school sent a team: the principal, two general education teachers, one special education teacher, and a paraprofessional. The school that sent the team accomplished so much more than the other schools during that first year that my colleague and I began requiring the team structure, with the principal as a key member. We saw that with a well-functioning team that included the administrator, schools could just fly.

Over the years, we have depended more and more on this team-based structure to drive the *Foundations* process, but we've also learned that the team alone is not enough—the team must engage the entire staff in the improvement efforts. Without staff engagement and buy-in to the process, the team might accomplish some things, such as improving one common area, but longitudinal progress really requires involvement of the entire staff.

If staff and administration do not communicate well or support each other, the *Foundations* processes will be more difficult to implement. When some staff members think administrators are part of the problem ("If the principal would just do this, we wouldn't have this problem") or if administrators think that the teachers are the problem ("If teachers would just . . ."), there are gaps in communication. Part of developing staff engagement and unity involves reducing communication gaps between staff and administration.

You also might have gaps within the staff—between certified and noncertified staff, for example. If children perceive a difference between the level of authority of paraprofessionals who supervise the playground and certified teachers, some students might not take the paraprofessionals seriously and you'll have misbehavior on the playground.

Another example is the relationship between special education and general education. If the general education teachers expect the special education staff to just fix their problem students for them, there is a gap. Similarly, teachers might think that support staff such as school psychologists, counselors, social workers, and so on should just fix their students. Gaps in communication from between levels—intermediate and primary teachers who rarely interact—or departments—the science department doesn't talk with the art department, for example, even though the teachers share the hallways and supply rooms.

All of these gaps make developing staff buy-in, engagement, and unity and implementing the *Foundations* processes more difficult. Staff need to support and work with each other; there should be a feeling of "we're all in this together."

Staff engagement can also be affected if the Foundations Team loses focus or moves too fast. If your team stops meeting for a 4-month period in the middle of the year—losing focus—the *Foundations* processes will stop. If this happens, the team needs to ask, Were we doing everything we could to engage staff? What can we do to keep the staff involved in these issues? Conversely, if the team tries to work on too many priorities at once and places too much pressure on staff, staff may inadvertently resist just because it's too much, too fast.

The Foundation Team's main responsibility is the maintenance of the Improvement Cycle. The Improvement Cycle does not end after you've identified a problem, developed solutions, and implemented them. It's bigger than that. It begins with the **Review** step; the team summarizes data and presents them to entire staff so the staff can set the priorities for what to work on next. In the **Revise** step, the team or a special task force asks for opinions and recommendations from the staff as they prepare a proposal for new policies or procedures, and the entire staff votes on whether to adopt the proposal. If it's adopted, the staff implement the policies or procedures. And here's where the engagement of the entire staff really pays off—when everyone has been involved in the whole Improvement Cycle, everyone feels some ownership of the new policy and will likely do his or her best to implement it with fidelity. No subset of the staff can implement a schoolwide policy by themselves. The entire staff must be on board.

Implementation of the Improvement Cycle will eliminate many of the gaps and issues surrounding staff engagement, but you will still have to continually strive for staff engagement and unity. Conscious attention to staff buy-in to the *Foundations* process is essential.

Task 1: Promote Staff Buy-In by Using Staff Incentives and Rituals shares a range of ideas for enhancing staff buy-in that *Foundations* schools have shared with us. These strategies can increase the odds that staff are active participants in the Improvement Cycle, so when revision proposals are adopted and implemented, most staff will be on board and unified in their support of the new policies and procedures.

Figure 5a   Improvement Cycle

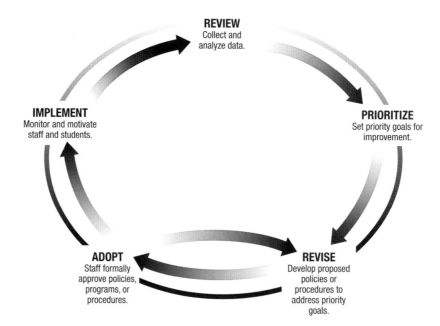

The entire team should probably work through this task, with the Staff Liaison paying particular attention to these ideas. The Staff Liaison's major responsibility is to ensure that the team continually involves the entire staff in the decision-making process and promotes staff unity.

Task 2: Administrators—Be an Effective Leader and Model for the *Foundations* Process shares tips and lessons we've received from some wonderful administrators about how to ensure staff unity and engagement in the improvement process. This task is designed to be a self-reflection piece for building and district administrators, although the Foundations Team might read and view it as well.

Task 3: Engage Reluctant Staff Members is geared mainly to administrators and offers strategies for engaging reluctant staff members. When you are close to unity but two or three individual staff members are not actively participating, what can the administrator do? We share some of the lessons we've learned from some great administrators.

This presentation concludes Module A, the base of the entire behavior support continuum that includes:

- A team that actively represents and unifies the entire staff.
- A continuous Improvement Cycle that results in behavior support—climate, safety, behavior, discipline, motivation, connectedness—that gets better every single year.
- Using data to drive the focus and direction of that improvement.

All of the other modules in *Foundations* are content pieces that can assist your team in addressing your identified priorities, such as common areas and schoolwide policies, inviting climate, consistency in responding to misbehavior, enhancing safety, reducing bullying, reducing conflict, supporting classroom management, and creating seamless support for staff and students when dealing with individual students with challenging behavior. Although each of these content pieces contributes to the continuum of behavior support, full implementation requires an entire staff working every day to make the school a safe, consistent, positive environment and working to make it even better every year.

TASK 1

Promote staff buy-in by using staff incentives and rituals

Part of the Foundations Team's job is to promote and enhance staff buy-in to the *Foundations* process. If buy-in is an issue with a few staff members, the Staff Liaison might review this task and use some of the suggested activities. If many staff members are reluctant or hesitant to implement *Foundations* strategies, consider having the entire team read or view this task. You are more likely to succeed with *Foundations* if you do some activities and tasks to promote staff buy-in and engagement. Also consider offering some staff incentives during the early stages of the program.

Why might staff buy-in be a problem? Adult behavior change is always a challenge in *Foundations*. Changing student behavior can be difficult; changing staff behavior can be even more difficult. It isn't that the new behaviors are difficult to learn—it's just that most people are more comfortable doing what they've always done. Moving away from the status quo takes work and time and can even be a little intimidating, so staff may be hesitant to do so. You probably know how difficult it can be to change your own behavior—to switch to a weight-loss diet, to begin a new exercise routine, or to stop smoking. Changing adult behavior will be a challenge.

Albert Einstein said that the definition of insanity is doing something over and over again and expecting a different result. Staff need to change what they are doing if they want different results—that is, better student behavior. Encouraging staff buy-in will encourage staff behavior change, which in turn will lead students to make more responsible, motivated decisions in school.

In this task, we suggest a wide range of activities and strategies that you (the principal) and the team can use to build staff buy-in to *Foundations*. Consider rotating these ideas to keep your buy-in program fresh and interesting. Staff incentives used during the initial stage of implementation can capture the staff's attention and set them up to buy in to the process. Once *Foundations* is well established and staff members have seen the positive outcomes, you may fade the incentives and replace them with intermittent celebrations. Keep using staff buy-in strategies even in the third and fourth year of *Foundations.* The long-term goal is that your new, improved procedures for common areas and schoolwide policies become such a part of the school culture and the school norm that the staff will say, "That's just the way we do things here at Morehead School."

These general long-term strategies promote and enhance staff buy-in and engagement:

- Provide frequent positive feedback to your staff and students.

- Keep *Foundations* activities and procedures in front of the staff by featuring them at staff meetings, in your staff newsletters, and in emails from the principal and from the team.

- Share data (common area observations, incident referrals, suspensions, and so on) that show improvement so staff can get a sense of the outcomes from the different initiatives you're implementing.

- Implement staff incentives to reinforce certain behaviors.

The remainder of this task describes more specific strategies for fostering staff buy-in and engagement. Feel free to modify and adapt them as needed, and of course use your own ideas to promote staff buy-in.

Review and celebrate.

Reviewing how the school is operating and celebrating your successes is crucial. The principal and Foundations Team should always be on the lookout for successes, both large and small, to celebrate.

Routinely review staff expectations for common areas and schoolwide policies such as effective supervision skills. Ask different teachers, perhaps your master teachers, to conduct the reviews. When you or team members observe staff members supervising well in the hallways or during recess—interacting positively with students, correcting fluently, and so on—compliment them. Make sure they know their efforts are noticed and appreciated. You might institute a *Foundations* leader recognition program, where the team publicly recognizes a staff member who is doing an exceptional job interacting and connecting with students or ensuring safety on the playground, for example. Award a small prize to the recognized *Foundations* leader, such as a special parking space for a week. (See "Ideas for Incentives for Staff Support of Foundations" on p. 181.)

Create more staff involvement.

Create staff task forces to assist the Foundations Team in developing common area and schoolwide policies, writing lesson plans for teaching behavioral expectations, and creating videos for teaching, re-teaching, and reviewing student behavioral expectations for hallways, the playground, recess, arrival, and so on.

Encourage teachers to share information with parents about policies and programs such as Guidelines for Success, schoolwide incentives for reducing tardies, and field trip expectations. Through email, newsletters, or website postings, teachers can share information about new procedures and the improvements they've seen. They can also discuss how parents can help their children recognize the importance of following the school's expectations.

Provide ongoing professional development activities.

Professional development activities can provide opportunities to work with the staff in a more relaxed setting and talk about important skill sets that can contribute to your success. For example:

- Ask a local business to provide a staff pizza meal once a month and have the staff stay after school for a brief (15–20 minutes) training session and pizza.

- Form staff study groups to address different *Foundations* topics. For example, ask groups to think about ways to promote better behavior during passing periods or to orient new students and staff members new to the school. The study groups can share their ideas with the staff at a staff meeting.

- Arrange a series of learning lunches. Bring in some catered food (or perhaps food prepared by the PTA) and have a 15-minute presentation on one or two current issues or *Foundations* topics, followed by a 15-minute open discussion. For example, have an experienced teacher present on addressing students who leave class before the bell rings, or have a team member present on increasing the frequency of positive interactions inside and outside the classroom.

- Arrange inservice dinners. Provide a nice dinner (again, perhaps the PTA can help) and have a guest speaker share some information of interest to the staff, such as ideas and tips for mentoring students.

Promote and encourage effective supervision skills.

The following suggestions can help encourage staff to adopt effective supervisory skills.

- It's very important for the school leadership—the principal and assistant principals—to model effective supervisory skills. They should also be prepared to give tactful reminders about the expectations when they see staff who aren't actively supervising their assigned area.

- Develop 3- or 5-minute reviews that focus on particular sets of supervisory skills, such as increasing ratios of positive interactions. Conduct the review during staff meeting. You also might focus on particular groups of students (seventh graders, primary grades) or common areas (the playground, the second-floor boys' restroom). To enhance buy-in, have teaching staff lead the training.

- Review the sample job descriptions for area supervisors on the Module B CD and consider modifying them for use in your school.

- Give the staff a list of key supervisory skills and ask them to identify those they could improve as individuals and as an entire staff. (You might use the Supervisory Skills Checklist from Module B, Presentations 4 and 5, or "The Art of Supervising Secondary School Hallways" from Module B, Presentation 6.) Clarify that you are not interested in individual names; you're looking at the big picture.

Encourage and promote CHAMPS and DSC.

Form a study group of staff members to work through relevant components of *CHAMPS* or *Discipline in the Secondary Classroom* (DSC). Ask teachers to try the recommended approaches and share their successes and frustrations with the group. If possible, offer professional credit to the participants.

Arrange for teachers to visit other teachers' classrooms to observe effective use of opportunities to respond and ratios of interactions, displays of expectations and Guidelines for Success, and *CHAMPS* or *DSC* activities. Nothing beats seeing another teacher doing a great job. The observing teachers are motivated to implement or modify what they saw for their classrooms.

Use staff incentives.

Staff incentives are useful tools to increase staff buy-in and promote staff engagement in the *Foundations* process. Teachers appreciate recognition for doing a good job, and they sure don't mind earning a small incentive, a privilege, an opportunity, or a small gift from the school (see "Ideas for Incentives for Staff Support of Foundations" below).

Remember that you are more likely to change adult behavior with positive strategies than with corrective, negative strategies. Incentives connect to adult motivation by affecting both the adult's expectancy of success and the extrinsic value of being successful.

Some readers might be thinking, "I don't believe in bribery." But remember that bribery is an incentive to do something illegal, immoral, or unethical. Rewarding and motivating adults to make good decisions and exhibit behavior that helps students be successful is not illegal, immoral, or unethical. It's good professional practice.

We suggest that the Foundations Team identify staff incentive programs currently in place and staff behaviors that are targeted for recognition. Then discuss how effective the incentives have been in your school. The team Recorder should document your decisions and discussion; the goal is to identify incentives that you want to keep and

Ideas for Incentives for Staff Support of Foundations

- Extra prep time
- Preferred parking space
- Privilege of wearing jeans on Friday
- Free lunch
- Miss a faculty meeting
- Come in 2 hours late on a teacher workday
- Leave 2 hours early on a teacher workday
- Extra 30 minutes for lunch (class coverage provided)
- Set of papers graded
- Include staff names on student reward tickets; if student wins, staff member also gets prize
- Positive notes in staff mailbox for active participation in *Foundations* efforts
- Coffee and doughnut delivered to teacher during class
- Handwritten note from principal that describes how the staff member's efforts are having a positive impact on *Foundations*
- Relieved of extra duties for a day
- Coupons from community businesses for coffee, movies, lunch, etc.
- Tickets to school athletic events, concerts, or plays

incentives that need to be tweaked to make them more effective. Be sure the incentives are used to recognize and reward staff behavior related to your schoolwide *Foundations* efforts. We've seen the following incentives used effectively in *Foundations* schools.

Foundations Super Staff Member. The principal or assistant principal writes notes to staff members who demonstrate the *Foundations* expectations in common areas with, for example, exemplary hallway supervision, interactions with students, or fluent corrections. Copies of the notes go into a bowl in the office, and a drawing is held each week. The winning staff member receives a small prize, such as a gift certificate to a local store or a pass to leave early one day.

Love Notes From the Principal. An elementary school principal in Texas told us about this incentive. Write a note (handwritten, not typed) to the staff member to compliment him or her for demonstrating an expectation required to improve student behavior—dealing with a challenging student, providing lots of positive attention, or circulating through the cafeteria, for example. Attach a coupon to the note for a simple reward, such as an extra 30 minutes of planning time, an extra 30 minutes of lunch, or a pass to wear jeans on Friday. Staff loved the Love Notes at this elementary school. (If the name Love Notes doesn't fit your personality, substitute another name: Commendations From the Principal or Compliments From the Principal, for example.)

You can get even more specific and have team members survey particular common areas to determine exactly what is needed to improve behavior, then tell staff about the expectations during a staff meeting. The Love Notes can relate specifically to those expectations.

We know of a high school in California that surveyed staff about incentives they valued, and many staff members said they would like to get a handwritten note from the principal. Not a text, an email, or a typed note, but a handwritten note. That personal communication from the principal can be a very powerful tool, and it doesn't cost a cent.

Caught You Caring! Staff members identify other staff members—teachers, paraprofessionals, school nurses, custodians—who actively engage and connect with students. The office staff prepare the blank Caught You Caring! forms (Figure 5b). Staff pick up the forms near the staff mailboxes, write the names of the staff members they are nominating and what each one did, and place the forms into a Caught You Caring! container. Three forms are drawn weekly for small prizes. Each month, all 12 winning names are put into a bowl to draw for one winner who receives a larger prize, such as an extra hour of prep time. The weekly Caught You Caring! forms are displayed in a window or on a board near the office. This idea came from a school in San Diego, California.

Caught You Caring!
Staff Incentive Program

This program is similar to our Caught You Being Good lottery ticket program for students, but it's for the amazing adults on our campus.

How It Works

- Watch for staff members you would like to recognize for their positive interactions with students.
- Pick up a nomination form near the staff mailboxes and fill it out.
- Place the form in the Caught You Caring! basket near the staff mailboxes.

Recognition Ceremony

- A drawing will be held each Monday during morning assembly.
- Three names will be drawn each week for small school-supply prizes.
- On the last Monday of each month, the 12 winners' names will be placed into a basket and one lucky grand-prize winner will be drawn.
- The winner receives an hour of prep time (with classes covered) or something equivalent to be arranged with the principal.

The Caught You Caring! Display

Each week, all the nomination forms will be displayed in the window of the Student Center. Be sure to stop by and check them out!

CAUGHT YOU CARING! NOMINATION FORM

Who did you catch? _____ Date _____

What did he or she do?

_____

_____

_____

Your name (optional) _____

This sample can be printed from the Module A CD.

Friday Free Lunch. Each week, the Foundations Team nominates staff members who have actively monitored and connected with students during passing periods. The nomination forms are placed into a bowl for a drawing, and the winning staff member gets a lunch delivered to his or her classroom on Friday. At the Fresno, California, high school where we heard about this program, the school's culinary arts students prepare the meal and deliver it with a tablecloth and nice china. The winning teachers are able to select from a menu on Thursday.

Shining Stars. At an elementary school in Wichita, Kansas, the staff had an incentive program for fifth-grade students to motivate them to make more responsible choices. The program was very successful. Then the fifth graders went to the principal and asked if they could give coupons to their teachers. The students created coupons called Shining Stars and nominated teachers who helped them be successful in class. The students turned the coupons in to the office, and each week they held a drawing for a small prize. Because students took it upon themselves to recognize teachers, this was a very powerful staff incentive.

Develop staff rituals.

Rituals can be a very powerful tool for promoting staff buy-in and creating a joyful, fun climate. They can also give staff the sense that they are valued and that they belong. When teachers feel valued, they are more likely to put energy into creating and maintaining school programs. The rituals and traditions you foster can help build a sense of ownership and pride in your school.

We suggest that the Foundations Team identify any staff rituals that are currently in place and the staff behaviors or events that are targeted for recognition. Then discuss how effective and fun the rituals are. The team Recorder should document your decisions and discussion; the goal is to identify rituals that you want to keep as well as rituals you might want to add (see "Guidelines for Creating School Rituals and Traditions" on the next page). Creative rituals can contribute greatly to a fun, congenial school atmosphere. Here are some ideas for staff rituals.

First day of school. Set a positive tone for a new school year by gathering the staff together at the end of the first day to toast the great beginning to a wonderful year. A sparkling cider toast is a delightful and appropriate way to celebrate. Use the library or another appropriate room and prepare a table complete with fancy tablecloth, stemware (from your prop collection) filled with sparkling cider, a flower arrangement, and snacks. The principal may start the proceedings with a toast to the school's quality staff and the promise of a wonderful year, but don't hesitate to invite other staff members to join in the toasting. A lively staff can turn this into a memorable event by exchanging humorous toasts to their colleagues.

Guidelines for Creating School Rituals and Traditions

Determine significant events that can and should be recognized (first day of school, staff retirements, staff marriages, births, holidays, last day of school, completion of higher education degrees, and improved performance on standardized tests). The idea is to have ritual celebrations at regularly scheduled times and on special occasions.

Develop a system for finding out when important events will occur. Use a calendar reminder application or have the school secretary track the dates and remind you.

Keep an eye out for props and small gifts that can be used as part of your celebrations. Items that can come in handy include punch bowls, stemware, old trophies and rosettes (that can be relabeled with staff accomplishments), and graduation caps and gowns (for ceremonies celebrating the completion of advanced degrees).

Remember the basic rule for orchestrating a celebration: Keep it simple, short, sweet, and sincere. Although a short, heartfelt, and dignified toast is generally always appreciated, long events tend to be viewed not as reinforcing, but rather as uncomfortable and annoying wastes of time.

Seize the moment! Timing is everything. Tie celebrations to existing events that everyone is already expected to attend. Incorporating short celebrations into your staff meetings is perfect because everyone has already planned to give up the time and is not likely to begrudge a brief diversion.

Last day of school. The last day of school also provides an excellent opportunity to celebrate, acknowledge a successful school year, and recognize staff members who are relocating or retiring. A parade of departing staff members wearing banners and crowns can be lots of fun. You might also want to decorate the office chairs of retiring staff members like floats and wheel them (people included) down the hall with musical accompaniment. For more outlandish fun, follow the parade with a staff line dance—the more challenging the year, the livelier the dance!

Educational degrees. Honor a staff member who completes a higher education degree by holding a formal cap-and-gown ceremony during a staff meeting. While a recording of "Pomp and Circumstance" plays, present the gowned staff member with a rosette or medal in the colors of his or her school. Have the rest of the staff join in a standing ovation. Other ideas include placing a congratulatory message on the school reader board or in the school newsletter.

Childbirth and adoptions. Celebrate and acknowledge these important events in the lives of your fellow staff members. Prepare a work apron that contains diapers, wipes, pacifiers, and other baby accessories (the gaudier the props, the better!) and have the parent-to-be (or new parent) come to a staff meeting wearing it. The staff can sing some lullabies and, if appropriate, present a gift to the staff member. Staff members can also offer the new parent some choice and humorous advice about parenting.

Staff retirements—the formal ceremony. The entire school community should recognize retiring staff members. During an assembly, stage a short, formal, and dignified ceremony that includes past and present students of the staff members. You might begin with a trumpet fanfare to announce the staff member, followed by a short speech by the principal about the staff member's accomplishments. The school chorus or band can perform, and the retiring staff members can give brief farewell speeches.

For a particularly touching conclusion, consider a flower presentation by students to end the ceremony. Students representing every grade line both sides of a red carpet (made of red butcher paper), each holding a single flower. As the entire audience sings a farewell song, the retiring staff member walks down the carpet, collecting the flowers from the children. With this type of tribute, you can be sure that there won't be a dry eye in the room.

Staff marriages. A staff member's wedding provides a perfect opportunity to celebrate and acknowledge a coworker's important life event. During a staff meeting, deck the bride out in a veil (made from an old curtain attached to a crown of paper flowers) and a plastic flower bouquet, or dress the groom in a top hat and a plastic or paper boutonnière. Get the staff to sing an appropriate song and possibly present a gift. It can also be fun to let staff members take turns offering the newlywed some humorous advice about marriage.

Improved school test scores. Good test scores reflect the efforts of an entire staff working together to ensure well-prepared and competent students. These efforts should always be recognized and reinforced! Hang a banner in the staff room that congratulates everyone on a job well done, give each staff member a flower or thank-you card, or arrange a small reception where you can lead a sparkling cider toast.

Valentine's Day. Valentine's Day is a perfect time to let your staff know that you care about them. For example, decorate the staff room table with hearts and flowers and provide a fruit or vegetable tray. Staff members may appreciate a personalized valentine in their mailbox. It can be as simple as a note of appreciation on a heart-shaped piece of paper or as involved as an individualized rhyming poem. Or hang a large valentine with a written poem about the staff in the staff room.

Income tax day. Income tax day is a good excuse for a staff party at the principal's home. You and the Foundations Team can plan a soup-kitchen menu and provide prizes for a staff drawing. Encourage anyone who had to pay additional income tax to wear black, or have black armbands available at the party. Sometime during the evening, draw names and award prizes to those in the tax-paying group, (a sack of potatoes or flour, cans of beans, piggy banks, or calendars with April 15 circled in red).

Special honors. Publicly acknowledge and celebrate staff members' professional accomplishments such as service awards, Fulbright Scholarships, National Science Foundation Awards, and so on.

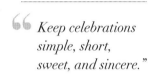

Keep celebrations simple, short, sweet, and sincere."

Note: If the principal did not attend the team meeting or meetings about reviewing staff buy-in, staff incentives, and staff rituals, be sure to update him or her as soon as possible. Tell the principal the strategies that the team thinks will promote staff buy-in to *Foundations*, appropriate incentives, and appealing staff rituals. Ensure that the principal and the team are all on the same page and working toward the same goal.

Also, if your school already has a social committee that organizes celebrations and rituals, be sure to include this team in reviewing, planning, and implementing new programs. Including an existing group helps to promote greater staff involvement in *Foundations* while reducing the workload for the Foundations Team Plan to evaluate staff incentives and rituals regularly.

Plan to regularly include discussions about staff rituals and incentives on the team meeting agendas. Talk about whether the incentives are enhancing staff buy-in and engagement. Do you need to tweak anything to increase effectiveness, or add or eliminate any programs or rituals? Consider creating a yearly (or semester) plan for using the incentives. You might also designate a team member as the Staff Buy-in Coordinator. This person will ensure that incentive programs and rituals take place and will lead discussions about adding, eliminating, and rotating the programs and rituals.

Task 1 Action Steps & Evidence of Implementation

Action Steps	Evidence of Implementation
1. Identify staff incentive programs and rituals already in place in your school, and identify any you would like to add. 2. If the team does most of the discussion about incentives and rituals, ensure that the principal is informed of any recommendations and is included in all decisions.	Foundations Process: Presentations/ Communications With Staff
3. Create a yearly (or semester) plan for using incentives to enhance staff buy-in.	Foundations Archive: Presentations/ Communications With Staff
4. Consider designating a team member as the Staff Buy-in Coordinator (a logical choice might be your Staff Liaison). This person will ensure that incentive programs and rituals take place and will lead discussions about adding, eliminating, and rotating the programs and rituals.	Foundations Process: Team Composition, Presentations/ Communications With Staff

TASK 2

Administrators: Be an effective leader and model for the Foundations process

This task includes suggestions for you, the administrator, on providing positive leadership for the *Foundations* processes.

A very successful principal of a large high school, one of the first high schools to implement *Foundations* in the late 1980s, discussed with us the difficulties of maintaining the daily functioning of the school while keeping a focus on long-term improvement. She said that all building administrators have so many immediate demands on their time that they sometimes feel like Yosemite Sam, the old cartoon character, shooting down problems with a pistol in each hand. Principals make decisions and problem-solve all day long. (She was a high school principal, but the same can be said of elementary and middle school principals.)

This principal always has a small part of her attention focused on assessing the magnitude of each problem—does it occur often enough that more energy put into prevention would be worthwhile? She was committed to the *Foundations* process because she realized the long-term benefits. Improving behavior takes time and energy initially to get staff buy-in and establish effective procedures. But if in the long run there are fewer fights, if in the long run all staff intervene with dress code consistently first thing in the morning every single morning, the principal has fewer decisions to make.

We—Randy and all the *Safe & Civil Schools* trainers—have collectively worked with thousands of schools that have implemented *Foundations* successfully, and we've noted the strategies and techniques that the most effective principals and assistant principals use to guide the process. We've also seen that when schools falter, it can often be attributed to administrators who do *not* employ the strategies and techniques we suggest in this task. As you read the following recommendations, reflect on those strategies you use easily and automatically and those you may need to make more of a conscious effort to implement.

Clarify your role and function on the Foundations Team.

Remember, one administrator must be on the Foundations Team. If there is only one administrator—you—in your building, you need to be on the team. In a larger school, an assistant principal may serve on the team instead of the principal, so you may or may not be on the team. Even when you are not on the team, you still play an important role and need to be very visibly supportive. If you don't fully support the process, the likelihood of long-term improvement is reduced tremendously.

Here's an example of visible support. During a staff meeting, when it is time for the Foundations Team to present, do more than just introduce the presenter. Let everyone know you are behind the team 100%.

> *We're about to hear from the Foundations Team. They want your input on the schoolwide personal electronics policy. Please give them your full attention. And please know that once we have adopted revised policies related to electronics, it is my job as the instructional leader of this building to ensure that we are all on the same page.*

Without this kind of public and visible support, there is too great a risk that a percentage of your staff will think, "Well, the assistant principal cares about this stuff but the principal really doesn't, so we don't have to take it very seriously."

We also recommend that the administrator on the team, whether it's you or an assistant principal, be a consistent presence throughout the *Foundations* processes. We've worked with some large schools that have tried to have different assistant principals work on different aspects of *Foundations*, but the absence of a single, stable administrative representative makes it difficult for the nonadministrative team members.

As you remember from Presentation 2, "Team Processes," we recommend that you serve as cochair of the team along with a nonadministrative team member. Be sure that you work directly with that person so that you come across as coleaders of the team. Your goal is to be as nondirective as possible while ensuring that team meetings are functional and that the continuous Improvement Cycle is maintained. You and your cochair might want to review or establish ground rules for the meetings.

One of you needs to be an "on-task and on-time nag." We recommend that you gently encourage the nonadministrative cochair to take this important job. Then ask team members to request that the cochair really nag them so he or she has no qualms about doing the job well. "Sharon, for the year that you are the cochair, we want you to nag us about staying on task and being on time. One of us will take that role next year, but please help us stay focused this year!" It can be difficult for the administrator to take on the slightly annoying role of keeping people on task and focused, so it's better if a direct colleague of the team members perform this role.

As the administrator on the team, you need to remind the team about bigger issues: board policy, community concerns, teacher union issues or concerns. You need to be the voice for the bigger picture and keep everyone aware of those issues.

Seek input from the quieter members of the team, and ensure that no team members monopolize discussions. If you aren't vigilant about ensuring parity, you might end up with three of the six team members doing 90% of the talking and the work. Gently seek everyone's opinions. "Hakim, you represent all of the language arts teachers and the custodial staff. What do you think the custodial staff will think of this idea?" Create an atmosphere in which all team members feel their opinions are valued and all team members are expected and encouraged to actively participate.

Know whether a decision or topic is site based or administrative.

Some decisions must be made by the administrator, while others can be site based. This issue is bigger than just the *Foundations* process. Be very clear with the team when a decision must be administrative—for example, whether to work on a safety issue or when school board policy, state law, or federal law dictates what needs to be done. Most staff members recognize that not everything can be site based.

Manage agendas for staff meetings.

There are four basic types of agenda items. You can make staff meetings more organized and efficient by clarifying the decision-making process for each agenda item. You might even formally label each item on the agenda with one of these four categories.

- **For information only (FYI).** Sometimes a decision must be administrative because it is related to board policy or state or federal law. Label the agenda item FYI to let team members know about the issue or decision and so they understand it's not a site-based issue.

- **Administrative decision with staff input.** You will make the decision, but you want recommendations and opinions from the staff.

- **Staff discussion for team consideration.** The Foundations Team wants staff recommendations and opinions about this issue or decision so they can work on a revision proposal. "Staff, we are going to be working on morning arrival procedures. For 10 minutes, let's discuss your concerns, comments, thoughts, revision ideas, and anything else about morning arrival that you want the team to consider as we work on the revision proposal."

- **Staff decision.** Discuss a decision or issue and then vote. For example, hold a 10-minute discussion about the proposed new arrival procedures, then have the staff vote on whether to adopt it.

Give the Foundations Team time at staff meetings.

At staff meetings, be sure to give time to the Foundations Team. If *Foundations* is often bumped from the agenda by more urgent business, staff engagement cannot happen. The Foundations Team must be able to seek staff input and update staff about data, progress, and priorities. Staff will also need opportunities to vote on adopting new policies and procedures.

Create opportunities for staff to make decisions.

The adoption process is covered in detail in Module A, Presentation 3, "The Improvement Cycle." You should thoroughly review Task 3 about the **Adopt** step because you need to model and guide the adoption process.

We recommend the Five Levels of Satisfaction voting system: Staff members show support or lack of support for a proposal by rating it on a 5-point scale. They use their fingers to indicate their rating publicly during staff meetings (see Figure 5c on the next page).

A fun way to introduce this voting method to the staff (and give them an idea of their involvement in all *Foundations* decisions) is to lead a vote on the important topic of snacks. Pose this question to the staff: "Should I, the principal, bring snacks to the next staff meeting?" Then display a voting rubric (several are available on the Module A CD; one is illustrated in Figure 5c) and explain the rating system as it relates to snacks.

5 = I not only want snacks at the next staff meeting, but I'm also willing to help accomplish that task. I'll help decide what kind of snacks to have, help you carry the snacks into the meeting, and set them out on the table.

4 = I would love to have snacks at the next meeting, but I'm not volunteering to help. I'll certainly eat them if they are there.

3 = I don't care one way or the other. I might eat some snacks, I might not. I do not object to having snacks at the next staff meeting.

2 = I have some concerns. We have too many sweets in the staff room all day long, and some people are trying to diet. Healthy snacks might be OK. If everyone else wants snacks, I won't roadblock the idea.

1 = I absolutely do not want snacks at the next meeting.

Explain the adoption criteria: If just one person votes 1, or if 10% or more of the staff vote 2, the proposal is rejected. So if one person votes 1, you will not bring snacks to the next meeting, but that person will assist you in making future decisions about snacks at staff meetings.

Figure 5c   *Five Levels of Satisfaction voting rubric (A-13)*

So you model the decision-making process with a nonthreatening, easy-to-implement decision. And by leading the first vote, you are demonstrating that you actively support this way of doing business that recognizes minority opinions but also forces a level of responsibility. People who vote 1 have to be part of the group that will work on the issue at hand.

Early in the *Foundations* process, also tell staff about the limit on votes when making decisions. If staff vote to reject a proposal three times (the initial proposal and two revisions), it becomes your job to decide what the final policy will be. This limit keeps the team and staff from getting stuck on issues (no one has time to discuss the pros and cons of allowing hats in the building for 17 staff meetings), and divisive issues are often best resolved by an administrator who has the courage to just say, "This is what we are going to do, and here's why."

If this situation comes up, be sure to frame your decision successfully: "Staff, because you have some strong opinions on this issue, and because we have voted on it at three staff meetings without consensus, I (or we, the administrative team) have decided that the policy is going to be . . ."

In his book *Good to Great*, Jim Collins (2001) writes about the importance of staff unity as it relates to business. He finds that one of the features of truly great businesses is that, no matter whether a whole staff or a CEO makes a policy decision, everyone rallies together to try to make it work. Even people who voted for a different policy support the adopted policy; their attitude is: I am so devoted to my fellow staff members and the company that I will try to make it work.

Your goal should be to establish that attitude. Benjamin Franklin wrote a speech that was read at the Constitutional Convention in 1787, just before the delegates signed the U.S. Constitution. (At age 81, Franklin was too weak to read it himself.) Consider reading excerpts from this speech to the staff. For example:

> *I confess that there are several parts of this Constitution which I do not at present approve, but I'm not sure I shall never approve them: For having lived long, I have experienced many instances of being obliged by better information, or fuller consideration, to change opinions even on important subjects, which I once thought right, but found to be otherwise.*

Franklin goes on to say that if he could have written the Constitution by himself, he thinks it would have been better, but he also knows that others' contributions add strength to the document:

> *I agree to this Constitution with all its faults, if they are such . . . For when you assemble a number of men to have the advantage of their joint wisdom, you inevitably assemble with those men, all their prejudices, their passions, their errors of opinions, their local interests, and their selfish views. . . . The opinions I have had of its errors I sacrifice to the public good. . . . On the whole, Sir, I cannot help expressing a wish that every member of the Convention who may still have objections to it, would with me, on this occasion doubt a little of his own infallibility, and to make manifest our unanimity, put his name to this instrument.*

The key phrase here is "to doubt a little of his own infallibility." When all stakeholders can sacrifice some of their own views for the common good, great things can be achieved.

Be an inspirational coach.

When you are ready to implement a newly adopted policy or procedure, model enthusiasm and a willingness to work hard to make that implementation work. Function like an inspirational sports coach might. Create energy.

*Next Monday, we're going to implement the new cafeteria proce-
dures that you voted to adopt. I'm excited to see how these procedures
improve the lunch period for our students and for the entire staff. We
can anticipate shorter lines and better behavior. With all of us united in
making this implementation work, I'm sure it will be a great success.*

Remind people why the common area or schoolwide policy became a priority.

*Our data show that students are frustrated by the current cafeteria
procedures and don't always feel safe in that setting. So remember, our
goal is to reduce the amount of time that students are waiting, which
should reduce misbehavior, and increase the quality of supervision so
that we can prevent the bullying behavior that students have reported.*

Model the behaviors you want to see from staff.

Examples of this leadership strategy come from secondary schools that have done a
great job of improving hallway supervision. To succeed in improving hallway behavior and reducing tardies, you need to have many adults in the hallways between
classes. The most successful schools always have principals and assistant principals
in the hallways as often as possible, modeling the behavior they want to see from
staff. They model active observation, checking blind corners, continuous scanning,
and being aware of other adults who might need support. They model high ratios of
positive interactions with students—greeting students, asking students their names,
and supporting new students. "Hey, Jamal, how are you today? Enjoying the school
so far? Good. Let me know if you need anything." They also model how to correct
fluently: calmly, consistently, briefly, and immediately.

Monitor your ratios of positive interactions with staff.

A strategy embedded in many of the *Foundations* modules is maintaining a high
ratio of positive interactions with students. We recommend that all adults interact
positively with students when they're behaving appropriately at least three times
more often than they correct students. You need to use the same strategy with your
staff. Greet staff members by name, interact with them positively, and give them
meaningful, positive feedback.

Be aware that the 3:1 positive to corrective ratio is probably not adequate with a staff
member you have had a rocky relationship with or a staff member who needs lots of
corrective feedback. Strive for a 5:1 or even 8:1 ratio with those people.

By paying attention to your ratios of positive interactions with staff, you are modeling how a person in authority should interact with people more frequently during times of strength than at times when errors must be corrected.

Conclusion

Exhibit with your staff all the strategies and techniques you want your teachers to implement with students. Let's review the STOIC acronym:

Structure: Organize your staff meetings. Structure your agendas with clarity.

Teach: Teach your expectations for staff behavior. Tell staff whether it's OK to read a newspaper or grade papers during a staff meeting. Tell them the process for deciding on policies and procedures.

Observe: Do you want your playground supervisors to actively observe students and circulate throughout the setting? Then visit the playground frequently to observe the supervisors because they need to know that the principal sees them doing a good job.

Interact positively: Thank staff for their efforts to implement *Foundations* processes, and provide noncontingent attention that shows you value staff as fellow human beings, too.

Correct: Whenever staff behavior is not what it needs to be, correct it in the same way you want teachers to correct students: calmly, consistently, immediately, briefly, respectfully, and as privately as possible.

Task 2 Action Steps

1. Reflect on these leadership suggestions and identify the strategies that seem most useful for your own continuous improvement efforts. In other words, what strategies do you need to make more of a conscious effort to implement?

2. Mark in your planning calendar a couple of times during the year when you will remind yourself to review this presentation (the video, book, or both) to continue your continuous improvement process of self-reflection.

TASK 3

Engage reluctant staff members

A few staff members may be reluctant to buy in to the *Foundations* process. Even staff members who voted in favor of a particular schoolwide policy or common area procedure might be reluctant to change their behavior to meet the new expectations— for example, a teacher who has always stayed in her classroom during passing periods might want to continue staying there during passing periods rather than assist with hallway supervision. Some staff members might not want to work on boosting their ratios of positive interactions or participate in a student incentive program. If 80 out of 100 staff members voted 3, 4, or 5 (on the Five Levels of Satisfaction voting scale) to adopt a procedure, that means 20 staff members voted 2 and didn't completely buy in to the new procedure. That's quite a few people who could undermine your attempts to change student behavior. And if they don't actively participate in the process, other staff members might think, "Why am I out here in the hallway while they stay in their classrooms?"

Staff buy-in activities, incentives, and rituals, as well as strong leadership from administrators, will convince many to get on board, but you might have a few staff members who require some additional effort. Consider analyzing a staff member's reluctance just as you might analyze a student who is hesitant about changing her behavior, by looking at the possible reasons for or functions of the behavior. Is the staff member saying or possibly thinking statements like the following?

- Hey, this is not my job, and I don't see how it's going to benefit me.
- I don't believe there's a problem with student behavior in the cafeteria.
- According to what I know, we need to punish these kids more.
- I don't think these kids will ever change.
- I'm not sure what you want me to do.

When a staff member has a nonsupportive attitude, others might want the principal to just make him do his job. But as with challenging students, if you rely on a reactive, consequence-based approach, the reluctant staff member might become passive-aggressive in dealing with your attempts to change his behavior or become openly resistant, proclaiming that the school should not be implementing *Foundations* at all. A negative, confrontational approach to trying to change a person's behavior usually results in a lose-lose situation, so consider using the following positive approach.

- Recognize and acknowledge that some staff members are reluctant to buy in to *Foundations* and to do their part. Don't ignore the fact or talk around it—deal with it openly, directly, and calmly.

- Use the STOIC framework with the entire staff:
  - **Structure:** Ensure that expectations are clear—everyone knows what they need to do for the policy or procedure to be successful and that working collaboratively with other staff members is essential.

  - **Teach:** Teach and review the skills and tools that staff need. What do the expected staff behaviors look like and sound like?

  - **Observe and monitor:** Collect data on the impact of the new policies and procedures on student behavior and share them with all staff, including reluctant staff members.

  - **Interact positively:** Boost your ratios of positive interactions with the reluctant staff members by nonverbally reinforcing them when they display appropriate behaviors. Acknowledge and support their efforts. When appropriate, offer some incentives at first to encourage adult behavior change. Celebrate the success when adults change their behavior to positively affect students.

  - **Correct fluently:** Some subtle corrections by the administrator might be needed—proximity management, for example. If a person has not been to her supervision assignment for two days in a row, be there the third day and remind her that being on time to supervise is crucial for promoting responsible student behavior. See if a slight schedule change might help the staff member get to her assignment more easily. Model how to actively monitor, acknowledge, and connect with students, and correct fluently, then encourage the staff member to practice these skills. Coach the staff member.

This positive approach should prompt reluctant staff members to buy in to *Foundations* and begin to meet the expectations for staff behavior. For any remaining reluctant staff members, consider the following seven steps that we've learned from some very skillful principals. These steps address possible functions of the resistant behavior and guide you in manipulating the STOIC variables to gain buy-in and compliance. As you review them, determine whether any are potentially helpful for your work with reluctant staff members. Modify and revise as necessary to fit your situation.

The first four steps are more or less interchangeable—you do not have to follow them in order.

Step 1: Remind all staff members, and reluctant staff members in particular, about their agreed-upon commitments to implement specific activities, policies, or procedures. For example, if a staff member chose not to re-teach the expectations for hallway behavior after winter break, privately remind the staff member that he made a commitment to do so, and you expect him to teach that review lesson plan as scheduled.

Step 2: Arrange sharing activities for staff, specifically sharing that relates to the skills or assignment of the reluctant staff member. In particular, ask highly respected staff members to share. Sometimes when a reluctant staff member hears others discuss their successes with improving student behavior, she begins to realize that the skill set, procedure, or program can benefit her and the school. So staff sharing about successes can sometimes help the staff member buy in to *Foundations*.

Step 3: Model the desired staff behaviors. Show with great clarity what the behaviors look like and sound like. You shouldn't assume that the staff members know. Often just a simple demonstration of "looks like, sounds like" can give them the clarification they need.

Step 4: Reinforce growth by recognizing both effort and progress, no matter how small or gradual. This reinforcement consists of lots of positive feedback and high ratios of positive interactions. To boost the ratio, use noncontingent attention along with the contingent recognition of any slight (or dramatic) behavior changes related to the skill or behaviors you want to see improved.

Step 5: Offer the assistance of a peer coach. This coach can be a skilled colleague who provides the reluctant staff member a chance to observe crucial skills such as delivering fluent correction, positive feedback, and noncontingent attention. The coach might also observe the staff member as he supervises and provide feedback and guidance.

Step 6: Schedule and conduct a nonevaluative observation of the staff member doing an activity or a skill related to her reluctance. For example, if the staff member does not want to circulate around the playground as she supervises, tell her you plan to observe her supervisory skills just to get an overall idea of how she's doing and how the students respond to her.

Step 7: Schedule a formal conference with the reluctant staff member. You, the principal, do the following:

- Identify what the staff member is doing correctly. Always begin with some positive observations and positive feedback.

  Beth, you do such a good job of visually scanning when supervising your location in the morning. You frequently look down all the intersecting hallways. Constant visual monitoring is just what we need in that location because of the heavy traffic. And you always stay in your location until the passing period has ended.

- Clarify the expectations for staff behavior and identify how the staff member is not meeting the expectations.

  Sometimes, however, you are late to your station. I observed on both Tuesday and Thursday that you were about 2 minutes late. If you aren't there before the bell rings, many students move through that intersection with no adult present to monitor behavior and interact positively with them. Last year, when students were going to first-period classes, we had 17 office referrals from that area alone. That's why the team and I decided to create a supervisory position there this year. Also, when you finally arrived, you seemed harried, and you reacted to misbehavior by loudly and emotionally correcting the students.

- Give a detailed description of what needs to be done to successfully execute the specific activity or action. Describe what it looks like and sounds like, so there's no confusion about what you're asking the staff member to do.

  I need you to arrive at your location every day before the bell rings. Get there 15–30 seconds before the bell rings so you can settle in and students will see you immediately as they enter the area. Keep up the visual scanning of all directions of the intersection. Whenever you see or hear any inappropriate behavior, you need to respond by delivering a verbal redirect. If the misbehaving student is more than 3–4 feet from you, ask him to come back to you or to stop so you can walk to him. Remember to deliver the redirect calmly, quietly, briefly, and respectfully by stating what you need the student to do. End by nodding your head and telling the student to have a good day. This approach will be especially effective if you also boost your ratio of positive interactions. You can do that by smiling, greeting students, calling students by name and asking how they are, nodding your head to students who are walking and talking, or giving a thumbs-up to a student who is helping another student. During the passing period, try to deliver at least 20 positive interactions. When I observed you today, you delivered only three positive interactions.

- Use a problem-solving approach to develop a plan to help the staff member change his behavior. Talk about what the staff member needs to begin doing and stop doing; ask what you can do to help, and be sure to emphasize what the staff member is doing correctly. Develop a detailed game plan to promote that behavior change.

  You're doing a good job of being alert and scanning the entire area, but your supervision will be more effective and easier if you arrive before the bell rings, boost your positive interactions, and deliver fluent corrections. If boosting your positive interactions to at least 20 seems high, realize that 20 per passing period translates to an average of five positive interactions per minute. That's doable.

Many of them can be quick nonverbal interactions such as a smile, head nod, or wave.

What positive interactions, verbal and nonverbal, do you feel comfortable delivering? What will you try to deliver more of starting tomorrow? What's your game plan for arriving on time—how will you avoid being sidetracked or losing track of time until you hear the bell?

That sounds great. What, if anything, can the assistant principal or I do to help you get there on time?

Please begin your plan tomorrow morning and follow it every day for the rest of the week. I'll walk by later this week to see how it's going. I also want to conduct an observation next Tuesday. I'll count your positive interactions and see how you respond to any inappropriate behavior. Is there a time later on Tuesday when we can meet and debrief, or would you prefer we meet on Wednesday during your planning period?

Task 3 Action Steps

1. Identify staff members who seem reluctant to buy in to *Foundations* and analyze why they are hesitant about changing their behavior.

2. Ensure that you are using positive universal procedures with all staff by following the STOIC framework.

3. If necessary, target individual staff members by reminding them of their commitments, modeling desired behavior, providing positive reinforcement, offering peer coaching, observing and providing constructive feedback, or conducting a private conference.

BIBLIOGRAPHY

Adams, C. (2011). Recess makes kids smarter. *Instructor, 120*(5), 55–59. Retrieved from http://www.scholastic.com/teachers/article/recess-makes-kids-smarter

Allensworth, E. M., & Easton, J. Q. (2007). *What matters for staying on track and graduating in Chicago public schools: A close look at course grades, failures, and attendance in the freshman year.* Retrieved from http://ccsr.uchicago.edu/sites/default/files/publications/07%20What%20Matters%20Final.pdf

American Lung Association, Epidemiology and Statistics Unit, Research and Health Education Division (2012). *Trends in asthma morbidity and mortality.* Retrieved from http://www.lung.org/finding-cures/our-research/trend-reports/asthma-trend-report.pdf

Applied Survey Research and Attendance Works (2011). *Attendance in early elementary grades: Associations with student characteristics, school readiness and third grade outcomes* (mini-report). Retrieved from http://www.attendanceworks.org/wordpress/wp-content/uploads/2010/04/ASR-Mini-Report-Attendance-Readiness-and-Third-Grade-Outcomes-7-8-11.pdf

Archer, A., & Gleason, M. (1990). *Skills for school success.* North Billerica, MA: Curriculum Associates.

Baker, M. L., Sigmon, N., & Nugent, M. E. (2001). *Truancy reduction: Keeping students in school* (Juvenile Justice Bulletin). Retrieved from U.S. Department of Justice, National Criminal Justice Reference Service website: http://www.ncjrs.gov/pdffiles1/ojjdp/188947.pdf

Balfanz, R., Bridgeland, J. M., Fox, J. H., DePaoli, J. L., Ingram, E. S., Maushard, M. (2014). *Building a grad nation: Progress and challenge in ending the high school dropout epidemic.* Retrieved from http://diplomasnow.org/wp-content/uploads/2014/04/BGN-Report-2014_Full.pdf

Balfanz, R., & Byrnes, V. (2012). *Chronic absenteeism: Summarizing what we know from nationally available data.* Retrieved from Johns Hopkins University Center for Social Organization of Schools website: http://new.every1graduates.org/wp-content/uploads/2012/05/FINALChronicAbsenteeismReport_May16.pdf

Balfanz, R., & Byrnes, V. (2013). *Meeting the challenge of combating chronic absenteeism: Impact of the NYC mayor's interagency task force on chronic absenteeism and school attendance and its implications for other cities.* Retrieved from Johns Hopkins School of Education website: http://new.every1graduates.org/wp-content/uploads/2013/11/NYM-Chronic-Absenteeism-Impact-Report.pdf

Becker, W. C., & Engelmann, S. (1971). *Teaching: A course in applied psychology.* Columbus, OH: Science Research Associates.

Brophy, J. E. (1980). *Teacher praise: A functional analysis.* East Lansing, MI: Institute for Research on Teaching.

Brophy, J. E. (1986). Teacher influences on student achievement. *American Psychologist, 4*(10), 1069–1077.

Brophy, J. (1987). Synthesis of research on strategies for motivating students to learn. *Educational Leadership, 45*(2), 40–48.

Bruner, C., Discher, A., & Chang, H. (2011). *Chronic elementary absenteeism: A problem hidden in plain sight.* Retrieved from http://www.attendanceworks.org/wordpress/wp-content/uploads/2010/04/ChronicAbsence.pdf

Cameron, J., & Pierce, W. D. (1994). Reinforcement, reward, and intrinsic motivation: A meta-analysis. *Review of Educational Research, 64*(3), 363–423.

Chang, H., & Romero, M. (2008). *Present, engaged, and accounted for: The critical importance of addressing chronic absence in the early grades.* New York, NY: National Center for Children in Poverty.

Collins, J. (2001). *Good to great: Why some companies make the leap . . . and others don't.* New York, NY: HarperCollins Publishers.

Colvin, G. (Writer/Producer). (1992). *Managing acting-out behavior: A staff development program* [video]. Longmont, CO: Sopris West.

Colvin, G. (2004). *Managing the cycle of acting-out behavior in the classroom.* Eugene, OR: Behavior Associates.

Cooper, J. O., Heron, T. E., & Heward, W. L. (2007). *Applied behavior analysis* (2nd ed.). Upper Saddle River, NJ: Pearson.

Cotton, K. (1990). *Schoolwide and classroom discipline* (Close-Up #9). Portland, OR: Northwest Regional Educational Laboratory.

Donovan, M. S., & Cross, C. T. (Eds.) (2002). *Minority students in special education and gifted education.* Washington, DC: National Academy Press.

Emmer, E. T., & Evertson, C. M. (2012). *Classroom management for middle and high school teachers* (9th ed.). Upper Saddle River, NJ: Pearson.

Esler, A., Godber, Y., & Christenson, S. (2008). Best practices in supporting school-family partnerships. In A. Thomas & J. Grimes (Eds.), *Best practices in school psychology V* (pp. 917–936). Bethesda, MD: National Association of School Psychologists.

Evertson, C. M., & Emmer, E. T. (2012). *Classroom management for elementary teachers* (9th ed.). Upper Saddle River, NJ: Pearson.

Fabelo, T., Thompson, M. D., Plotkin, M., Carmichael, D., Marchbanks, M. P. III, & Booth, E. A. (2011). *Breaking schools' rules: A statewide study of how school discipline relates to students' success and juvenile justice involvement.* Retrieved from http://csgjusticecenter.org/wp-content/uploads/2012/08/Breaking_Schools_Rules_Report_Final.pdf

Feather, N. T. (1982). Expectancy-value approaches: Present status and future directions. In N. T. Feather (Ed.), *Expectations and actions: Expectancy-value models in psychology.* Hillsdale NJ: Erlbaum.

Furlong, M., Felix, E. D., Sharkey, J. D., & Larson, J. (2005). Preventing school violence: A plan for safe and engaging schools. *Principal Leadership, 6*(1), 11–15. Retrieved from http://www.nasponline.org/resources/principals/Student%20Counseling%20Violence%20Prevention.pdf

Get Schooled and Hart Research (2012). *Skipping to nowhere: Students share their views about missing school.* Retrieved from https://getschooled.com/system/assets/assets/203/original/Hart_Research_report_final.pdf

Glossary of Education Reform for Journalists, Parents, and Community Members. Retrieved from http://edglossary.org/school-culture/

Gottfredson, D. C., Gottfredson, G. D., & Hybl, L. G. (1993). Managing adolescent behavior: A multiyear, multischool study. *American Educational Research Journal, 30*(1), 179–215.

Jensen, E. (2009). *Teaching with poverty in mind: What being poor does to kids' brains and what schools can do about it.* Alexandria, VA: Association for Supervision and Curriculum Development.

Jenson, W., Rhode, G., & Reavis, H. K. (2009). *The Tough Kid tool box.* Eugene, OR: Pacific Northwest Publishing.

Kerr, J., & Nelson, C. (2002). *Strategies for addressing behavior problems in the classroom* (4th ed.). Englewood Cliffs, NJ: Merrill/Prentice Hall.

Kerr, J., Price, M., Kotch, J., Willis, S., Fisher, M., & Silva, S. (2012). Does contact by a family nurse practitioner decrease early school absence? *Journal of School Nursing, 28,* 38–46.

Kim, C. Y., Losen, D. J., and Hewitt, D. T. (2010). *The school-to-prison pipeline: Structuring legal reform.* New York, NY: New York University Press.

Klem, A. M., & Connell, J. P. (2004). Relationships matter: Linking teacher support to student engagement and achievement. *Journal of School Health, 74*(7), 262–273.

Kounin, J. S. (1977). *Discipline and group management in classrooms.* Huntington, NY: Krieger Publishing.

Losen, D. J. (2011). *Discipline policies, successful schools, and racial justice.* Boulder, CO: National Education Policy Center. Retrieved from http://nepc.colorado.edu/publication/discipline-policies

Losen, D. J., & Martinez, T. E. (2013). *Out of school & off track: The overuse of suspension in American middle and high schools.* Retrieved from http://civilrightsproject.ucla.edu/resources/projects/center-for-civil-rights-remedies/school-to-prison-folder/federal-reports/out-of-school-and-off-track-the-overuse-of-suspensions-in-american-middle-and-high-schools/OutofSchool-OffTrack_UCLA_4-8.pdf

Maag, J. (2001). *Powerful struggles: Managing resistance, building rapport.* Longmont, CO: Sopris West.

Marzano, R. J. (2003). *Classroom management that works: Research-based strategies for every teacher.* Alexandria, VA: Association for Supervision and Curriculum Development.

Maslow, A. H. (1962). Some basic propositions of a growth and self-actualization psychology. In A. W. Combs (Ed.), *Perceiving, behaving, becoming: A new focus for education* (pp. 34–49). Washington, D.C: Association for Supervision and Curriculum Development.

McNeely, C. A., Nonnemaker, J. A., & Blum, R. W. (2002). Promoting school connectedness: Evidence from the National Longitudinal Study of Adolescent Health. *Journal of School Health, 72*(4), 138–146.

National Association for Sport and Physical Education (2006). *Recess for elementary school children* (Position Statement). Retrieved from http://www.eric.ed.gov/PDFS/ED541609.pdf

National Center for Education Statistics (2012). *Digest of Education Statistics* (NCES 2014-015). Retrieved from http://nces.ed.gov/programs/digest/d12/ and http://nces.ed.gov/programs/digest/d12/tables/dt12_122.asp

O'Leary, K. D., & O'Leary, S. G. (1977). *Classroom management: The successful use of behavior modification* (2nd ed.). New York, NY: Pergamon Press.

O'Neill, R. E., Horner, R. H., Albin, R. W., Storey, K., & Sprague, J. R. (1996). *Functional assessment and program development for problem behavior: A practical handbook* (2nd ed.). Belmont, CA: Cengage.

Payne, C. (2008). *So much reform, so little change: The persistence of failure in urban schools.* Boston, MA: Harvard Education Press.

Purkey, W. W., & Novak, J. M. (2005). *Inviting school success: A self-concept approach to teaching, learning, and democratic practice in a connected world* (4th ed.). New York, NY: Wadsworth Publishing.

Ready, D. (2010). Socioeconomic disadvantage, school attendance, and early cognitive development: The differential effects of school exposure. *Sociology of Education, 83*(4), 271–289.

Rhode, G. R., Jenson, W. R., & Reavis, H. K. (2010). *The Tough Kid book: Practical classroom management strategies* (2nd ed.). Eugene, OR: Pacific Northwest Publishing.

Sheets, R. H., & Gay, G. (1996). Student perceptions of disciplinary conflicts in ethnically diverse classrooms. *NASSP Bulletin, 80*(580), 84–94.

Skiba, R. J., Horner, R. H., Chung, C.-G., Rausch, M. K., May, S. L., & Tobin, T. (2011). Race is not neutral: A national investigation of African American and Latino disproportionality in school discipline. *School Psychology Review, 40*(1), pp. 85–107.

Skiba, R. J., Michael, R. S., Nardo, A. C., & Peterson, R. L. (2002). The color of discipline: Sources of racial and gender disproportionality in school punishment. *Urban Review, 34*(4), 317–342.

Skiba, R., & Peterson, R. (2003). Teaching the social curriculum: School discipline as instruction. *Preventing School Failure, 47,* 66–73.

Sparks, S. D. (2010). Districts begin looking harder at absenteeism. *Education Week, 30*(6), 1, 12–13.

Spinks, S. (n.d.). Adolescent brains are works in progress. *Frontline.* Retrieved from http://www.pbs.org/wgbh/pages/frontline/shows/teenbrain/work/adolescent.html

Sprague, J. R., & Walker, H. M. (2005). *Safe and healthy schools: Practical prevention strategies.* New York, NY: Guilford Press.

Sprague, J. R., & Walker, H. M. (2010). Building safe and healthy schools to promote school success: Critical issues, current challenges, and promising approaches. In M. R. Shinn, H. M. Walker, & G. Stoner (Eds.), *Interventions for achievement and behavior problems in a three-tier model including RTI* (pp. 225–258). Bethesda, MD: National Association of School Psychologists.

Sprick, R. S. (1995). School-wide discipline and policies: An instructional classroom management approach. In E. Kame'enui & C. B. Darch (Eds.), *Instructional classroom management: A proactive approach to managing behavior* (pp. 234–267). White Plains, NY: Longman Press.

Sprick, R. S. (2009a). *CHAMPS: A proactive and positive approach to classroom management* (2nd ed.). Eugene, OR: Pacific Northwest Publishing.

Sprick, R. S. (2009b). *Stepping in: A substitute's guide to managing classroom behavior.* Eugene, OR: Pacific Northwest Publishing.

Sprick, R. S. (2009c). *Structuring success for substitutes.* Eugene, OR: Pacific Northwest Publishing.

Sprick, R. S. (2012). *Teacher's encyclopedia of behavior management: 100+ problems/500+ plans* (2nd ed.). Eugene, OR: Pacific Northwest Publishing.

Sprick, R. S. (2014). *Discipline in the secondary classroom: A positive approach to behavior management* (3rd ed.). San Francisco: Jossey-Bass.

Sprick, R. S., & Garrison, M. (2000). *ParaPro: Supporting the instructional process.* Eugene, OR: Pacific Northwest Publishing.

Sprick, R. S., & Garrison, M. (2008). *Interventions: Evidence-based behavior strategies for individual students* (2nd ed.). Eugene, OR: Pacific Northwest Publishing.

Sprick, R. S., Howard, L., Wise, B. J., Marcum, K., & Haykin, M. (1998). *Administrator's desk reference of behavior management.* Longmont, CO: Sopris West.

Sprick, R. S., Swartz, L., & Glang, A. (2005). *On the playground: A guide to playground management* [CD program]. Eugene, OR: Pacific Northwest Publishing and Oregon Center for Applied Sciences.

Sprick, R. S., Swartz, L., & Schroeder, S. (2006). *In the driver's seat: A roadmap to managing student behavior on the bus* [CD and DVD program]. Eugene, OR: Pacific Northwest Publishing and Oregon Center for Applied Sciences.

Sugai, G., Horner, R. H., Dunlap, G., Hieneman, M., Lewis, T., Nelson, C. M., & Wilcox, B. (2000). Applying positive behavior support and functional behavioral assessment in schools. *Journal of Positive Behavioral Interventions, 2,* 131–143.

U.S. Department of Education. (2000). *Safeguarding our children: An action guide.* Retrieved from http://www2.ed.gov/admins/lead/safety/actguide/action_guide.pdf

U.S. Department of Health and Human Services, Centers for Disease Control and Prevention (2009). *Fostering school connectedness: Improving student health and academic achievement.* Retrieved from http://www.cdc.gov/healthyyouth/protective/pdf/connectedness_administrators.pdf

U.S. Department of Health and Human Services, Centers for Disease Control and Prevention. (2012). *Youth violence: Facts at a glance.* Retrieved from http://www.cdc.gov/violenceprevention/pdf/yv_datasheet_2012-a.pdf

U.S. Department of Health and Human Services, Centers for Disease Control and Prevention. (2013a). *Asthma and schools.* Retrieved from http://www.cdc.gov/healthyyouth/asthma/index.htm

U.S. Department of Health and Human Services, Centers for Disease Control and Prevention. (2013b). *State and program examples: Healthy youth.* Retrieved from http://www.cdc.gov/chronicdisease/states/examples/pdfs/healthy-youth.pdf

U.S. Department of Justice, Office of Justice Programs, Office of Juvenile Justice and Delinquency Prevention. (2006). *Statistical briefing book.* Retrieved from http://www.ojjdp.gov/ojstatbb/offenders/qa03301.asp

University of Utah, Utah Education Policy Center. (2012). *Research brief: Chronic absenteeism.* Retrieved from Utah Data Alliance website: http://www.utahdataalliance.org/downloads/ChronicAbsenteeismResearchBrief.pdf

Wald, J., & Losen, D. J. (2003). Defining and redirecting a school-to-prison pipeline. *New Directions for Youth Development, 99,* 9–15. doi:10.1002/yd.51

Walker, H. (1995). *The acting-out child: Coping with classroom disruption.* Longmont, CO: Sopris West.

Walker, H. M., Colvin, G., & Ramsey, E. (1995). *Antisocial behavior in school: Strategies and best practices.* Pacific Grove, CA: Brooks/Cole.

Walker, H., Ramsey, E., & Gresham, F. M. (2003–2004a). Heading off disruptive behavior: How early intervention can reduce defiant behavior—and win back teaching time. *American Educator, Winter,* 6–21, 45–46.

Walker, H., Ramsey, E., & Gresham, F. M. (2003–2004b). How disruptive students escalate hostility and disorder—and how teachers can avoid it. *American Educator, Winter,* 22–27, 47–48.

Walker, H. M., Ramsey, E., & Gresham, F. M. (2004). *Antisocial behavior in school: Evidence-based practices* (2nd ed.). Belmont, CA: Cengage Learning.

Walker, H. M., Severson, H. H., & Feil, E. F. (2014). *Systematic screening for behavior disorders* (2nd ed.). Eugene, OR: Pacific Northwest Publishing.

Walker, H., & Walker, J. (1991). *Coping with noncompliance in the classroom: A positive approach for teachers.* Austin, TX: Pro-Ed.

Wentzel, K. R., & Brophy, J. E. (2013). *Motivating Students to Learn* (4th ed.). New York, NY: Taylor & Francis.

Wise, B. J., Marcum, K., Haykin, M., Sprick, R. S., & Sprick, M. (2011). *Meaningful work: Changing student behavior with school jobs.* Eugene, OR: Pacific Northwest Publishing.

Wright, A. (n.d.). Limbic system: Amgdala. In J. H. Byrne (Ed.). *Neuroscience online.* Retrieved from http://neuroscience.uth.tmc.edu/s4/chapter06.html

APPENDIX A
Foundations Implementation Rubric and Summary

The rubric is a relatively quick way for the Foundations Team to self-reflect on the implementation status of each of the modules. If you are just beginning *Foundations*, you might use this rubric toward the end of your first year of implementation. There-after, work through the rubric each year in the spring and consider using it in mid- to late fall to guide your work during the winter.

Each column—Preparing, Getting Started, Moving Along, and In Place—represents a different implementation status. The text in each row describes what that status looks like for each *Foundations* presentation. For each presentation, read the four descriptions from left to right. If the statements in the description are true, check the box. Each description assumes that the activities preceding it in the row have been attained. Stop working through the row when you reach a description that you cannot check off because you haven't implemented those tasks.

Notice that the descriptions for the In Place status include a section about evidence, which suggests where to find objective evidence that the described work is truly in place. If no documentation exists, think about whether the work has really been thoroughly completed. Throughout *Foundations*, we recommend archiving all your work so that policies and procedures are not forgotten or lost when staff changes occur.

When you've worked through every row, summarize your assessment on the Rubric Summary. If any items are rated as less than In Place, or if it has been more than 3 years since you have done so, work through the Implementation Checklist for that module. Of course, if you know that you need to begin work on a module or presentation, you can go directly to the corresponding content.

> Print the summary and rubric (Form A-01) from the Module A CD.

For Module B, evaluate (separately) the common areas and schoolwide policies that you have implemented—that is, you've structured them for success and taught students the behavioral expectations. Use the rows labeled Other for your school's common areas and schoolwide policies that do not appear on the rubric by default.

Figure A-1 shows a summary form completed by an imaginary school in the spring of their second year of *Foundations* implementation. They have highlighted the check-boxes to create a horizontal bar graph, giving the evaluation an effective visual com-ponent. They've done a great job on most of Module A, the common areas they've prioritized so far (hallways and cafeteria), and Welcoming New Staff, Students, and Families (C7). They need to work a bit more on staff engagement and unity (A5) and most of Module C, which they began in Year 2. Modules D, E, and F are blank because they plan to work on them in future years.

Figure A-1   *Sample Foundations Rubric Summary*

Date _____

Foundations Implementation Rubric and Summary (p. 8 of 8)

	Preparing (1)	Getting Started (2)	Moving Along (3)	In Place (4)
Module A Presentations				
A1. Foundations: A Multi-Tiered System of Behavior Support	X	X	X	X
A2. Team Processes	X	X	X	X
A3. The Improvement Cycle	X	X	X	X
A4. Data-Driven Processes	X	X	X	X
A5. Developing Staff Engagement and Unity	X	X		
Module B Presentations				
Hallways	X	X	X	X
Restrooms				
Cafeteria	X	X	X	X
Playground, Courtyard, or Commons				
Arrival				
Dismissal				
Dress Code				
Other:				
Other:				
Other:				
Other:				
Module C Presentations				
C2. Guidelines for Success	X	X	X	
C3. Ratios of Positive Interactions	X	X		
C4. Improving Attendance	X	X	X	
C5 & C6. School Connectedness and Programs and Strategies for Meeting Needs	X	X		
C7. Welcoming New Staff, Students, and Families	X	X	X	X
Module D Presentations				
D1. Proactive Procedures, Corrective Procedures, and Individual Interventions				
D2. Developing Three Levels of Misbehavior				
D3. Staff Responsibilities for Responding to Misbehavior				
D4. Administrator Responsibilities for Responding to Misbehavior				
D5. Preventing the Misbehavior That Leads to Referrals and Suspensions				
Module E Presentations				
E1. Ensuring a Safe Environment for Students				
E2. Attributes of Safe and Unsafe Schools				
E3. Teaching Conflict Resolution				
E4. Analyzing Bullying Behaviors, Policies, and School Needs				
E5. Schoolwide Bullying Prevention and Intervention				
Module F Presentations				
F2. Supporting Classroom Behavior: The Three-Legged Stool				
F3. Articulating Staff Beliefs and Solidifying Universal Procedures				
F4. Early-Stage Interventions for General Education Classrooms				
F5. Matching the Intensity of Your Resources to the Intensity of Your Needs				
F6. Problem-Solving Processes and Intervention Design				
F7. Sustainability and District Support				

Additional information about the rubric appears in Module F, Presentation 7, Task 1.

Thanks to Carolyn Novelly and Kathleen Bowles of Duval County Public Schools in Florida. We modeled the Foundations Implementation Rubric on a wonderful document they developed called the School Climate/Conditions for Learning Checklist. Thanks also to Pete Davis of Long Beach, California, for sharing samples of rubrics and innovation configuration scales.

Foundations Implementation Rubric and Summary (p. 1 of 8)

Directions: In each row, check off each description that is true for your *Foundations* implementation. Then summarize your assessment on the Rubric Summary form. For Module B, evaluate each common area and schoolwide policy separately, and use the rows labeled Other for common areas and schoolwide policies that do not appear on the rubric by default. *Note:* Each block assumes that the activities in previous blocks in the row have been attained.

Presentation	Preparing (1)	Getting Started (2)	Moving Along (3)	In Place (4)
A1 Foundations: A Multi-Tiered System of Behavior Support	☐ Staff are aware of the *Foundations* approach and basic beliefs, including that *Foundations* is a process for guiding the entire staff in the construction and implementation of a comprehensive approach to behavior support.	☐ *Foundations* multi-tiered system of support (MTSS) processes are coordinated with academic MTSS (RTI) processes, and team organization has been determined (e.g., one MTSS Team with a behavior task force and an academic task force).	☐ Staff have been introduced to the STOIC acronym and understand that student behavior and motivation can be continuously improved by manipulating the STOIC variables: Structure, Teach, Observe, Interact positively, and Correct fluently.	☐ A preliminary plan has been developed for using the *Foundations* modules. For a school just beginning the process, the plan includes working through all the modules sequentially. For a school that has implemented aspects of positive behavior support, the team has self-assessed strengths, weaknesses, and needs using this rubric. **Evidence:** Foundations Implementation Rubric
A2 Team Processes	☐ Foundations Team members have been identified. They directly represent specific faculty and staff groups, and they have assigned roles and responsibilities.	☐ Foundations Team attends trainings, meets at school, and has established and maintains a Foundations Process Notebook and Foundations Archive.	☐ Foundations Team members present regularly to faculty and communicate with the entire staff. They draft proposals and engage staff in the decision-making process regarding school climate, behavior, and discipline.	☐ Foundations Team is known by all staff and is highly involved in all aspects of climate, safety, behavior, motivation, and student connectedness. **Evidence:** Staff members represented by Foundations Team members and presentations to staff are documented in the Foundations Process Notebook.
A3 The Improvement Cycle	☐ Foundations Team is aware of the Improvement Cycle and keeps staff informed of team activities.	☐ Foundations Team involves staff in setting priorities and in implementing improvements.	☐ Foundations Team involves staff in using multiple data sources to establish a hierarchical list of priorities and adopt new policies. Team members seek input from staff regarding their satisfaction with the efficacy of recently adopted policies and procedures.	☐ All staff actively participate in all aspects of the Improvement Cycle, such as setting priorities, developing revisions, adopting new policies and procedures, and implementation. Foundation Team presents to staff at least monthly. **Evidence:** Memos to staff and PowerPoint presentation files are documented in the Foundations Process Notebook.
A4 Data-Driven Processes	☐ Administrators and Foundations Team review discipline data and establish baselines.	☐ Common area observations and student, staff, and parent climate surveys are conducted yearly.	☐ Discipline, climate survey, and common area observation data are reviewed and analyzed regularly.	☐ Based on the data, school policies, procedures, and guidelines are reviewed and modified as needed (maintaining the Improvement Cycle).
A5 Developing Staff Engagement and Unity	☐ Foundations Team regularly communicates with staff through staff meetings, scheduled professional development, memos, and so on.	☐ Foundations Team members understand that they play a key role in staff unity. They periodically assess whether any factions of staff are disengaged and how they can develop greater staff engagement in the *Foundations* process.	☐ A building-based administrator attends most *Foundations* trainings and plays an active role in team meetings and in assisting the team in unifying staff.	☐ For districts with more than five or six schools, a district-based team meets at least once per quarter to keep the *Foundations* continuous improvement processes active in all schools. **Evidence:** Meeting minutes and staff presentations are documented in the Foundations Process Notebook.

If any items are rated as less than In Place or if it has been more than 3 years since you have done so, work through the Module A Implementation Checklist.

Foundations Implementation Rubric and Summary (p. 2 of 8)

Common Area	Preparing (1)	Getting Started (2)	Moving Along (3)	In Place (4)
Hallways	☐ Common area observations are conducted and data from multiple sources are collected and analyzed.	☐ Current structures and procedures have been evaluated and protected, modified, or eliminated.	☐ Lesson plans have been developed, taught, practiced, and re-taught, when necessary.	☐ Common area supervisory procedures are communicated to staff and monitored for implementation **Evidence:** Policies, procedures, and lessons are documented in the Foundations Archive and, as appropriate, in the Staff Handbook.
Restrooms	☐ Common area observations are conducted and data from multiple sources are collected and analyzed.	☐ Current structures and procedures have been evaluated and protected, modified, or eliminated.	☐ Lesson plans have been developed, taught, practiced, and re-taught, when necessary.	☐ Common area supervisory procedures are communicated to staff and monitored for implementation **Evidence:** Policies, procedures, and lessons are documented in the Foundations Archive and, as appropriate, in the Staff Handbook.
Cafeteria	☐ Common area observations are conducted and data from multiple sources are collected and analyzed.	☐ Current structures and procedures have been evaluated and protected, modified, or eliminated.	☐ Lesson plans have been developed, taught, practiced, and re-taught, when necessary.	☐ Common area supervisory procedures are communicated to staff and monitored for implementation **Evidence:** Policies, procedures, and lessons are documented in the Foundations Archive and, as appropriate, in the Staff Handbook.
Playground, Courtyard, or Commons	☐ Common area observations are conducted and data from multiple sources are collected and analyzed.	☐ Current structures and procedures have been evaluated and protected, modified, or eliminated.	☐ Lesson plans have been developed, taught, practiced, and re-taught, when necessary.	☐ Common area supervisory procedures are communicated to staff and monitored for implementation **Evidence:** Policies, procedures, and lessons are documented in the Foundations Archive and, as appropriate, in the Staff Handbook.
Arrival	☐ Common area observations are conducted and data from multiple sources are collected and analyzed.	☐ Current structures and procedures have been evaluated and protected, modified, or eliminated.	☐ Lesson plans have been developed, taught, practiced, and re-taught, when necessary.	☐ Common area supervisory procedures are communicated to staff and monitored for implementation **Evidence:** Policies, procedures, and lessons are documented in the Foundations Archive and, as appropriate, in the Staff Handbook.
Dismissal	☐ Common area observations are conducted and data from multiple sources are collected and analyzed.	☐ Current structures and procedures have been evaluated and protected, modified, or eliminated.	☐ Lesson plans have been developed, taught, practiced, and re-taught, when necessary.	☐ Common area supervisory procedures are communicated to staff and monitored for implementation **Evidence:** Policies, procedures, and lessons are documented in the Foundations Archive and, as appropriate, in the Staff Handbook.
Other: _____	☐ Common area observations are conducted and data from multiple sources are collected and analyzed.	☐ Current structures and procedures have been evaluated and protected, modified, or eliminated.	☐ Lesson plans have been developed, taught, practiced, and re-taught, when necessary.	☐ Common area supervisory procedures are communicated to staff and monitored for implementation **Evidence:** Policies, procedures, and lessons are documented in the Foundations Archive and, as appropriate, in the Staff Handbook.
Other: _____	☐ Common area observations are conducted and data from multiple sources are collected and analyzed.	☐ Current structures and procedures have been evaluated and protected, modified, or eliminated.	☐ Lesson plans have been developed, taught, practiced, and re-taught, when necessary.	☐ Common area supervisory procedures are communicated to staff and monitored for implementation **Evidence:** Policies, procedures, and lessons are documented in the Foundations Archive and, as appropriate, in the Staff Handbook.

If any items are rated as less than In Place or if it has been more than 3 years since you have done so, work through the Module B Implementation Checklist.

Foundations Implementation Rubric and Summary (p. 3 of 8)

Schoolwide Policy	Preparing (1)	Getting Started (2)	Moving Along (3)	In Place (4)
Dress Code	☐ Foundations Team has discussed the clarity and consistency of the current schoolwide policy.	☐ Data from multiple sources about the efficacy of the policy have been gathered and analyzed.	☐ The policy has been analyzed for clarity, efficacy, and consistency of enforcement.	☐ Schoolwide policies, lessons, and procedures have been written and are reviewed as needed with staff, students, and parents. **Evidence:** Policies, lessons, and procedures are documented in the Foundations Archive and, as appropriate, in the Staff Handbook.
Other: _____	☐ Foundations Team has discussed the clarity and consistency of the current schoolwide policy.	☐ Data from multiple sources about the efficacy of the policy have been gathered and analyzed.	☐ The policy has been analyzed for clarity, efficacy, and consistency of enforcement.	☐ Schoolwide policies, lessons, and procedures have been written and are reviewed as needed with staff, students, and parents. **Evidence:** Policies, lessons, and procedures are documented in the Foundations Archive and, as appropriate, in the Staff Handbook.
Other: _____	☐ Foundations Team has discussed the clarity and consistency of the current schoolwide policy.	☐ Data from multiple sources about the efficacy of the policy have been gathered and analyzed.	☐ The policy has been analyzed for clarity, efficacy, and consistency of enforcement.	☐ Schoolwide policies, lessons, and procedures have been written and are reviewed as needed with staff, students, and parents. **Evidence:** Policies, lessons, and procedures are documented in the Foundations Archive and, as appropriate, in the Staff Handbook.
Other: _____	☐ Foundations Team has discussed the clarity and consistency of the current schoolwide policy.	☐ Data from multiple sources about the efficacy of the policy have been gathered and analyzed.	☐ The policy has been analyzed for clarity, efficacy, and consistency of enforcement.	☐ Schoolwide policies, lessons, and procedures have been written and are reviewed as needed with staff, students, and parents. **Evidence:** Policies, lessons, and procedures are documented in the Foundations Archive and, as appropriate, in the Staff Handbook.
Other: _____	☐ Foundations Team has discussed the clarity and consistency of the current schoolwide policy.	☐ Data from multiple sources about the efficacy of the policy have been gathered and analyzed.	☐ The policy has been analyzed for clarity, efficacy, and consistency of enforcement.	☐ Schoolwide policies, lessons, and procedures have been written and are reviewed as needed with staff, students, and parents. **Evidence:** Policies, lessons, and procedures are documented in the Foundations Archive and, as appropriate, in the Staff Handbook.
Other: _____	☐ Foundations Team has discussed the clarity and consistency of the current schoolwide policy.	☐ Data from multiple sources about the efficacy of the policy have been gathered and analyzed.	☐ The policy has been analyzed for clarity, efficacy, and consistency of enforcement.	☐ Schoolwide policies, lessons, and procedures have been written and are reviewed as needed with staff, students, and parents. **Evidence:** Policies, lessons, and procedures are documented in the Foundations Archive and, as appropriate, in the Staff Handbook.
Other: _____	☐ Foundations Team has discussed the clarity and consistency of the current schoolwide policy.	☐ Data from multiple sources about the efficacy of the policy have been gathered and analyzed.	☐ The policy has been analyzed for clarity, efficacy, and consistency of enforcement.	☐ Schoolwide policies, lessons, and procedures have been written and are reviewed as needed with staff, students, and parents. **Evidence:** Policies, lessons, and procedures are documented in the Foundations Archive and, as appropriate, in the Staff Handbook.
Other: _____	☐ Foundations Team has discussed the clarity and consistency of the current schoolwide policy.	☐ Data from multiple sources about the efficacy of the policy have been gathered and analyzed.	☐ The policy has been analyzed for clarity, efficacy, and consistency of enforcement.	☐ Schoolwide policies, lessons, and procedures have been written and are reviewed as needed with staff, students, and parents. **Evidence:** Policies, lessons, and procedures are documented in the Foundations Archive and, as appropriate, in the Staff Handbook.

If any items are rated as less than In Place or if it has been more than 3 years since you have done so, work through the Module B Implementation Checklist.

Foundations Implementation Rubric and Summary (p. 4 of 8)

Presentation	Preparing (1)	Getting Started (2)	Moving Along (3)	In Place (4)
C2 Guidelines for Success (GFS)	☐ All staff understand what Guidelines for Success (GFS) are and why they are important.	☐ Foundations Team has drafted proposals and engaged all stakeholders in the decision-making process of developing GFS.	☐ GFS have been finalized and posted and are reviewed regularly.	☐ GFS are embedded into the culture and are part of the common language of the school. **Evidence:** Procedures for teaching and motivating students about GFS are documented in the Foundations Archive, Staff Handbook, and Student and Parent Handbook.
C3 Ratios of Positive Interactions	☐ Staff have been taught the concept of 3:1 ratios of positive interactions and the importance of creating a positive climate and improving student behavior.	☐ Staff have been taught how to monitor ratios of positive interactions and are encouraged to evaluate their interactions with students.	☐ Administrator plans for teachers to observe and calculate other teachers' classroom ratios of interactions; the teachers involved meet to discuss outcomes.	☐ Observation data show that most staff at most times strive to interact with students at least three times more often than when students are behaving responsibly than when they are misbehaving. **Evidence:** Procedures for teaching and motivating staff are documented in the Foundations Archive and Staff Handbook.
C4 Improving Attendance	☐ Average daily attendance is monitored to view long-term trends and patterns. Faculty and staff have been made aware of the importance of encouraging regular attendance by all students.	☐ All students with chronic absenteeism (absent 10% or more of school days) are identified at least quarterly; Foundations Team determines whether universal intervention is warranted.	☐ Each student with chronic absenteeism is identified and assigned one school-based support person who monitors whether additional support is needed. Foundations Team has analyzed attendance data and analyzed policies for clarity and efficacy.	☐ Every student with chronic absenteeism that has been resistant to universal and Tier 2 supports becomes the focus of a multidisciplinary team effort. **Evidence:** Data on average daily attendance and chronic absenteeism as well as efforts to improve attendance (e.g., parent newsletters) are documented in the Foundations Process Notebook.
C5 & C6 School Connectedness and Programs and Strategies for Meeting Needs	☐ Foundations Team has analyzed the degree to which current programs and practices meet the needs of all students (outstanding, average, and at risk).	☐ Foundations Team has developed proposals for programs and practices that might help meet unmet needs of students (e.g., the average student's need for purpose and belonging).	☐ Faculty and staff have implemented programs and practices designed to meet basic needs of all students (e.g., Mentorship, Student of the Week, Meaningful Work).	☐ Programs to meet students' basic needs are in place and analyzed at least once per year to determine their effectiveness and assess whether the needs of any student groups are not being met. **Evidence:** Analysis is documented in the Foundations Process Notebook, and programs and practices for meeting needs are documented in the Foundations Archive.
C7 Welcoming New Staff, Students, and Families	☐ Foundations Team has reviewed the welcoming aspects of the school, such as signage, website, and phone and front office procedures, and has suggested improvements.	☐ Foundations Team has analyzed procedures and suggested improvements for welcoming and orienting new students and families at the beginning of the school year. (New students include those in a new grade-level cohort [e.g., ninth graders in high school] and students who are not part of that cohort.)	☐ Foundations Team has analyzed procedures and suggested improvements for welcoming new students and families who arrive during the school year. Improvements might include written information about rules, procedures, GFS, and so on.	☐ Foundations Team has analyzed procedures and suggested improvements for welcoming new staff members, both professional and nonprofessional, at the beginning of the year. New staff members are oriented to essential procedures and the culture and climate defined by the school's behavior support procedures. **Evidence:** All policies and procedures for welcoming and orienting staff, students, and families are documented in the Foundations Archive.

If any items are rated as less than In Place or if it has been more than 3 years since you have done so, work through the Module C Implementation Checklist.

Foundations Implementation Rubric and Summary (p. 5 of 8)

Presentation	Preparing (1)	Getting Started (2)	Moving Along (3)	In Place (4)
D1 Proactive Procedures, Corrective Procedures, and Individual Interventions	☐ Foundations Team is aware of data and staff opinions about consistency in correcting misbehavior, including clarity of staff roles in discipline compared with administrative roles.	☐ Staff understand the potential limitations of office referral as a corrective procedure and avoid using it whenever possible.	☐ Staff have been made aware of the limited benefits and potential drawbacks (including disparate impact) of out-of-school suspension (OSS) as a corrective consequence.	☐ Staff avoid pressuring administrators to use OSS. Staff perceptions of consistency and administrative support for disciplinary actions are documented in staff survey results. **Evidence:** Discussions on these topics are documented in the Foundations Process Notebook.
D2 Developing Three Levels of Misbehavior	☐ Staff are aware of the concept of three levels of misbehavior: Level 1 (mild), Level 2 (moderate), and Level 3 (severe) misbehavior.	☐ Annually, staff discuss and agree on what behavior *must* be sent to the administrator, what can be sent to the administrator, and what should be handled in the setting in which the infraction occurred (3-level system for responding to misbehavior).	☐ A referral form that reflects the agreed-upon definition of Level 3 misbehavior has been developed. A notification form that reflects the agreed-upon definition of Level 2 misbehavior has been developed. (Alternatively, both Level 2 and Level 3 may be on one form.) Accurate data are kept and analyzed quarterly for all Level 2 and Level 3 misbehaviors and consequences.	☐ Data are collected on the implementation of the 3-level system for responding to misbehavior and on staff and administrator satisfaction with the system. **Evidence:** All aspects of the policy are documented in the Foundations Archive and Staff Handbook.
D3 Staff Responsibilities for Responding to Misbehavior	☐ Staff have generated and administrators have approved a menu of corrective consequences for use in common areas.	☐ Staff have generated and administrators have approved a menu of corrective consequences for use in classrooms.	☐ Staff have been trained in how to use Level 2 notifications as a process for moving toward collaborative planning for severe or chronic behavior problems.	☐ Staff have been trained in writing objective and appropriate office referrals for Level 3 misbehavior. **Evidence:** Menus and procedures are documented in the Foundations Archive and Staff Handbook.
D4 Administrator Responsibilities for Responding to Misbehavior	☐ Procedures have been developed for responding to Level 2 notifications to ensure that the reporting staff member receives timely feedback and that administrators and support staff take appropriate actions.	☐ Office procedures for dealing with students sent to the office have been analyzed and streamlined. Students do not get too much attention from office staff or staff members who visit the office	☐ Administrators are familiar with the game plan for dealing with Level 3 incidents. The game plan includes a menu of alternative consequences to out-of-school suspension.	☐ If the school has an ISS program, that program has been analyzed and revised as needed to ensure that it is highly structured and includes an instructional component. **Evidence:** All procedures for Level 2 and Level 3 infractions are documented in the Foundations Archive.
D5 Preventing the Misbehavior That Leads to Referrals and Suspensions	☐ Foundations Team has examined data on Level 2 and Level 3 infractions to determine what misbehaviors get students into trouble.	☐ Foundations Team has reviewed the lessons in Module D (how to interact appropriately with adults) and discussed whether they might reduce misbehaviors that get students into trouble.	☐ To avoid duplication, the Foundations Team has compared the Module D lessons with other social skills or social-emotional curricula currently in use. Staff have agreed on a plan for when and how to teach expected behaviors to all students.	☐ Foundations Team has discussed whether re-teaching the Module D lessons (or similar) in ISS or detention settings would be beneficial; if so, the team has planned when and how to re-teach. **Evidence:** Lesson plans and teaching logistics and schedule are documented in the Foundations Archive.

If any items are rated as less than In Place or if it has been more than 3 years since you have done so, work through the Module D Implementation Checklist.

Foundations Implementation Rubric and Summary (p. 6 of 8)

Module E

Presentation	Preparing (1)	Getting Started (2)	Moving Along (3)	In Place (4)
E1 Ensuring a Safe Environment for Students	☐ Team members are aware of their responsibilities for overseeing school safety efforts. The team coordinates with other teams or task forces that may be doing similar work and avoids duplicating other efforts.	☐ Foundations Team has viewed or read Module E and has compared that content with the school's current efforts toward safety, managing conflict, and bullying prevention. The team has developed a proposal for closing any gaps in the current efforts.	☐ Foundations Team has made staff aware of the importance of a comprehensive view of safety that includes preparing for outside attackers as well as the more common occurrences of playground injuries, student fights, bullying, and so on.	☐ Foundations Team has assessed problems with safety, conflict, and bullying within the last 3 years. If problems exist, a plan for using or adapting information from this module and integrating them with current curriculum or procedures has been completed. **Evidence:** Data analyses are documented in the Foundations Process Notebook, and final policies and procedures are documented in the Foundations Archive.
E2 Attributes of Safe and Unsafe Schools	☐ Team members and other staff directly involved with safety concerns have viewed or read Presentation 2 and have completed (individually) the form Understanding the Attributes of Safe and Unsafe Schools.	☐ Foundations Team has compiled individual responses to Understanding Attributes of Safe and Unsafe Schools and correlated those data with safety assessments completed in the last 3 years. Information about strengths and concerns has been shared with staff, and priorities have been set.	☐ Foundations Team and other staff involved with safety concerns have completed the form Assessing Emergency Preparedness, evaluated current plans for natural disasters and man-made emergencies, revised any weak procedures, including training on policies regarding seclusion and restraint.	☐ Foundations Team has completed the form Lessons to Increase Safety and Belonging, reviewed the Module E sample lessons, and evaluated whether current problems and policies address all features of the sample lessons. If there are gaps, a plan to teach some or all of the *Foundations* lessons is established. **Evidence:** Lesson plans and procedures are documented in the Foundations Archive.
E3 Teaching Conflict Resolution	☐ Foundations Team has assessed whether the school has a conflict resolution strategy that students and staff use when necessary. If so, document the effective procedures in the Foundations Archive (and skip the rest of this row).	☐ Foundations Team has reviewed the concepts and lessons in the Stop-Think-Plan (STP) approach and has prepared an implementation plan for staff.	☐ With staff input, lessons have been revised, an implementation plan has been established, and a process is in place for training all staff in how to encourage students to use the conflict-resolution strategy.	☐ Foundations Team has established a process for evaluating the effectiveness of STP by analyzing multiple data sources. The policy and lessons are revised and staff are retrained when necessary, and successes are celebrated. **Evidence:** Data analyses are documented in the Foundations Process Notebook, and lessons and teaching procedures are documented in the Foundations Archive.
E4 Analyzing Bullying Behavior, Policies, and School Needs	☐ Foundations Team is aware of the content of this presentation and can compare it with current policies and procedures related to bullying.	☐ Foundations Team has completed the form School-Based Analysis of Bullying Data and has identified whether new or revised procedures need to be implemented to enhance the current use of data related to bullying.	☐ Foundations Team has completed the form School-Based Analysis of Bullying Policies and has identified whether new or revised policies need to be implemented to enhance current policies related to bullying.	☐ Quarterly, the Foundations Team reviews data related to bullying. Annually, the team uses those data to answer each of the questions in the form STOIC Analysis for Universal Prevention of Bullying (or an equivalent process), and improvement priorities are established. **Evidence:** Data analyses are documented in the Foundations Process Notebook.
E5 Schoolwide Bullying Prevention and Intervention	☐ Foundations Team has completed the form Staff Training in Preventing and Responding to Bullying and has developed and implemented a plan to fill in any identified gaps in current practices.	☐ Foundations Team has completed the form Student Training in Preventing and Responding to Bullying. As part of a previously adopted bullying curriculum or through the *Foundations* lessons, students are taught about bullying prevention.	☐ Foundations Team has completed the form Family Training in Preventing and Responding to Bullying and has developed an implementation plan to fill in any identified gaps in current practices.	☐ Foundations Team has completed the form Active Engagement for the Prevention of Bullying and has developed an implementation plan to fill in any gaps in current practices. Bullying issues are a regular part of the team's work and are integrated into staff development efforts. **Evidence:** Ongoing discussions are documented in the Foundations Process Notebook. Established programs to enhance student engagement are documented in the Foundations Archive.

If any items are rated as less than In Place or if it has been more than 3 years since you have done so, work through the Module E Implementation Checklist.

Foundations Implementation Rubric and Summary (p. 7 of 8)

Presentation	Preparing (1)	Getting Started (2)	Moving Along (3)	In Place (4)
F2 Supporting Classroom Behavior: The Three-Legged Stool	A research-based model for classroom management has been adopted at the building or district level. All teachers have access to training, and teachers new to the building or district receive the same training.	School and district personnel are identified as resources for teachers who would like observations, feedback, and coaching. An effort is made to actively market the benefits of coaching support.	The administrator has communicated clear outcomes and goals of effective classroom management: • 90% engagement • 95% respectful interactions • 95% of behavior matches posted expectations	The model creates a common language among teachers, support staff, coaches, and administrators for problem solving and intervention. Data are collected and analyzed to evaluate classroom management efforts. **Evidence:** Information on the model, administrative walk-through visits, and coaching supports is included in the Foundations Archive and Staff Handbook.
F3 Articulating Staff Beliefs and Solidifying Universal Procedures	Foundations Team has reviewed sample staff beliefs about behavior management.	In faculty and staff meetings, faculty and staff have examined and discussed sample staff beliefs about behavior management.	All staff have developed and adopted a set of written staff beliefs regarding discipline and behavior, and ensured that it aligned with the school's mission statement.	To solidify the culture of the school and to guide the ongoing development of school policies and procedures, staff beliefs are reviewed, discussed, and revised as needed at least annually. **Evidence:** Staff beliefs and the review process are documented in the Foundations Archive and Staff Handbook.
F4 Early-Stage Interventions for General Education Classrooms	Foundations Team and support staff (counselor, school psychologist, and so on) understand the concept of early-stage intervention.	Foundations Team, support staff, and principal (or district administrators) agree on the interventions that should be included in the early-stage protocol.	All teachers and support staff have been trained on the interventions in the school or district early-stage protocol, including how and why to keep records of each intervention.	Data Collection and Debriefing (or an equivalent) is adopted as a required intervention for most chronic behavioral problems. Data must be charted before assistance is requested from support staff or problem-solving teams. **Evidence:** Expectations about when and how to get assistance are included in the Foundations Archive and Staff Handbook.
F5 Matching the Intensity of Your Resources to the Intensity of Your Needs	Foundations Team and support staff (counselor, psychologist, and so on) have identified a set of red-flag criteria and (if possible) have conducted universal screening to identify students who may need individual behavior support.	Foundations Team, support staff, and principal (or district administrators) agree on who can serve as advocates for students who need additional support.	The advocates meet regularly to discuss progress and case studies to ensure that each student's needs are being met. Patterns of need are communicated to the Foundations Team so prevention efforts can be implemented.	All support staff and problem-solving teams have written brief job descriptions that outline the services they can provide. The documents are shared with staff to inform them about available resources. **Evidence:** Suggestions for accessing these services are in the Foundations Archive and Staff Handbook.
F6 Problem-Solving Processes and Intervention Design	Foundations Team understands that it will not conduct staffings (team-based problem solving) on individual students, but the team should examine current processes for supporting students and staff.	Foundations Team and support staff (counselor, school psychologist, and so on) have discussed the range of problem-solving support (individuals and teams) currently available to students and staff.	Foundations Team and support staff have discussed the problem-solving processes suggested in *Foundations* (e.g., the 25-Minute Planning Process), and have determined whether the processes would strengthen current practices.	A flowchart or description of how the school meets the needs of students and staff has been created. It clarifies how the intensity of student needs matches the intensity of both problem-solving processes and intervention design and implementation. **Evidence:** This information is documented in the Foundations Archive and summarized in the Staff Handbook.
F7 Sustainability and District Support	Foundations Team archives data, in-process work, and all completed policies and procedures, and builds on this work each year.	Foundations Team orients new staff and re-energizes returning staff about all policies and procedures, and emphasizes unity and consistency.	Foundations Team uses the rubric annually and the Implementation Checklists as individual modules near completion and every 3 years thereafter. The team uses this information to guide staff in setting improvement priorities.	In larger districts (more than four schools), a district-based team works on sustainability. The team reminds schools about important milestones (e.g., surveys, year-end tasks, etc.) and ongoing staff development opportunities on behavior support. **Evidence:** This information can be found in district communications (e.g., emails) to schools and agenda items for principals' meetings.

If any items are rated as less than In Place or if it has been more than 3 years since you have done so, work through the Module F Implementation Checklist.

Foundations Implementation Rubric and Summary (p. 8 of 8)

	Preparing (1)	Getting Started (2)	Moving Along (3)	In Place (4)
Module A Presentations				
A1. Foundations: A Multi-Tiered System of Behavior Support				
A2. Team Processes				
A3. The Improvement Cycle				
A4. Data-Driven Processes				
A5. Developing Staff Engagement and Unity				
Module B Presentations				
Hallways				
Restrooms				
Cafeteria				
Playground, Courtyard, or Commons				
Arrival				
Dismissal				
Dress Code				
Other:				
Other:				
Other:				
Other:				
Module C Presentations				
C2. Guidelines for Success				
C3. Ratios of Positive Interactions				
C4. Improving Attendance				
C5 & C6. School Connectedness and Programs and Strategies for Meeting Needs				
C7. Welcoming New Staff, Students, and Families				
Module D Presentations				
D1. Proactive Procedures, Corrective Procedures, and Individual Interventions				
D2. Developing Three Levels of Misbehavior				
D3. Staff Responsibilities for Responding to Misbehavior				
D4. Administrator Responsibilities for Responding to Misbehavior				
D5. Preventing the Misbehavior That Leads to Referrals and Suspensions				
Module E Presentations				
E1. Ensuring a Safe Environment for Students				
E2. Attributes of Safe and Unsafe Schools				
E3. Teaching Conflict Resolution				
E4. Analyzing Bullying Behaviors, Policies, and School Needs				
E5. Schoolwide Bullying Prevention and Intervention				
Module F Presentations				
F2. Supporting Classroom Behavior: The Three-Legged Stool				
F3. Articulating Staff Beliefs and Solidifying Universal Procedures				
F4. Early-Stage Interventions for General Education Classrooms				
F5. Matching the Intensity of Your Resources to the Intensity of Your Needs				
F6. Problem-Solving Processes and Intervention Design				
F7. Sustainability and District Support				

APPENDIX B
Module A Implementation Checklist

The Implementation Checklist is a detailed checklist of the processes and objectives in each *Foundations* module. The Module A checklist (Form A-02) appears in this appendix and can be printed from the Module A CD.

As you near completion on the module, use the Implementation Checklist to ensure that you have fully implemented all recommendations. If you've decided not to follow some recommendations—you've adapted the procedures for your school—indicate the reason on the checklist. If data show problems later, this record of what you implemented and what you chose not to implement could be helpful in deciding how to address the problem.

In addition to using the checklists as needed, plan to work through all *Foundations* checklists every 3 years or so. See the sample schedule below. Additional information about Implementation Checklists appears in Module F, Presentation 7, Task 1.

Sample Long-Term Schedule: Improvement Priorities, Data Review & Monitoring

Year 1	Work on:

- Modules A and B (continuous improvement process, common areas and schoolwide policies)
- Cafeteria
- Guidelines for Success

In late spring, work through the Foundations Implementation Rubric for Modules A, B (cafeteria), and C2 (Guidelines for Success).

Use the Modules A and B Implementation Checklists to assess status as you near completion of those modules.

Year 2	Work on:

- Module C (inviting climate)
- Hallways

In the fall, evaluate cafeteria data.

In late spring, work through the Foundations Implementation Rubric for Modules A, B (cafeteria and hallways), and C.

Use the Module C Implementation Checklist to assess status as you near completion of Module C.

Year 3	Work on:
	• Module D (responding to misbehavior) • Playground
	In the fall, evaluate hallway data.
	In late spring, work through the Foundations Implementation Rubric for Modules A, B (cafeteria, hallways, and playground), C, and D.
	Use the Module D Implementation Checklist to assess status as you near completion of Module D.
Year 4	Work on:
	• Module E (safety, conflict, bullying prevention) • Arrival and dismissal
	In the fall, evaluate playground data.
	In late spring, work through the Foundations Implementation Rubric for Modules A, B (cafeteria, hallways, arrival and dismissal), C, D, and E.
	Use the Module E Implementation Checklist to assess status as you near completion of Module E.
	Monitor Year 1 priorities:
	• Module A Implementation Checklist • Module B Implementation Checklist for cafeteria • Module C Implementation Checklist for Guidelines for Success (C2 only)
Year 5	Work on:
	• Module F (classroom management and sustaining *Foundations*) • Assemblies • Guest teachers
	In the fall, evaluate arrival and dismissal data.
	In late spring, work through the Foundations Implementation Rubric for Modules A, B (playground, arrival and dismissal, assemblies, guest teachers), C, D, E, and F.
	Use the Module F Implementation Checklist to assess status as you near completion of Module F.
	Monitor Year 2 priorities:
	• Module B Implementation Checklist for hallways • Module C Implementation Checklist

Module A: Foundations of Behavior Support—A Continuous Improvement Process

Year 6	In the fall, evaluate assemblies and guest teacher data.

Year 6 — In the fall, evaluate assemblies and guest teacher data.

Work through the Foundations Implementation Rubric for all modules.

Monitor Year 3 priorities:

- Module B Implementation Checklist for playground
- Module D Implementation Checklist

Year 7 — In the fall, work through the Foundations Implementation Rubric for all modules and all common areas and schoolwide policies.

Monitor Year 4 priorities:

- Module A Implementation Checklist
- Module B Implementation Checklist for arrival, dismissal, and cafeteria
- Module C Implementation Checklist for Guidelines for Success (C2 only)
- Module E Implementation Checklist

Year 8 — In the fall, work through the Foundations Implementation Rubric for all modules and all common areas and schoolwide policies.

Monitor Year 5 priorities:

- Module B Implementation Checklist for assemblies, guest teachers, and hallways
- Module B Implementation Checklist for hallways
- Module C Implementation Checklist
- Module F Implementation Checklist

Year 9 — In the fall, work through the Foundations Implementation Rubric for all modules and all common areas and schoolwide policies.

Monitor Year 6 priorities:

- Module B Implementation Checklist for playground
- Module D Implementation Checklist

Implementation Actions	Completed Y/N	Evidence of Implementation	Evidence Y/N
Presentation 1: Foundations—A Multi-Tiered System of Behavior Support	✓		✓
1. Decisions have been made about how to integrate a multi-tiered approach to behavior (*Foundations*/PBIS) with a multi-tiered approach to academic and instructional improvement. You may use one team, two separate teams, or one large team with two separate task forces.	☐	Foundations Process Notebook: Team Composition*	☐
2. Information has has been presented to staff about *Foundations*, including, but not limited to, the following basic beliefs: • Punitive and corrective techniques are necessary, but have significant limitations; misbehavior is a teaching opportunity. • In common areas and with schoolwide policies, clear expectations and consistent enforcement are essential. • Staff behavior creates the climate of the school; a positive, welcoming, and inviting climate should be intentionally created and continuously maintained. • All students should have equal access to good instruction and behavior support, regardless of their skills or background. • All student behaviors necessary for success must be overtly and directly articulated and taught to mastery. "If you want it, teach it!" • Everyone (even students who make poor choices) should be treated with respect.	☐	Foundations Archive: Presentations/Communications With Staff* *These notebooks are discussed in Presentation 2. Documentation of Presentation 1 tasks can be added to the notebooks when record-keeping procedures are established.	☐
Presentation 2: Team Processes			
1. The Foundations Team has been established by modifying an existing team or forming a new team. • Team composition includes an administrator, classroom teachers, and others. • The team formally represents the entire staff. Each team member knows the staff members he or she represents, and staff members know who represents them on the team. *(continued)*	☐	Foundations Process Notebook: Team Composition	☐

Implementation Actions	Completed Y/N	Evidence of Implementation	Evidence Y/N
Presentation 2 (*continued*)	✓		✓
2. The team meets regularly for a minimum of 4 hours per quarter.	☐	Foundations Process Notebook: Meeting Minutes	☐
3. Team members have assigned roles, such as: • Chair or Cochair • Recorder • Data/Evaluation Coordinator • Materials Manager • Keeper of the List • Staff Liaison • Equity and Student Liaison • Family Engagement Coordinator	☐	Foundations Process Notebook: Team Composition	☐
4. The team creates processes for orienting new team members.	☐	Foundations Archive: New Staff Orientation	☐
5. At least once per month, the team communicates to staff about the *Foundations* implementation by (for example) sharing data, reminding staff about some aspect of implementation, sharing strategies, or celebrating successes.	☐	Foundations Process Notebook: Presentations/ Communications With Staff	☐
6. Record-keeping and archiving procedures have been established, including a Foundations Process Notebook, Foundations Archive, Staff Handbook, and Student and Parent Handbook. The Foundations Process Notebook is for working documents and includes at least the following (or similar) sections. • Team Composition • Planning Calendar • Meeting Minutes • Data Summaries • Current Priorities (with record of the data that led to the area or policy becoming a priority) • Safety • Guidelines for Success • Presentations/Communications With Staff • Communications With Parents • 3-Level System for Responding to Misbehavior • Foundations Implementation Rubric and Summary and Implementation Checklists *(continued)*	☐	See the four notebooks (listed for items 1–5 above).	☐

Implementation Actions	Completed Y/N	Evidence of Implementation	Evidence Y/N
Presentation 2 (*continued*)	✓		✓
The Foundations Archive is for finalized documents and includes at least the following (or similar) sections: • Long-Term Planning Calendar • Guidelines for Success • 3-Level System for Responding to Misbehavior • Job Descriptions for Common Area Supervisors • Schoolwide Policies • Common Area Policies and Procedures • Safety Policies • Lesson Plans for Teaching Common Area and Schoolwide Policy Expectations • Lesson Plans for Teaching Safety Expectations • Lesson Plans for Teaching Guidelines for Success • Lesson Plans for Teaching Expectations for Interacting With Adults			
7. The team has chosen a team name.	☐	Foundations Process: Team Composition, Meeting Minutes	☐
8. Team meeting ground rules have been established, such as: • An established minimum number of members must be present. • Meetings will start and end on time. • No side conversations during the meeting. • All team discussions and disagreements will be respectful. • Before speaking, team members will paraphrase what the speaker before them said. • A cochair will serve as the on-task and on-time "nag." • Meeting minutes will identify specific tasks to be accomplished with responsible staff and timelines; these tasks will be highlighted. • Meetings will follow an agreed-upon agenda.	☐	Foundations Process Notebook: Meeting Minutes	☐
9. Annually, team members reflect on their roles as team members, perhaps by using the Are You an Effective Team Builder? self-assessment tool.	☐	Foundations Process Notebook: Meeting Minutes	☐

Implementation Actions	Completed Y/N	Evidence of Implementation	Evidence Y/N
Presentation 3: The Improvement Cycle	✓		✓
1. The team annually **reviews** multiple data sources about climate, discipline, and safety (some data sources are reviewed more frequently).	☐	Foundations Process Notebook: Data Summaries	☐
2. The team presents summaries of the data for staff (and for students and parents, as appropriate).	☐	Foundations Process Notebook: Presentations/ Communications With Staff presentations	☐
3. At least once per semester, the staff **prioritizes** one to three problem areas or concerns for improvement.	☐	Foundations Process Notebook: Current Priorities	☐
4. The team (or a special task force) develops a comprehensive proposal to **revise** policies and procedures to address the prioritized problem or concern and presents the proposal to staff for feedback.	☐	Foundations Process Notebook: Current Priorities	☐
5. The staff **adopts** or rejects the proposal using a consensus-based process such as the Five Levels of Satisfaction Voting System. • If the proposal is rejected, the team or task force reworks it and presents it to staff again (as many as two revision cycles). • If the staff rejects the initial and two revised proposals, the principal determines the final policy or procedure.	☐	Foundations Process Notebook: Meeting Minutes	☐
6. When a policy or procedure is finalized, all staff are provided guidance in how to **implement** it.	☐	Foundations Process Notebook: Presentations/ Communications With Staff	☐
7. The team and building-based administrators monitor the fidelity of implementation and efficacy of the policy, making adjustments as needed.	☐	Foundations Process Notebook: Current Priorities	☐

Implementation Actions	Completed Y/N	Evidence of Implementation	Evidence Y/N
Presentation 4: Data-Driven Processes	✓		✓
1. A plan for data review is in place and includes the range of data sources to be used, the frequency of review, due dates, and responsible team members. The following data sources have been considered:	☐	Foundations Process Notebook: Planning Calendar, Meeting Minutes, Data Summaries	☐

- Anonymous surveys of staff, students, and parents to assess their perceptions of school safety, climate, connectedness, bullying, and so on (administered at least annually).
- Formal observations of both student and staff behavior in common areas (conducted in winter and spring).
- Trends and patterns of incident reports, including both office referrals and Level 2 Notifications (explained in Module D; review at least quarterly).
- Data to assess the *Foundations* suggestions about 90% Thresholds (review at least annually).

  ○ Every family helps children attend at least 90% of school days, on time and ready to learn.
  ○ Every administrator ensures that at least 90% of school minutes (minus lunch) are instructional.
  ○ Every teacher uses at least 90% of instructional time for instructional activities.
  ○ At least 90% of students are engaged during every instructional activity.
  ○ Every student is engaged at least 90% of instructional minutes.

- Other pre-existing data sources (review at least annually and some, such as chronic absenteeism, at least monthly). Sources include:

  ○ Average daily attendance and absence rates
  ○ Tardiness rates
  ○ Suspensions, expulsions, and referrals to alternative education placements
  ○ Referrals to special education
  ○ Number of students referred to special education who did not qualify
  ○ Instances of vandalism and graffiti
  ○ Instances of other illegal activities
  ○ Injury reports
  ○ Feedback from staff

(continued)

Implementation Actions	Completed Y/N	Evidence of Implementation	Evidence Y/N
Presentation 4 (*continued*)	✓		✓

1. (*continued*)
   ◦ Focus groups
   ◦ Social-emotional support (information from counselors, social workers, school psychologists)
   ◦ Red flags
   ◦ Summaries of universal screening			

2. The team collects, analyzes, and presents summaries and findings to staff at least quarterly.	☐	Foundations Process Notebook: Presentations/ Communications With Staff	☐
3. The staff uses these data summaries to identify a manageable number of priorities for improvement.	☐	Foundations Process Notebook: Meeting Minutes, Current Priorities	☐
4. The team uses data to assess the implementation of revised policies and procedures. Is behavior in prioritized common areas and related to schoolwide policies improving?	☐	Foundations Process Notebook: Data Summaries, Current Priorities	☐
Presentation 5: Developing Staff Engagement and Unity			

1. At least quarterly, the team discusses activities, programs, and strategies for motivating staff and increasing the degree to which staff buy in to and actively implement and support policies and procedures that support student behavior.
   • If some staff members are reluctant to buy into *Foundations*, the team discusses ways to encourage and include those staff.
   • The team discussses rituals and incentives for motivating staff, and they implement any that are appropriate.
	☐	Foundations Process Notebook: Meeting Minutes	☐

2. The principal and assistant principals have reviewed the content in Task 2, reflected on the leadership suggestions, and identified the skills that seem most useful to facilitate continuous improvement efforts in your school.	☐	Interview with administrators	☐

APPENDIX C
Guide to Module A
Reproducible Forms and Samples

The CD provided with this book contains many materials to help you implement *Foundations*. A thumbnail of the first page of each form, figure, or sample on the CD appears in this appendix. Most forms can be completed electronically. See the Using the CD file for more information about using fillable forms. Unless otherwise noted, all files are in PDF format.

Folders included on the CD are:

- Forms (A-01 through A-09)
  - Fillable Forms
  - Print Forms
- Other Resources (A-10 through A-14)
- Samples (A-15 through A-31)
- PowerPoint Presentations (A1 through A5)
  - A1 Introduction.pptx
  - A2 Team Processes.pptx
  - A3 Improvement Cycle.pptx
  - A4 Data.pptx
  - A5 Engagement.pptx

DOWNLOAD CD CONTENT

Go to cdcontent.pacificnwpublish.com and enter access code
59909-069-6-forms to download forms, PowerPoints, and other resources.
Enter access code **59909-069-6-samples** to download samples.

Forms
(A-01 to A-09)

A-01 Foundations Implementation Rubric and Summary (8 pages)

A-02 Module A Implementation Checklist (6 pages)

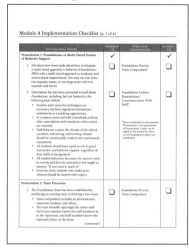

Form A-03 Foundations Team Meeting: Agenda and Minutes (2 pages; 3 versions)

Form A-04 Are You an Effective Team Builder?

Form A-05 Data Summary Form and Instructions (5 pages)

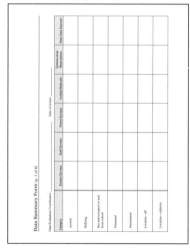

Form A-06 Common Area Observation and Instructions (5 pages)

Form A-07 Behavior Incicdent Referral Form (2 pages; Word format)

A-08 Referral Forms (2 pages)

Form A-09 *Behavior Incident Notification Form (2 pages; Word format)*

A-10 *Foundations Continuum Graphic*

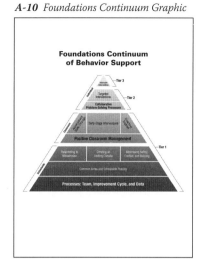

Other Resources
(A-10 to A-14)

A-11 *Traditional Discipline vs. the Safe & Civil Schools Approach to PBIS (3 pages)*

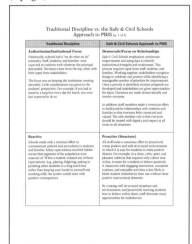

A-12 *Improvement Cycle Graphic*

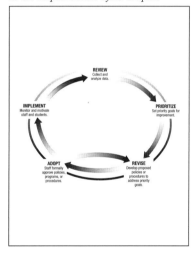

A-13 *Voting Rubrics (4 versions)*

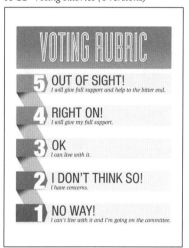

A-14 *Evaluation Flow Chart*

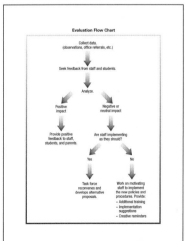

Samples
(A-15 to A-30)

A-15 *STOIC Poster*

A-16 *Record of Team Composition and Representation*

A-17 *Team Purpose Statement*

A-18 *Team Logo and Team Purpose Statement*

A-19 *CRUISE Team Fall Staff Inservice (adapted from PowerPoint)*

A-20 *Documentation of Meeting Rules*

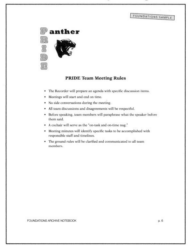

A-21 *Evidence of Decision-Making Process and Revision Policy Communicated to Staff*

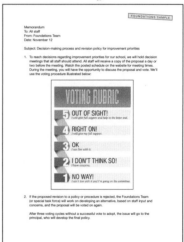

A-22 *Evidence That New Policies and Procedures Have Been Evaluated and Results Conveyed to Staff*

A-23 *Foundations Archive: Plans and Policies in Place*

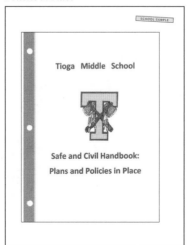

A-24 *Data Review Summary*

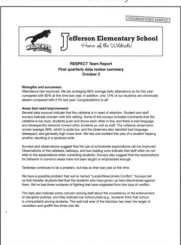

A-25 *Documentation of Improvement Priority Sequence*

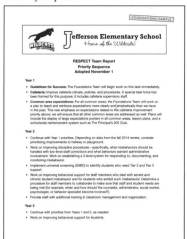

A-26 *Sample Survey*

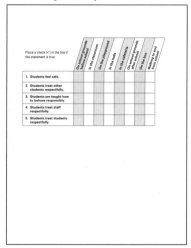

A-27 *Letter About Surveys to Parents*

A-28 *Letter to Parents About Survey Results*

A-29 *Documentation That Data Were Shared With Staff*

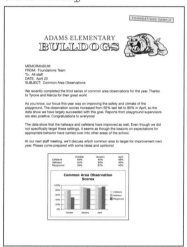

A-30 *Caught You Caring! instructions and nomination form*

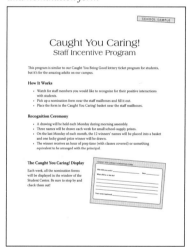

A-31 *Engaging Staff in the Prioritize Step (2 pages)*

PowerPoint Presentations
(A1 to A5)

For Single-School Use Only

Permission to copy and use the *Foundations* reproducibles is granted only to staff members who work in schools that have purchased the *Foundations* module.

DOWNLOAD CD CONTENT

Go to cdcontent.pacificnwpublish.com and enter access code
59909-069-6-forms to download forms, PowerPoints, and other resources.
Enter access code **59909-069-6-samples** to download samples.
